CH

from. BARBARA , DANNY &
LEIGH-ANN & SARAH

DOWN
A COUNTRY ROAD

DOWN
A COUNTRY ROAD

By Roy G. Taylor

First Edition

Printed in the United States

Published by J Mark
203 North Cone Street
Wilson, N.C. 27893

Library of Congress Catalog Card Number 86-90422
ISBN 0-9613485-1-8

*To Kay, Marshall,
Jason and Andy*

Index

Introduction

Eighteen-wheelers, foreign compacts, luxury U.S.-made cars and millions of outdated automobiles travel along the highways of America every day, clogging the interstates as they speed toward their destinations. Across hills, dipping down into valleys, they follow the terrain, observing the beauty of this nation's rich heritage.

Along seashores, through desolate swamps, along rural settings, across scenic regions. Parkways give panoramic views of awe-inspiring scenes from lofty mountains. Huge objects that become miniature due to sharp drops in elevation show waterfalls that appear to be within the grasp of the hand; where millions of trees appear as children's playthings. Americans on the move see these things — busy and anxious to arrive — wherever people are going.

Truckers haul produce and other goods coast-to-coast day and night, criss-crossing major highways North, South, East and West. Businessmen and women hurry to meet appointments, finding home any place they visit. Tourists travel year-round, visiting thousands of places in every state.

Maps become the best-read publications for the traveling public. Routes are mapped out and followed carefully to keep the traveler informed of his whereabouts. Maps are comparable to the circulatory system. The interstates represent the major arteries and other insignificant highways the lesser arteries. And from these arteries the smaller capillaries fan out in all directions.

From the wide, red markings used for the interstates the artist uses the finest pinpoints to mark the almost-unknown roads and highways that branch out in every direction, appearing as mere hairlines on the map. They seem almost without purpose and appear to have little bearing in traveling across America.

Travelers who take the main routes see a good cross-section of the nation, but they don't see the real America. It is along the thousands and thousands of fine lines on the map that seemingly lead to nowhere that the greatest drama of life is played out every day. Far from the hustle and bustle of the fast-paced life of the 1980s, the pace is slower there.

* * *

I am directing traffic off the interstate, inviting the travelers to see a minute part of America in a setting they will find unbelievable. It is a visit to the past. There will be no light lines, no telephone poles, no fancy brick homes, no landscaped premises, nothing of a modern trend until the 1940s. It is a look at a rural setting from 50 to 60 years ago.

Please take it easy as you come off the interstate. Drive slowly and carefully. There might be hens and biddies in the road and a cow might have jumped over the fence to try the corn across the road. You'll be entering a dirt road and you'll get dust on yourselves and your vehicles.

Stay as close together as you can, for I'll have to give you the details about the little area I am familiar with. I'm using one of Pa's old fox horns to carry the sound.

I will walk along slowly and identify the places. I want you to know about my little paradise.

Ready? Then take a look to the left. That's Hood Swamp School, where all us young'uns around here learned our ABC's (and a lot of things we had no business learning, too). I walked to and from this school every day during the school term, along with hundreds of other young'uns, unless the weather was too bad to travel.

Over to your right is the cotton gin where we take our loose cotton to be ginned and baled. And that little road over there going back through the woods is where hundreds of people live and come out on Sad'dy to go to town.

See that clay hill to the left? I slid down that thing a thousand times when I went to school and got my butt tore down too when I got clay on my overhalls. And I won't the only one.

A few farmers own most of the land in here, and they have a lot of sharecroppers and tenants. See them old houses scattered back in the fields? That's where a lot of them live. And please don't be unkind about this little place. It's home to us and we love it. Best something to eat you ever tasted is cooked in them old houses. The most laughing I ever heard came from them houses and yards along this road.

We used to be something else. We'd find baby birds on the ground and climb the trees and put them back in their nests, but we'd take the little birds out of their nests at other times and kill them. We'd find baby rabbits in little holes and take one out and try to make it drink milk, and it always died. We'd catch lightning bugs and tear off one wing and throw them up and watch as they fell to the ground with the little signals of light showing when they breathed. We were cruel in a sense, yet, at other times we were filled with compassion for our animal friends. Boys my age have outgrown that now, but the younger ones are still doing the same things.

There's Miss Lany's house, and she's one fine woman. She don't think nothing but something good. She is a walking saint if there ever was one.

I ain't going to say much about that house back yander in the field. Some of the carryings-on there are funny, and you can see a lot of men coming and going from the house. I've been told several things about that place. I know that a right pretty woman lives there and there's been talk that she sells whisky. But others use the term "loose" to describe her. I always wanted to ask what they meant, but was scared to broach the subject to a grown-up. It is mostly the womenfolks that say "loose" all the time when they talk about her.

We've plowed and chopped and sowed soda in these fields more times than I can tell you. We've crapped and looped and put in backer in the fields six to eight weeks a summer all my life. We've near 'bout worked ourselves down in them backer patches, let me tell you. But along with all the hard work, we've had a lot of fun around all these backer barns you see scattered everywhere.

I could tell you a story about every barn, every hog pasture, every backer barn, every swimming hole, every path around here, but some of them would make you and me red-faced, so I won't go into all that.

Us boys back here behind these piney woods had to "learn" about life just like boys in Montana and Texas and Ohio and everywhere else across this nation, and I mean "learn," no humming and hawing and beating around the bush and saying we "knowed" when we didn't. We were as rank as a boar and filled to the brim with whatever it is that makes men and boys like they are. But until we "knowed" we won't nothing but a pack of wishful thinkers.

You ain't never seen anything as revealing as "knowing" and the effect it has on a pack of boys. Each one in his own way and his own time, and the respect each one gains upon knowing that he "knows." Nor the envy among the rest of them who are still not "initiated." That's why every place is special for us. Pastures or barns or backer shelters or back fields or the woods become places that will live forever in our thoughts when we remember our teen years and learning about life.

Miss Lettie won't let no young'uns go in her yard. She's curious. She lives by herself and they say she has a shotgun sitting just inside her kitchen door. She hates young'uns and don't mind letting anybody know it. She's got that old dog you see lying in the yard trained, too. She'll sic him on anything that enters her yard.

But Miss Dora's, right over there, is just the opposite. She's got boys, and she lets other young'uns go and play with them and she always finds tea cakes or muffins or something to give all of them and they can romp and play all they want to, just so they stay on the outside. She won't let them traipse through her house.

See that little creek there? It has always been muddy looking, like it looks right now, and we hain't never been able to git in it to swim and bathe, but we have had more fun there than you can imagine. We've caught a hundred toad frogs and played with them (and they say if frog pee gits on your hand it'll make warts, and we've got them too, so it must be true) but we don't never let that stop us.

And I feel more like a man every time I go in that store over there. They have just about "educated" all us boys in the neighborhood. I still can't believe some of the things they tell. If I said we just loved the stores I wouldn't be saying it strong enough. We actually worship the stores. If our Ma's and Pa's knowed what we was picking up there, they'd have fits.

Look at them corner rooms on the front of the houses as we pass. In some of them front rooms the neighborhood young folks gather on Sad'dy night and Sunday evening and do their courting. I mean a whole gang of 'em. They have to git chairs out of the dining room to seat everybody, but you darn sure better not sit on one of them girls' armchairs. Them old men and women are curious, let me tell you.

But all of it seems like heaven on earth to me. I see all the things about me and I go into a trance sometimes. I look at the stars at night and the moon when it makes the night near 'bout bright enough to read, and the clouds when they form and lightning flashes and loud claps of thunder come and the rain splashes down, and I know the same things happen everywhere else, but I don't know about other places. I just know about this little spot in all the world.

I know one thing. Ain't nothing in the world sounds better than rain falling on them tin roofs at night. It'll put you to sleep before you can say "Now I lay me down to sleep."

I look at the bright sunshine in the morning when the clouds have all passed away and I see the raindrops on everything sparkling like diamonds and hear the birds singing and see people moving about and I just know I'd never be happy anywhere else.

Whatever you do, don't say nothing sassy right now. Mr. Clee and Miss Rosa quote scriptures all the time and don't have no such thoughts as us boys have. They're on Glory Road and headed for heaven. This is hallowed ground. We're approaching the church and that makes it all the more hallowed. And we know about church, for we have to go, whether we want to or not. And our Ma's and Pa's are there, too, so there ain't no way of gitting out of going. But we're proud of our church.

Mr. Luby keeps a boar or two in his pasture, and most of us don't have no boars, for it's hard enough to feed hogs for a year at best. So we do like a lot of people do when something is available for free; we take our sows to Mr. Luby's boar to be mated. We tie a slip-knot in a rope and put it around one of the sows' hind legs and just march them to Mr. Luby's and go on to the hog pasture back in the woods and git the work done.

Across over there a little piece is the hard-surfaced road that takes you to town. And between here and town there are two or three groups of Burma Shave signs as you whiz by on your old mobiles. And we read the signs every time we go by. They rhyme, you know. We couldn't help from reading them to save our lives. Sometimes we start out saying we ain't going to read them. Instead, we'll count the birds on the signs. But we've just got to read the signs every time.

And that old camel on the side of the store is gitting old and faded out. I remember when he looked like life standing there with his old hump and his lips puckered out. Seems like the sign-painters don't come around no more like they used to.

Did any of you ever go up in the woods and find cocoons on bushes and pull them and take them to a shed room or some place where they wouldn't be messed with and just leave them til they hatched into the prettiest moths you ever seen? Well, they's a thousand cocoons in them woods.

And the trees have a special meaning for us. By day they form our horizon and provide boundaries to our world. By night they take on special forms as we watch them under darkening skies. The trees stand darker than the night and give us silhouettes that are familiar to us. Some appear as statues against the skyline. Some form the shapes of human faces. They give shelter to wild creatures that give their cries in the night. Sometimes there's a howl that sounds eerie. A shrill cry from a bird sends chills down the spine. The whip-poor-wills call and are answered by their mates and a silvery moon shining down on us gives radiance to the night and intensifies shadows that give the effect of black-and-white over the neighborhood.

The waters catch the glow of the sun by day and send sparkling beams of light across the expanse of the little lakes and streams and ponds and the sunbeams move with the ripple of the water. The banks and wooded areas beside streams provide a lovers' paradise and a little world within a world to get away from the cares of life.

I could never tell you all the things that happen along this country road. I don't even know all that happens. But it is life, lived to the fullest every day of the week — from Sunday morning when there is a quietness over the neighborhood until singing erupts in the churches and preaching and amens are heard; to quiet Sunday dinners (and especially quiet if company comes for dinner) and young'uns waiting forever to git the "scraps" of chicken and all the other mess the high and mighty company and the old folks don't want; to Sunday night with its peacefulness and the last few hours before a full week in the fields; to hitching up mules at daybreak and facing 12 hours under a hot summer sun and then the fall when cooling breezes make you feel like a new person after sweating for months and wilting down in the summer heat. The blue skies of autumn and the turning of the leaves and harvesting the crops is a sight to behold. And the winter months when everything freezes over and winter winds blow and snow comes sometimes and whitens everything and young'uns romp and play.

This is my world, travelers. This is the only life I've ever known. Maybe it ain't nothing special for you, but it will live in my heart for as long as I live. And I want to invite you to stick around for a while. I'm telling you about a lot of little things that happened along this country road. Nothing earth-shaking, mind you. Just plain, ordinary things that make up most of our lives.

There are reflections on specific families and stories about rural life and there is the Crebbins family that represents all of us. Most of us can see ourselves in old Zebedee Crebbins and Kizzie, his wife, and their brood of children — Hank, Fuzz, Shine, Lizzie Mae, Little Bud, Sarah and Sis. The best is yet to come, so go with me Down A Country Road.

Sharecroppers Go Home

T he holiday season is here and it will be Christmas almost before we know it. Thanksgiving is already past and even the newspapers are numbering the days to Christmas. What a joyous season to anticipate!

I am thinking about the "SHARECROPPERS" and their new status this year. They have spread out among the public, even to many states and a few to foreign countries. And I know that many are in average homes, but some find themselves among the high and mighty, and I find it a little hard to imagine their awe at being treated so royally and in such surroundings.

Picture, if you will, glistening chandeliers in some of the places, the plush carpeting that the sharecroppers could easily misinterpret as being pallets; the fine furniture in rich mahogany, birch, pine, walnut, maple and other woods polished to a mellow glow; elaborate curtains and valances at windows overlooking settings that would be considered ethereal by the sharecroppers. There they are amid the Baldwins, the Uprights, the Baby Grand pianos and the credenzas and the tester beds and Martha Washington bedspreads and chairs comfortable enough to serve as beds.

There they are amid the microwaves, the dishwashers, the rotisseries, the large dining tables with padded chairs and arm rests. They are in another world and no doubt reveling in all it has to offer.

The ease with which the holiday meal is prepared will certainly appeal to the women who worked for days in getting things ready. There will be no arms worn out from beating cake batters; not with the electric beaters on the market today. There will be no basting of the turkey over and over with modern basting material implanted deeply within the birds. And there are electric graters for the coconut and blenders for potatoes and many other things. There are prepared dressings and ready-made pies and frostings. It will be a cinch for the sharecroppers to partake in the traditional feast without having to turn their hands in the preparation of all the food.

The gaiety and glitter of the season will delight the group who grew up without all the niceties of the present generations. The elaborate, yet tasteful decorations, will have a very special appeal to them. They will marvel at the ingenuity of the modern world.

But you will pardon them, I'm sure, if it takes a little time for them to adjust fully to their new surroundings. They perhaps feel they are in Heaven and they may have to pinch themselves to make reality out of the things they perceive.

And when Christmas Eve arrives, it will be easy to imagine that the sharecroppers will gaze out the windows of their new homes upon avenues of evergreens and manicured lawns or overlooking busy interstates and bumper-to-bumper traffic and revert in their thoughts to winding roads that seemingly lead to nowhere and humble abodes that speak no message to the modern world; to naked trees stretching heavenward in the midst of a winter landscape with leaden skies and chimneys sending white smoke into the atmosphere; to scenes far removed from the land as we know it today.

They may draw air into their lungs in search of the smell of onions in the preparation of the dressing, or the spices used generously in preparing pumpkin and potato pies and the smell of the wood burning in the open fireplaces.

But knowing them as I do, I can truthfully say they will not see the beauty around them as they gaze out upon the setting. And please allow them this indulgence, for you see, they are willing to forgo the beauty of the present-day yuletide season to flock back to their humble past and see it all in memory. It's a yearly ritual, and nothing against the "now" generation.

They will be seeing back porches piled high with wood and signs of people meandering around the places. They'll smell the burning leaves after the yards are swept and their ears will be keen for the pop of the acorns among the burning leaves.

The smell of vinegar and hot pepper will invade the premises as the pork is baked in the ovens and the aroma of sage will fill their nostrils as dressing is made for the Christmas feast. Their appetites will be whetted and they'll feel the yearning for food in their "craws."

They'll see the open hearth and logs burning brightly in the fireplace and the front of the fireplace under the mantel where soot has darkened the wood and it will appear as an artistic etching and that little bit of holly on the mantle will be illuminated with berries redder than Santa Claus' suit and the insignificant tree will be brighter than the one decorating Times Square in New York.

Large unadorned pine cones will rest among the wreaths of holly and they appear as miniature Christmas trees. The oil lamp will shed a soft radiance over the room. The odor of delicious apples - each covered in its own piece of tissue paper and resting in the closet — along with the other fruits and nuts, will fill the house. Someone will play Christmas carols on the hand-pedaled organ and there will be singing and laughter and merriment.

The fresh-scoured floors will appear to have been bleached and the clean smell will permeate the house. Outside, the north winds will blow and the gray skies of winter will be welcomed at this particular time.

They'll all gather around the fireplace on Christmas morning for the annual ritual with the children but no one will capture the radiance on the children's faces, for there is no camera to preserve the picture for posterity.

And soon will come the traditional feast — the feast of Christmas. They'll all be there, the young and the old, and they'll be happy just to be together, to share the beauty of the season.

When Christmas is over, the sharecroppers will be happy to return to their new homes to become a part of other families. And I know that every one of you will forgive them for this one special time to retreat to their heritage, for you see, many of you live on the pages of "SHARECROPPERS" and you are really the sharecroppers themselves. You understand, I'm sure.

The Night Of Christ's Birth

T he road was dusty from the throng trudging wearily toward its destination. Never mind the personal sacrifices. It was not by choice they were making the journey. A decree had been issued by Caesar Augustus that all the world should be taxed. And everyone was ordered to appear in his own city. There were no exceptions.

Joseph traveled from Galilee, along with Mary, out of the city of Nazareth, into Judea, unto the City of David, called Jerusalem, because he was of the house and lineage of David. And this had to be a strenuous journey for Mary, who was expecting a child at any moment.

In those days donkeys were used a lot in travel to carry supplies when journeys were made. And it is unlikely that Mary rode on the donkey's back in her condition. But she would have had to walk throughout the long journey otherwise, and it is easy to imagine the physical pain she felt as she carried her heavy burden along the road to Jerusalem.

Did they have ample food on the journey? According to Bible maps, the distance between Nazareth and Bethlehem appears to be some 70 miles. Did they have sleeping quarters along the way? What did they feed the donkey, if one was taken along? What did they eat? Did the most blessed among women have to sleep on the ground as they moved slowly along the dusty trail? There are so many questions and so few answers.

Were there holly trees with red berries along the way? Were there thickets or marshy places where mistletoe grew? Hardly so. Were there fir trees lining the road as they made their way slowly toward their destination? We associate those things with Christmas.

What was it like when they finally arrived in the little town of Bethlehem? There were crowds of people and it was perhaps total consternation for Joseph and Mary to find the inns crowded and no place to stay. What were they to do? And then Mary felt the pangs of labor and a place had to be found to deliver the baby.

How could it possibly have been a lowly stable where dung permeates the air and where sanitation is impossible? There would certainly be straw and other refuse on the ground. Was straw piled high for Mary to lie on in her travail? Did she have any kind of bed clothing with which to cover the straw?

Finally, when the baby was born, he was placed in a trough used to feed the animals that were quartered there. Was hay placed in the manger to cushion the hardness of the trough for the infant? He was wrapped in strips of cloth used in clothing babies at that time in history.

What must Mary have thought as she gave birth in a stable, when it was she who was chosen above all other women to be the mother of the Messiah? Surely it could have been carried out differently than in such a dismal setting.

Therein lies a lesson for mankind — the lesson of humility. There has never been a person born who even approached the status achieved by this son of a carpenter, begotten by the Holy Ghost, born in a stable, that changed the course of history. It didn't have to be that way. It was intended.

Thus a baby was born that few in the world even knew about.

But there were shepherds in the fields tending their flocks by night and the angel of the Lord appeared before them and made them aware of the Saviour's birth, whereupon they went into Bethlehem and saw the baby in the manager and proclaimed the news abroad.

And wise men from the east saw his star and determined to go to Bethlehem to worship him, but Herod privily called the wise men together and asked when the star had appeared and admonished them to go in search of the baby and bring him so that (Herod) could worship him also. And the star, which they had seen in the east, went before them until it stood over the manger where Christ lay. They showered him with gifts of gold, frankincense and myrrh. But they didn't return the Christ Child to Herod.

Now I have no problem with how the star got there. If that is naive, I accept that without apology. If the Bible said it, I can accept it totally.

And when the Christ Child was taken into Jerusalem to be presented to the Lord after Mary's days of purification were accomplished, according to the law of Moses, they took either a pair of turtledoves or two young pigeons, neither of which we associate with the Christmas season.

It was such an humble beginning in a setting so primitive we would consider it below human dignity today. There was little fanfare among the masses and very little was written, nor has ever been known, of all the events leading up to Christ's birth. Yet the light that appeared before the wisemen is even more magnificent 2000 years later in the hearts of Christian believers. He has transcended time and circumstances and has remained the eternal hope for Christendom. And the world could not know in those days the significance of this humble birth that would grow in its impact throughout the centuries.

But it all comes together as the most miraculous story ever written and the miracle still lives! If I could make one wish for this Christmas season it would be that every Christian concentrate on this one event in history and make it the centerpiece of the holiday season. Except for the creche and the bright lights, things which we associate with Christmas are not those that were in evidence at the time of Christ's birth. Think of a dusty road, a tiring journey, a manger scene, a shining star, turtledoves and pigeons and an humble setting, and above all, the Christ Child. That is the message and the magic of Christmas.

Christmas For The Elderly

What is there in Christmas for you when you are 66 years old; when the momentum is all downhill and at a faster pace than the legs can keep up with; when the fire burns down to embers and the only sound in the house is the tick-tock of the mantle clock; when a joyous season is approaching and all the things which have been traditional over a lifetime are something to ponder in the mind?

The days when you were young and when your little ones looked up to you with wonder in their eyes as if you were a god, who could not know all your imperfections and failings that you carried in your heart, yet, leaving a feeling of being a superman to a select few among the throngs of humanity.

The little tree stands lonely in its corner trying to impart the true spirit of Christmas with its miniature lights flashing on and off, lighting up the decorations that adorn the tree. The poinsettia adds its color to the setting and the clear lights at the windows make an impressive scene.

There is no odor of turkey roasting in the oven; no cakes with rich icings; no pies on the cabinets and no large array of gaily-wrapped presents under the tree.

There are thoughts of times when many who shared in the Christmas celebration are no longer among the living and a reminder that a time will come when you cannot count yourself among that group either. It's a way of saying, "old man, you've had it." It's a lot to think about.

Life is such a beautiful experience. From earliest recollections there is the wonder of it all, the mystery and the exploration and the challenge. There are the tender years when it is easy to believe in everything.

Remember the days when "Twinkle, twinkle little star, how I wonder what you are, up above the world so high, like a diamond in the sky" brought a sparkle to the eyes and a real question in a child's mind as to what a star really is? Remember the years of growing, of learning, of finding that some of our childish beliefs were only fairy tales that left a letdown feeling when the dream ended?

Remember the days of youth with its impetuosity? Days when young love bloomed and when Christmas came there was anguishing over selecting a present for your beloved? Remember all the gaiety of the season — the parties, the dances, the carolling?

Remember young adulthood and the desire to marry and start a family; the struggles of the newly married, the sacrifices, dodging bill-collectors, robbing Peter to pay Paul, the angelic cries of the first baby, the gray days with little hope for getting ahead and being able to live decently?

Remember the passing of the years and how they went by so swiftly? Remember when the first child left the nest and ventured out on its own, and the others that followed, leaving an emptiness in the home that would never again be filled?

Remember middle age and the realization that youth was eternally gone, that it had been such a short experience it was impossible to grasp in retrospect? Remember all the events that transpired to place you in this position at this particular time in history — Christmas 1984?

As you nod before the fire between periods of reality and a dream world all those thoughts flash before you in the dying embers and you wonder what it is all about. Then you reflect again on the Christmas season and a brilliant beacon of light shines before you. The new generation! You see yourself again through their eyes. You visualize their hopes, their dreams, their zest for life and the wonders of the world about them. They represent you and the future. They will carry on! Their exuberance will have its impact on you and you know that the future is in good hands; that the dream will never die; that our small contributions to society will merge with all others and that Christmas will live as long as time lasts. The young of today will in turn give way to future generations in a plan designed by God to ensure continuity.

Christmas is as beautiful at age 66 as it was at the age of six. It is only viewed differently. There is something about it that uplifts the spirit and places us on a higher plane than at other seasons of the year. It has a magical quality that inspires hope for the good life here as well as a life beyond this world.

If you doubt the real beauty of life at age 66 or beyond, look toward the sunset. Has there ever been a more beautiful picture than a golden sun at the end of day when all the brilliant hues paint the sky so magnificently it cannot be duplicated by man? Sunrise is beautiful with its promise of a sunshiny day and a world sparkling with dew. But something about a beautiful sunset brings out the poet in the human race.

I expect to enjoy all the beauties of Christmas with my loved ones just as most of you will do. I will partake in all the season has to offer and I will be happy and because the new generation lives and has high hopes for the future, I can face tomorrow and all the remaining tomorrows left for me without fear of a time when I can no longer participate in Yuletide activities. As beautiful as is the picturesque scene at sunset, it must be even more beautiful beyond, where man has not been able to penetrate.

Merry Christmas.

Hog-Killing Time Again

I t's that season again, so let's go back to an old-fashioned hog killing. I mean those from a long time ago when a hole was dug out for the barrel to be set slanting to scald the hogs in. And those were big barrels. They sure looked larger than these 50-gallon jobs. Maybe they had 100-gallon barrels in those days, for all I know.

After those hogs were drug up to be scalded the water was dipped boiling hot from the washpots and dumped into the barrel, for by the time the hog was put into the water it had cooled down considerably, since the barrel was cold and that decreased the temperature of the water quite a bit.

A lot of the hog-killing process was detailed in an earlier column, but there are post-hog-killing chores that didn't get attention in that article — like the liver hash, or hog hash as some people call it. And I ain't one of these nuts about hog liver. But liver hash was different. And all you oldsters and some a lot younger know all about liver hash, when they used the haslet and the lights that you can't buy no more and cooked them together in a big pot, added sage and hot pepper and cooked that stuff down to a slow gravy. And it was good.

But there are two textures to the liver and the lights, and I didn't like the texture of the lights. They were soft when done, whereas the liver had a grainy texture. So I'd just pick out the soft and eat the liver.

And did any of you ever hear of Norton Yam sweet taters? Well that's what they called those I grew up with, and I'd be willing to swear on a stack of bibles they were the best sweet taters that ever were grown. And they weren't dark red like you see today. They were nearer a natural to light tan color than red, and I still don't know how that much juice, or syrup, came out of a sweet tater. Slip that skin off and it was totally covered in that syrup, and if there were several on a plate the juice would run onto the dish. And sweet! Take one of those rascals and put it in that plate of liver hash and mash it into that gravy and eat it with those mouthfuls of liver that didn't taste like liver, and it was fit for a king.

And that souse meat wasn't anything to sneer at either. The noses and ears went into souse meat, and sometimes the feet, but most people wanted them cooked by themselves. And those home-cooked pigs feet were better'n anything on the market today. But they'd make that souse and add a sumptuous amount of red pepper and place it in a glass dish or an aluminum pan and let that stuff jell and then pickle it in vinegar, and that was good eating. They were careful not to put souse meat into anything galvanized, for folks said that would cause ptomaine poisoning.

Then there were the chitlins. And there's still a hassle about hog guts. Some people turn up their noses and say they never tasted of the things and others swear they're as good as barbecue and there is no reconciling the two. The way I always felt about chitlins was bless those that didn't like them, for it left more for me.

And nobody has to tell me that they stink up a house worse than anything in the world, even collards. And the tighter other room doors were shut the more that terrible odor penetrated every nook and crevice in a house. But heck, the way they smelled cooking didn't have anything to do with the way they tasted when they were cooked the way I like them, and in a few DAYS the odor finally went away. I like chitlins fried so they are reasonably brown, but not crisp. And I want cornbread in a hoecake cooked on top of the stove to eat with chitlins.

It always kind of bothered me to see somebody go up to the pot after the chitlins became tender and pull out a long one and cool it by blowing on the gut, then eating it in one string without bothering to cut it up. They don't look appetizing either when they're a sickly white. I have nothing agin chitlins, so long as I don't see a grain of corn nowhere around them. If I saw that, I'd puke.

But the kidneys and the heart are two things about a hog I never had any use for in the eating line. The long tongue, the sweet breads and melts are all right, and I could appreciate them more today than I did when I was a young'un, but don't feed me on heart, kidneys or hog jaw. Too many knots in that old fat jaw.

And the various meat packers have some good sausage today, and I have no complaint with it. But any of you who can remember can vouch for that sausage they used to save out and cook in patties. Oh boy! That was something good. That red pepper and sage just stood out when it was cooked to a golden brown in good-sized patties and it was sweet inside and a buttermilk biscuit wouldn't last no time with sausage and eggs.

I never was one to eat green sausage in the casings. It has such a fresh taste I just didn't like it until it hung up a couple of weeks and dried out a little. And some how or other, I was always thinking about when the chitlins were scraped and all that stuff scraped off and put into a pan or something and how gooey and pink it looked.

And some folks had heavy cast iron presses they used for stuffing sausage and pressing cracklings, and they were whiz-bangs in those days. They had a heavy lid that screwed down as sausage or cracklings were pressed. They saved a lot of time in stuffing sausage and pressed cracklings were really good, for a lot of that cholesterol-producing fat was taken out of them, yet leaving plenty of lard in the cracklings. Oh well, we'd never live to tell it if we did it like that now. But I'd love to have some liver hash and Norton yams for supper, or a good piece of crackling bread!

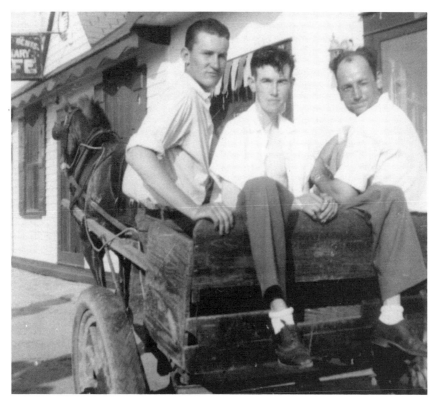

Riding In Hoover Cart In 1943
Courtesy Beulah Godwin Mercer

Oh, Those Old Hoover Carts!

We become accustomed to change to the extent we forget what the norm was in the past. And prices over the past decade have changed so much, we don't even dare let ourselves think back to what they were, especially when we go to the grocery store.

And we don't have to be very old to remember when nice homes were selling for around $16,000 to $17,000. And when I say nice, I mean NICE. Nice neighborhoods. Plenty of room. Well constructed. Just compare such prices with those of today, and we almost get nauseated. Mobile homes are far more expensive today than were the larger homes of yesterday. And $7,000 to $10,000 homes used to be fairly nice as far as that goes.

But knowing me as you do, my thoughts go a lot further back

than the days I have described. Heck, these are all modern days. I go back to the days when there just wasn't anything to brag about. I even remember the "Hoover Cart" days!

Now all the old codgers know that when Herbert Hoover was in the White House, we were at our poorest, and that continued even after he left office, and Hoover wasn't entirely responsible for the mess we were in those days, although I'm not going into the political aspect of the era.

Anyhow, whatever old automobiles we had during those days, many of them got off the roads during the Depression, for there was no money with which to purchase tires, make repairs and buy gasoline to run them. Let me tell you folks, there just wasn't any money, period. Whatever ain't, ain't.

So what did folks do? They built them Hoover Carts to do some running around in. There never was a time when people didn't like to favor their feet by having something to ride in. And the way they did it was this: They'd take the back wheels, axle and housing from those old "mobiles" that weren't running any more and build the cart and attach the housing to it. They'd buy a tube of tire patches and put them over the holes in the inntertubes and inflate the tires unless the rubber was rotten. If it was, they had to discard the idea, for as I said, there was no money for inner tubes and such things.

But since a Hoover Cart was a two-wheeled vehicle it was attached to the mule with two shafts, as is the case with other carts. And when a shaft is attached to the mule to pull the vehicle, the movement of the animal is felt by the rider. In other words, it ain't a really smooth ride.

Anybody that's ever used a cart in farming operations knows that riding in one is not too restful. Not only that, the floor of the cart is slanted. When a cart was used, the back of the cart had to be enclosed or whatever was being hauled would fall out.

But with few diversions in those days, some people built some pretty fancy Hoover Carts. I don't mean they'd paint them up bright colors and all that, for that's where money came into the picture again. So forget money. But I heard tell of some people building two-seaters, but I never saw one of them. As a matter of fact, we never built a Hoover Cart at my house, cause we didn't have the necessary "mobile" wheels.

And I've seen them where they took heavy canvas cloth, although I don't know where in the heck they got it, and used it for the foot of the carts. It would be attached at the bottom of the seats and to the front of the cart, and it would be a natural curve to the foot of the cart.

And let me tell you, people used to court in those old carts. On a Sunday afternoon, you'd see those country doods and their girlfriends riding around the countryside, laughing and carrying on and having as much fun as if they'd been in a Model-T or Model-A Ford. And they might have some bigger laughs in the Hoover Carts than they would have had in cars when those old mules decided to embarrass the boys and girls on their escapades. But why not use the Hoover Carts and those old tires? After all, the highways were there and cars were few and far between and it was better to have Hoover Carts traipsing up and down the roads than nothing.

But I don't know why I got into all this mess about Hoover Carts when a large percentage of the population today doesn't even know what I am talking about. I reckon one reason is that I merely mentioned Hoover Carts in "Looking Backward," and they were a part of our past.

But for the record, except for the fact that the horse and buggy age had gone by the wayside by then, it would have been more comfortable riding in the buggies, for they were four-wheeled vehicles and the seats were made more comfortable. By the time the buggy age ended we were ashamed of them anyway, and having to resort to Hoover Carts was a necessity in some cases and a pleasure in others, but it wasn't the same as it had been when buggies were the main mode of transportation.

And just think. I started out about $16,000 - $17,000 homes, and that was only yesterday compared to the Hoover Cart days. And chances are today's prices will only be a drop in the bucket to what they'll be a few years in the future.

Laughing At Silly Things

I nsignificant things that happened a long time ago sometimes bring a laugh or a smile when they are recalled. Some were not worth remembering, but they are a part of our past that lingers in the memory.

I wonder how many of you ever had to sleep at the foot of the bed? You know that 50 to 60 years ago, most every house was brimming full of young'uns, and young'uns will be young'uns. And we used to spend the night with each other occasionally. And there weren't empty bedrooms waiting for company. If it was summer, it was fine, and a pallet would suffice, but when the weather was cold, there might be three to sleep on one bed. And one of the three had to sleep at the foot. God forbid!

It always fell the lot of the youngest child that occupied the bed on a regular basis to sleep at the foot, while the two larger boys would have the length of the bed to wallow in, throw their arms in their sleep, and kick like a mule.

First, there was the matter of cover, and we needed several quilts to keep us warm in the cold rooms, and when three were sleeping on the bed the cover had to be pulled out from the foot. The two boys that were lying straight on the bed controlled the "kivver" and they'd pull it up around their shoulders and the poor boy at the foot got left out in the cold. Oh, he'd pull and pull and try to get further on the bed, but there were four legs that acted in a manner similar to a mule. You'd just about get your head kicked off at the foot of the bed.

And did you ever notice that the "kivver" at other people's houses had a little different smell than your own? It didn't stink, but it just smelled a little bit funny. But when you slept at the foot of the bed there wasn't time to really think about smell. Heck, you were trying to survive.

And I remember something that happened when I was about 14 years old that brings a laugh now when I think about it, although it wasn't a laughing matter at the time it happened.

My oldest brother had an old Model-A Ford that wouldn't start, and he wanted that baby fixed so he could go a courting. So my brother next to me hitched Gray and Zeb to the wagon and we set out to pull the Model A so we could start it. My brother was going to get on the running board and work on the engine while the car was being pulled, my other brother was going to drive the mules and a chain would be attached to the Ford and the back of the wagon, and I was going to guide the car and work the brakes if necessary.

Well, we got out on the paved road as had been planned, the mules were going at a trot, my brother eased out of the Ford and I moved over in the driver's seat to take command. But I tell you folks, I hadn't learned to drive a car then and didn't know a darn thing about the controls.

The first thing I did wrong was to turn the steering wheel too sharply, causing my brother to lose his balance on the running board and throwing him to the pavement. The old Ford's speed was greater than the wagon's and the car was moving up on the end of the wagon. My other brother was beating old Zeb and Gray like you wouldn't believe, trying to get the wagon out of danger and hollering at me to apply some pressure on the brakes to slow the car down.

But you know what I did. I applied ALL the pressure to those old brakes, and I can still see that old wagon suddenly going sideways and almost getting in the ditch and breaking the chain apart. It put a stop to Zeb and Gray too. And there was my other brother back on the highway, but I think he had come to by then and was sitting up. To tell the truth, I think he had a slight concussion, for it knocked him out for a few minutes. But he never went to a doctor and was laid up for a few days for he took a pretty good fall on that hard surface. And my other brother was sore and felt bad for a few days too.

But lucky me, there wasn't anything wrong with me except my stupidity. I was the cause of the whole mess due to my ignorance. But I paid for it. It was time to pick cotton, and in those days when there was work to be done you worked if you were able. I had to get out in the field with my cotton sack and pick cotton for several days all by my lonesome, for the other boys weren't up to it.

And youth is so cruel. Nothing has ever been more embarrassing than to be poked fun at by your peers. And those who have been victims of such cruelty would number in the millions. And I believe it was worse in the old days than it is today. Whatever could be found to knock another young person was used to its fullest extent.

I remember when I was in about the fourth grade at Hood Swamp School, a boy in one of the classes had an accident — an awful accident. He messed up his overalls! Now I don't know whether he asked to be excused or what the circumstances were. Maybe his Ma had given him Black Draught or castor oil the night before. Anyhow, that poor boy suffered the consequences of his act unmercifully. And youth never forgets.

That boy stood up beside the wall of the school, silent and forlorn looking, and it was only when his peers got near him they found out what had happened. He was the laughing stock of the school for weeks, and I'm sure that as long as he was in that school he was ribbed every day.

And I remember another student that was ribbed all through school because of a stupid question asked in his class: "What did you have for breakfast?" I guess he was being perfectly candid in saying, "goose eggs and coffee." And he might have broadcast it on CBS evening news. From that day forward, whenever he was referred to, you know what he was called. "Goose eggs and coffee."

What a life!

Thinking Old, Wanting to Live

I know some of you think of me as a pure nut to be eternally talking about something old, and maybe you've got a point. But I reckon when you're old it's a natural thing to think old.

But I also realize that this young crowd is forever searching for something old, too. And I just wonder why? They think of the older human race as a pack of nitwits a lot of times, and place no faith in what we say. Yet they traipse to every flea market they can find, rummage through countless yard sales and look everywhere for something from the era that we tell them about, but which they seem not to believe.

But maybe I have an answer in part. They've got all this new-fangled mess you can buy, and that hasn't hit the spot. So they want to take this new-fangled mess with their chintz curtains and fancy doodads in their kitchens and family rooms that have all the

marks of the modern age and display the old, ugly things we used to hate too. They'll take something that was dull as long as we knew it, polish it until it glitters, sand old wood that never boasted paint or shellac, and mellow it down and make them a dream world out of antiques and gloat over it and treasure it far more than we ever treasured it in the old days.

I even read in the Wall Street Journal this week that Sears Roebuck mail-order homes that were featured in its catalogs from 1909 to 1937 are considered chic today. During those years some 100,000 such homes were sold, ready-cut for assembly upon arrival.

The Journal says many of the homes are still standing, some in remarkably good condition. And preservationists are fighting to save the houses from demolition. Owners are nominating them for historical status.

Of course there were no Sears homes in my neck of the woods, and I have never seen one to my knowledge. You had to be pretty high up the ladder to buy a home of any kind in those days, and we didn't even have the ladder.

In the 1926 catalog, Sears Honor Bilt homes ranged from a modest cottage known as the Franklin, which sold for only $595, (imagine) to an elegant Southern-style mansion (get this) with Gothic columns, curving staircases and servants' quarters — the Magnolia, for $5,000. And you could get a matching outhouse for $39. Heck, we couldn't have bought the outhouse.

And I know this generation that throws away that much in a year's time (some of them) could never understand how with prices so very low, we couldn't wrangle somehow to buy one of those homes. The answer is that it's easier to wrangle a $100,000 loan today than it was $200 during those years. It doesn't matter how cheap the price if there is no money with which to purchase the merchandise.

But imagine a mansion for $5,000! And I reckon if such a thing were possible today, we wouldn't want it. It wouldn't be good enough for us. But I notice that a lot of the new houses today are taking on looks similar to bygone days.

But whatever I may say, I'm proud that today's generation cares enough about our junk of the past to pay high prices for it and make it a treasure in their homes. We'd take a gang of the mess we threw out umpteen years ago and treasure it for ourselves if we could. But we were scatterbrained too. We didn't want any part of it. And just the fact of it being old doesn't appeal to us all that much today, unless it is something from our own homes. We'd take anything in that category. I'd be proud to have a scarecrow Ma put in the chicken yard to try to run off the hawks if that were possible. And I wouldn't put it in no yard. I'd sit it right in the living room, and to heck with what anybody else thought. And the old chamber pot could rest under my bed, too.

But I swear that if I had some of those old ragged ladder-back chairs, I'd have new bottoms put in them. I don't feel like I could stand going through the anguish of having broken straw cutting into my arthritic legs again.

And if I had that old tin-front safe that sat in the kitchen, I'd scrape off all that accumulation of grease and scum over the sorry paint job before I even started applying paint remover to try to do a refinish job. That old safe needed redoing back there in the 30s and 40s, but it would have stood out like a sore thumb with everything else dull, if such a job had been contemplated in those days — which it wasn't.

And everybody that lived during the era I write about would give a chunk for the old earthenware churn that sat on the hearth and the wooden handle to go with it. But do you think we wanted that mess back then? The first milk we saw in the grocery stores (fresh milk) we determined the old churn was one eye-sore we'd haul up in the woods and git rid of forevermore. And we didn't just haul them up in the woods. We'd chunk them as hard as we could so they'd bust on impact. And we did the same thing with a lot of other junk that has become treasures over the years.

I reckon we were lacking in aesthetic values that society boasts today. But to be truthful, we weren't all that concerned with aesthetic values. We were happy to have one warm room to sit in in the winter, a good well or pump for our use, a warm bed at night, and three square meals a day. And all that meant an awful lot in those days. Many folks didn't have all those things, and they'd have given a right arm for what we poor folks out in the sticks had. They might laugh at our callousness and poke fun at us to our backs, but you'd better believe they sat down at our tables every chance they got. And talking about eating! That town crowd that was half-hungry could eat you out of house and home.

Spring In The Old Days

W hen I see the first budding of leaves after experiencing the harshness of winter, I get sort of a yearning to backtrack and see spring emerge as I saw it many years ago. And it isn't that spring differs today from those of "ancient" times. Rather, it's how we view it.

I remember so well the budding of the trees and the rushing of the water and the sudden growth out in the back fields and along the streams. One day it was all dead and drab, and suddenly there was the splash of color. The leaves were a softer green than they would become later, tender and immature, not yet shading the area around them.

Walking along the edges of the woods, there were the many species with their own distinguishable foliage, some later than others in awakening from their long winter sleep. And the March winds would send dust across the fields, dimming the view sometimes and where farmers were plowing thick dust rose into the atmosphere, creating a lonely scene along the back roads.

Along the banks of the little creek there was evidence of spring under foot. Plant life was emerging, along with early blooms where warm sunshine provided the atmosphere for growth. The violets bloomed earlier than expected, with the small, purple flowers shouting for recognition.

Water would run swiftly in the creek that had never been cleaned out, filled with debris that accumulated over the years — a fallen limb or sticks and other matter thrown into the water by children that always habitated the banks when spring came.

It was the same creek where we would later drive a mule and wagon to the water's edge and fill barrels for transplanting tobacco and for resetting after tender plants wilted and died soon after being set out. The barrels would be filled and guano sacks placed over the tops to help hold the water inside as it was transported to the fields.

And there was a new sound out in the country. The birds had arrived! From every direction there were chirps and songs and evidence of another breeding season. Twigs and moss and stray scraps of paper were being taken to nesting places and the birds would pitch nearby and peck at things unseen by the human eye. And at this season robins were predominant.

Winter rye added to the greenness of spring and it was a favorite place for barnyard fowl to gather and fill their crops with the rye and insects that congregated there in spring. It was a colorful sight to see the chickens meandering across the fields in a con-glomeration of colors and the crowing of the roosters added to the spring ritual.

A few more warm days would bring the fruit trees into bloom with the soft shades of pink and white dotting the countryside. And the buttercups would glisten with their yellow blossoms against the drabness of unpainted houses and mud-filled yards.

Children would get a hankering to shed their shoes and go barefoot, knowing that that would not be allowed before May, al-though there were a few parents who allowed this earlier than most, and this always caused children to complain about having to wear shoes when some children were barefooted.

And the spring smells were indescribable. There was a sweetness in the soil and the air was exhilarating and everything seemed clean, washed by a change of seasons and a purification of the atmosphere.

A few warm days would bring out feather beds on porches and clotheslines for airing after acquiring body odors during the long winter months. The feather beds were usually returned to their place in the closets upon the arrival of spring.

Folks took to the porches as soon as possible. They had been cramped inside for months and needed the fresh air and sunshine to renew their spirits. Doors would be opened so fresh air could circulate throughout the houses and the mothers were thinking about scalding in a few weeks.

Menfolks were checking on their tobacco beds almost daily, observing the growth of the plants and projecting a time for transplanting the plants to the fields. They had to have tobacco land prepared when the plants were ready to be set out. And the plant beds had to be picked often, for grass and weeds flourished in the rich soil where generous amounts of fertilizer had been ap-plied.

And boiling pots in the kitchens spread their aroma over the countryside. Where there was turnip salad it was cooked daily by someone in the community, and people in the fields became hungry just by smelling the boiling pots.

Farm folks had enjoyed the winter months with the cold and

snows and winds of winter, for each season has its unique qualities to give variety to life. But they were ready for a change.

It would all come a little later — the dotting of the forests with white as the dogwoods came into flower. They were only in the woods out in the sticks in those days. The annuals would sprout and decorate the plain premises, the climbing rosebushes would bloom and the shade would thicken on the trees. Bare feet would expose themselves to the perils of summer. The male gender would shed themselves of those long-handled union suits that had acquired a bluish or black tint from corduroy breeches worn during the winter months. Spring would reign supreme, just as it has done throughout the ages. And it would be no different than spring, 1985. It's a ritual as old as time itself.

Good Friday Gardening

I n the days (50 years or more ago) when the young crowd would say darkness was upon the land and we were roaming around like cave men, we managed to do a few things that have been traditional through the ages. And one was that when Good Friday came we planted a garden. That was the Friday before Easter, and it happened every year.

So, hitch up the mule to the one-horse plow, cause we don't need two mules in there. It would git crowded turning around with the fences and all that.

But first we got to pull up the collard stalks and tote them out. Somebody's got to set fire to the dried-up butterbean vines on the fence and that will git the grass around the edge of the garden, too.

But the old folks didn't exactly say "garden." Somehow they'd pronounce the word like it had a "U" in it and come up with something that sounded like "guarden." But don't you think that we hep cats of the 30s put a "U" in our gardens. We couldn't stand the way the "old man and the old lady" talked. If there was one thing disgusting to us it was the way our elders momicked up the English language.

Take a pitch fork and spread the fire so the fence will burn off in a hurry, and don't let the fire git away from you. And "far" would be a better word to say in those days than "fire."

Now git in there and break up the ground good. But first let me git some "far" and burn off the grass that grew everywhere during the summer. Heck, burn the whole durn "guarden" over.

Now run the rows and somebody start toting the chicken manure from the henhouse. Best fertilizer in the world fer a "guarden." Tote out the bag of guano too. We want the "guarden" to be rich.

That "far's" done spread to a ditch bank over yonder. Run over there and pick up some dirt and put it out. We'll burn ditchbanks after they've been shrubbed and the mess has dried.

No, no, don't go too near the end of the "guarden." Remember the sage bush and the parsley bed, and the old lady's flower mess at the ends — them big sunflowers at one end and them things that bloom in the fall and always git killed by the frost. Can't think of their name and couldn't say it if I could.

Ridge up the rows now and some of you start knocking off the top of the rows. Then take the end of the hoe and open up a shallow dip all the way down the rows. Mustard and kale have to be planted shallow. Beets too.

Don't ridge up the rows where "guarden" peas are going to be planted. They go deeper in the ground. Then throw the dirt over them sort of shallow with the plow. And plant the corn just like the rows are run.

Git the old lady out here to show us where she wants the cucumbers and mess like that planted. The chicken manure will have to be put nearer the top of the ground where they are planted. Put 'em in one place and she'll be complaining that they ought to have been planted somewhere else.

Don't you young'uns mess with the mustard and kale seed. Or the beets. Let a grown person git them cause they're small seeds.

Look at them butterbeans now and be sure you ain't planting the running ones where the bunch beans are supposed to go. If you plant the running ones there you'll be putting up a fence for them to climb on. Take about three beans and push them down about half an inch in the knocked off row (about this far apart).

Do the string beans the same way. And just drop the corn and take the hoe and cover it.

That young'un hain't put out that "far" on that ditch bank. Run over there and put it out 'fore we have to start fighting "far" stid of planting a "guarden."

And them old turnips that were turned up when the ground was broke ain't fitten to eat now. They're pure pethy. No, they won't hurt you, but they shore can't be good. Look at 'em wiping them off and using their teeth to peel off the skin.

Them mater plants on the backer bed big enough to set out? Run over there and see. If they are we'll just put them out and turn quart jars over them so if frost comes it won't kill them. Got to pull the cabbage plants too. Don't have to worry about a late freeze killing them. We'll set out the collards later.

Don't this dirt smell good? It's like a breath of spring. Time for everything to start budding out too. That mustard and kale will come up in no time and it'll be ready to eat before you know it. Grows fast. Wouldn't some be good right now?

No, we ain't planting "ish taters" in the "guarden." Ain't enough room for them. Takes a whole lot of taters. But it's time to buy the seed taters and we'll plant them in the next week or so.

I just don't see no need of using a row or so in the "guarden" for them whatchamacallit flowers. Zinners? Ain't never heard of nobody eating them. But knowing the old lady, might as well save a row on one edge for that mess. Just ridge up the row and let her look after them. She saved the seed anyhow and you know how she is about flowers. Sometimes I think she ought to be a florist or something, always messing with a bunch of mess that blooms.

Run and git the onion slips and the scallions. Liked to of forgot them. Trim off a stick and punch them down in the ground like a backer plant. Them little roots will give you something to push. Then take the stick and push dirt around them.

Git all the stuff up and growing good and it gives the terrapin bugs and the worms and the grasshoppers something to chew on and us something to fight. First thing you know we'll be painting everything white with Paris Green.

And don't ask me why Good Friday is the ideal time to plant a "guarden." Easter don't come the same time every year and it's weeks apart from one year to the next. But I know that everything I've ever heard about planting "guardens" is that Good Friday is the time they should be planted. And if there comes a freeze and kills the stuff off, we'll just plant it over, like we do anything else that don't come up with a good stand.

And to the best of my recollection, they'd plant things on Good Friday that they'd wait to plant at other times til the moon was right. Presumably they thought Good Friday was the ideal time to plant regardless of the moon or the signs. Uh oh, there's another word with the "U". They'd come up with "reguardless," or that's the way it sounded anyway.

Eating Habits Have Changed

O f all the changes that have come about since the days when I was a young fellow, I can think of none more drastic than the eating habits of Americans. I can make a comparison by my own eating habits, and many of those whom I know.

I think back to breakfast as a boy and the way we ate soon after getting out of bed. I don't know how we ate that much, but I can tell you breakfast was as large a meal as were dinner and supper. There would always be some kind of meat, whether sausage, ham, or fatback. (There was no bacon that I knew of in those days.) There would be buttermilk biscuits (a pan full of them) and rice and preserves or jelly or syrup or molasses, butter, coffee, and I suppose some families drank milk, although mine didn't even want to smell it.

And about those biscuits — nobody that I knew ever rolled out the dough and cut out the biscuits. They'd knead that dough in a deep bread tray and there'd be a good half-a-peck of it, and they'd flour their hands and catch up one end of the dough and cut it off in biscuit size with one hand until they had a dozen or so pieces of dough. They'd take up a piece of dough and roll it in their hands a few times, pat it and place it in the pan, and there wasn't a crack anywhere and they could make a biscuit before you could count to ten.

What do I eat for breakfast today? A bowl of instant grits over which I place a big hunk of margarine, and coffee. And I grew up using two teaspoons of sugar for every cup, and I couldn't stand all that sweetness now. And I did not grow up with grits. I don't know why, for they're considered a country food, but I never remember grits being served at Ma's house. But boy, we ate the rice, although not quite as much as they gobble down in South Carolina. Heck, they sell it by the 100-pound-sack down there.

And with big families and dirt poor, even the syrup would give out sometimes and after all the preserves and jelly were gone, we'd still want something sweet. It was not unusual at our house to see somebody put sugar in his plate and pour coffee over it and sop it with a biscuit. And sometimes we'd take biscuit crusts and put them in a saucer, spread sugar over them, then pour coffee over the mess and eat it like it was cake.

And you know as well as me that if we got fruit mostly at Christmas, there were no glasses of orange or pineapple or apple juice sitting by our plates.

I think about the way gravies are done today and how they used to be, and I can't think of what they call gravy today as being the same thing I used to sop with delight. We used to eat gravy for flavor, but today it's a concoction that has color and texture, but lacking the taste. If you've got to add coffee to ham gravy to make it brown, you ain't kidding yourself when you pour it over eggs or grits or rice. It's as far from ham gravy as the hog's nose is from its tail.

And I know different people had different ways of making gravy. I've read where in some places they'd take plain old fatback and make a thickened gravy — real thick — and eat it with relish. Well let me set the record straight about my crowd. We never ate thickened fatback gravy. We might fish out a spoonful of grease from the pan and put it over our rice, but I feel like I'd almost puke if I ate thickened fatback gravy. But to each his own. If you like it, it's fine with me.

I know when I was a young'un I'd dream about eating some kind of fancy food that I didn't even know what I was thinking about. Anyhow, it was something different than the country diet I grew up on. Maybe I was thinking then about the "lean quisine" diets of today or some of the other fancy foods they have all packaged up that the public is supposed to relish, and I reckon a lot of them do. If that mess was what I was thinking about, I'm glad I didn't get to sample it back then.

To many of today's generation, for food to be good it has to be commercially prepared. And I can understand that. Most of them never knew about what we used to eat and the oven ain't used like it used to be, and when it is, in many cases commercially-prepared food is used. What you don't know don't hurt you.

At lunch time I eat whatever is there, with no plans made in advance to assure a full meal. That has gone on for so long now I don't even think anything about it. But I don't dwell on what was and what ain't now. I became so "sot" in my ways about country cooking so many years ago I've never been able to get it out of my system. I'd rather have the plainest foods, prepared at home and picked at the peak of their perfection than the fanciest meal you could give me at any restaurant of your choice. But millions of people would say I'm a fool and know nothing about culinary art. Good. I'm glad. But I do know my taste buds. I repeat: What you don't know don't hurt you.

But now by the time it's gitting dark, the old craw is getting kinda weak and there's got to be some food put in there. So what do I do? I usually eat something I like, all I want, with a very small menu. I never liked to mix up a lot of mess in my plate at one time and I'd rather have all I want of something good than to have to spread it thin to get in something not all that appealing to me.

I ain't going to worry about how you folks eat. Wine and dine out tonight if you like. And don't be surprised if I'm there too, for I do just that sometimes. I like good food, but I shore don't eat like in the old days. And I don't know of anybody who does. But I do know that some of those good cooks out there are still putting just the kind of food on their tables that I like, for I've eaten at a few of those tables, and what I tasted defies description. It was out of this world.

Easter Party Of Long Ago

I sit here with the ravages of old age setting in, yet letting my thoughts return to my humble beginnings that have kept me humble all my life. I'm thankful for those humble beginnings. I've plodded along down those rough roads that have many times been overcast and storm-filled, yet with many brilliant sunsets and star-filled skies. It has been most rewarding.

Tomorrow is Easter, and it brings to mind an Easter party I participated in when I was a child. That is because it was the most special party I have ever participated in. And that must have been about 1926.

The only way any of you can appreciate this fully is to remember that this happened 59 years ago! And being backwoods young'uns and having nothing of the finer things in life, we were treated to a party that would be as modern today as those that are being given across the nation. It was simply out of this world!

This is how it came about: There was a lady that grew up in the community named Miss Sadie. Now she was married but we

never used Mrs. with a woman's name. We called all of them
"miss." And Miss Sadie married Mr. Bill De Farley. And it don't
take no stretch of the imagination to know that there were no De
Farleys roaming around among those piney woods. We had plain
names.

Well, Miss Sadie De Farley decided to come home for Easter
and put on a party for the neighborhood young'uns. She didn't
have any children of her own. And she lived in Tampa, Florida.
I'm sure she came in on the train, for that was the way of most
long-distance travel in those days. And I'm sure she bought the
things for the party after she arrived.

And Mr. Foy had a pretty stretch of pine woods at the end of the
field behind his house, and that's where Miss Sadie held the party.
There was a lot of pine straw on the ground and not much
undergrowth, so it was an ideal place to have an Easter egg hunt.

Well, Miss Sadie put on the dog. And don't you think for one
minute that there weren't pretty toys and things like that in those
days. It was just the fact that us poor folks didn't have any money
to buy them with. And you've got another thought coming if you
think we had just old hen eggs to use for the hunt. No sir, she had
candy Easter eggs of every color in the rainbow, and plenty of
them.

Course we had some dyed boiled hen eggs too. They used to take
lye soap and rub over the eggs good, then put a piece of some colorful silk cloth that would bleed easily, wrap it around the eggs
and drop them in the pot and boil them and the colors would
transfer to the eggs. And some young'uns just took crayons and
scratched colors on them.

But I ain't even got started yet. There were these little carts to
which rabbits were hitched (toys) and there was all that colorful
shredded, dyed paper in the carts and smaller eggs lying among
the paper. There were Easter baskets with fuzzy baby chicks and
miniature hens and roosters inside (toys also) and little rabbits.

There were large Easter eggs made from paper that opened in
half, filled with candies (jelly beans as I recall it) and the eggs
had that fancy, lacy stuff where they opened. There were choco-
late-covered marshmallow candies in the shape of animals.

But one of the greatest treats was the fishing at the well. Mr.
Foy had a well in his front yard and Miss Sadie had taken backer
twine and attached it to celluloid toys and they dropped down in
the water. There was a string for every young'un, and you can
imagine the excitement as we gathered around the well curb
holding our strings until we were told to pull them up. And we had

to put down our other goodies while we pulled the strings from the well.

There were little boats, frogs, alligators, fishes and other toys and we were thrilled beyond description with our catches until we went back to our other treasures. Some of them were gone, or we got the wrong ones. And there was one of everything for each young'un. But heck, there was enough to go around even with a little bit gone.

We spent the entire afternoon at the Easter party and there has never been a more excited bunch of young'uns. It was as colorful as it would be today. There was a variety of things to play with. We'd get wash basins or tin tubs when we got home to float our celluloid toys in. We'd ration out the candy eggs and take special delight in choosing the colors to eat for their flavors. This was better than any Christmas we'd ever known.

And there was no person in the community loved more than Miss Sadie that Easter weekend, not even Miss Lillie, our Sunday school teacher.

It's still amazing to me how Miss Sadie was able to put on such a party during those hard times. But she and Mr. De Farley ran an employment agency in Tampa, and they shore must have got a lot more jobs for people than were available in eastern North Carolina in those days. That woman spent a lot of money on that party too. I'll bet she spent at least $10 or $15 for all that stuff. By comparison, I'll bet the same things would cost a minimum of $200 today.

It was a party I have remembered all my life, and I'll bet every one of the others who attended can remember it too.

But my feet are killing me, even sitting down, and here I am telling about things from another lifetime when I should be wondering whether I'll make it to the car. The ravages of old age!

S ince I work inside today, I am not exposed to the winds as in the old days. But when they blow hard like they have done recently, I still feel like there is some foreign object in my eyes. And everybody that lived out in the open in those days must have the same feeling.

I can still see us with eyes half-shut, running for somebody that could see a little better than us, asking them to get a piece of trash out of our eyes. If there were a clean pocket handkerchief around, they'd take a corner and make it as small as possible and put it in the eyes (and that didn't feel good either) and they'd work it around and usually come up with the culprit — a tiny piece of leaf or a grain of sand or something. And if it was the mother doing the probing she'd gather up a corner of her apron and perform the task with it. I tell you, they made use of those aprons and they served many purposes, from gathering the eggs and vegetables to holding their snuff boxes in their pockets, as well as keeping their dresses cleaner.

It was at such windy times they'd put us to threshing the peas that had been tied up in cotton sheets in the barn since early autumn. We had picked the peas from the cornfields where they had climbed on the stalks after eating the green ones and letting the others dry up. Dry peas were a staple in rural homes, and I just wish they'd taste now like they did then.

But I think maybe I go too far in comparing present-day tastes with those of the past. Ain't no way in the world anything could taste as good to an old person as it does to a growing young'un. And our taste buds change also. Just maybe somebody does cook peas "exactly" like they used to. And just maybe somewhere there's the same taste we used to know. But they'd have to get up before day to cook a pot of peas that would taste like those Ma used to cook when I was going to school.

They were cooked in a heavy iron pot and sat on the back eye of the stove and they were still warm when we got home from school. We'd take a passel in a saucer and they were good without anything else, although if there was sausage or side meat or sweet taters we'd eat all of it together, and if not, the peas in their brown liquor were good just so.

But back to threshing peas. We'd take part of the peas out of the full sheet and put them in another and tie it up. Then we'd take a passel in a saucer and they were good without anything else, although if there was sausage or side meat or sweet taters, we'd eat all of it together, and if not, the peas in their brown liquor were good just so.

But back to threshing peas. We'd take part of the peas out of the full sheet and put them in another and tie it up. Then we'd beat on the sheet with a pole or something until the peas came out of the pods. Then we'd open up the sheet and hold the hulls up and the wind would blow them away, leaving the peas in the sheet. And almost always we'd get something in our eyes.

But the way the wind would blow dust and grit over the area, something got in the eyes anyway.

Another thing I've done on a windy day was wash guano sacks. The tow bags were never thrown away, for many uses were found for them — from serving as cotton sacks to toting up watermelons or cantaloupes or other produce from the fields.

And on a windy day the particles of fertilizer left in the bags would get into the eyes sometimes. We'd turn the sacks inside out, then put them in a tub of water and swish them around to get out the remaining guano. Then we'd have to rinse them and hang them on the clothesline, or across a fence to dry.

And it is today just as it has always been. When windy, dry weather prevails, there is always forest fires to deal with. It was not at all unusual to see smoke rising in the distance, consuming many acres of woodsland and smoke gathering in the air and dimming the sun sometimes. I can almost hear the cracking of tree limbs and reed beds and see the gnashing flames as they crept near where people lived. But fortunately, I never remember a dwelling getting destroyed by a woods fire. But plenty of tobacco barns burned down during the curing season. And in those days, when a tobacco barn caught on fire it was always a total loss for there was no firefighting equipment in the country, not even if a house caught on fire.

At such times when there were scattered clouds around and with smoke in the atmosphere, the beauty of the flowering cherry, apple, peach, pear and plum trees was muted. In brilliant sunshine they stood out like paintings on the landscape. But even their patches of color against the drabness of the still-dormant trees failed to liven the spirits when chilly winds blew, and it seemed a pall was over the area.

It was too early for children to pull off their shoes on the way home from school and the water in the creek was too cool for wading. It was an in-between season with very warm days sometimes but with a deep chill at night. Children would play on the side of the house sheltered from the winds, but the way they blew in March and April sometimes, there was no real protection from them.

And carrying a lighted lamp from the front of the house, onto the porch and into the kitchen was almost impossible. The light would flicker and go out, and if darkness had descended there was a trip to the shelf near the stove to get a hard-stemmed match, or fumbling your way back to the mantle in the front room where the match supply was kept.

But we were not dismayed by the winds that blew over our domain, for we knew they would subside and total calmness would prevail later, and we would long for a cooling breeze to make the heat more bearable.

Back Side Of Photograph

I f a picture paints a thousand words, it only captures an instant in time that leaves its image for posterity. A picture can become priceless for those who cherish the image, no matter how inconsequential it may have been in the flash of a second in which it was captured. But the reverse side of the photograph is never exposed.

On page 97 of the "SHARECROPPERS" is a picture of three little children. They show a happiness experienced only by the very young who are without cares or worries or problems and who are able to live life at its fullest.

This picture is of children of the 1930s and 1940s. They are laughing and exuberant and unpretentious. They are rural children, free to explore their world about them and enjoy simple pleasures of their own creation. They show no concern about a depression or bad economic times or problems facing the world. They are filled with happiness.

They are up with the dawn, finding birds fallen from the nest, building toad frog houses when the sand is moist, using their feet to shape the soil, then bringing reality to their creations by placing toads in their new domain. They chase butterflies, fireflies, and flies. They wade in mudholes after the rains. Their minds and their hands are busy and they make work out of play.

They are precious to me, for you see, I have diapered them;

washed the tater ridges from their necks; combed their matted hair.

And no one could know in those happy years that each life was marked for tragedy.

First was Glenda, a red-haired freckle-faced charmer of five. Everybody was her friend. She loved everyone and knew no strangers. She was the youngest of the three, but she participated in all their games. And children in those days created their own entertainment.

They took a piece of tobacco wood and placed a board over it and a child would get on each end and one would jump and the other would become airborne for a moment.

Glenda was on one end and one of the other children on the other. And the board became dislodged somehow and struck Glenda in the mouth. It knocked several teeth up in the roof of her mouth. She was taken to the doctor and some of the teeth removed. She had apparently overcome the injury, but one night a few weeks later something happened. She began to breathe heavily and was taken to the hospital. Something had happened to her heart. She lived a day or two, but the damage to her heart was too great. And that was before there were antibiotics to treat such injuries. So a young life that had hardly begun was snuffed out in a matter of days.

Second was Janet, oldest of the three. She was a happy-go-lucky child who grew into a caring adult. She entered nursing school upon graduation from high school, and became a very efficient nurse and worked for years in the obstetrics department of two local hospitals. She married and had a son whom she worshipped.

Five years ago she lost her life as a result of a tragic house fire at her home. She was 45 at the time of her death.

Third was D.C., the clown of the three. As a young child — 4 or 5 years old — he would pretend he was a lion and mimic the mannerisms of the lion. And he could actually jump from the ground onto the porch on all-fours, a distance of about two feet. He was an outdoorsman and loved to roam the fields and streams and was an explorer of nature.

Before D.C. was old enough to join the Army on his own, he got someone to sign for him, and joined the Army and was sent to Germany. But his Army experience was total disillusionment, for he had an accident while there that cost him his legs. He jumped onto a train that was charged with electricity from an overhead wire, and the high voltage almost cost him his life.

The Army sent his father to Germany to be with him and in time D.C. was able to be transferred to Walter Reed Hospital in

Washington, D.C. where his legs were amputated and he was fitted with artificial limbs. It was almost a miracle that he survived the ordeal. But not too long after returning home he was married and in time became the father of four fine children.

After D.C.'s accident, life was difficult for him at best, but he made the best of the situation, although there had to be a lot of loneliness associated with his life. There was also depression and a feeling of hopelessness at times.

There were high points and low points in his life and he suffered in many ways as a result of the accident in Germany. Life was never a bed of roses for him after the accident and he was forced to give up many activities that had meant much to him. But for the most part, he was cheerful and became a dedicated father and husband and gained a new perception of life. He had a nice home and a workshop where he made pieces of furniture and other items.

But on Good Friday he suffered a massive heart attack and died instantly at the age of 47. Although he died from natural causes, an accident in Germany could have contributed to his death.

Strangely, all three died during the Easter season, either a few days before or a day or two after. The oldest was born in 1936, the second in 1938, and the third in 1939.

There is no need to question the wisdom of God where life and death are concerned. There is no answer as to why some families experience such tragedies while others do not. Glenda was only a baby, and Janet and D.C. were middle-aged. Two boys were born in later years and both survive. But three out of five children of my brother next to me in age have paid the supreme price. And tragedies are not new, but for three children in one family to experience different tragedies is unusual.

It is finished. All that is left are memories. It is well that the back side of the photograph was not exposed. But Janet, Glenda and D.C. will always live on the pages of "SHARECROPPERS" showing happy, laughing children during the innocence of childhood.

Tobacco Barns Tell Stories

T hey are everywhere in eastern North Carolina — old, decaying tobacco barns — only eyesores as the rural area becomes modern with large, handsome homes and landscapes. They are remnants of a past whose only claim to a former era are the barns, and old, uninhabited houses that appear to be waiting for a wind to strike them and scatter them into oblivion or nature to complete its process by returning them to dust to make room for the new.

Although they are of a general structure, there are many variations as to exterior finish. Some are tin — all rusty — some plywood finish, but many with rubber roofing as an exterior insulator. There are even old log barns. They serve no useful purpose today, for most tobacco barns today are in keeping with modern farming methods and bulk barns have become the trend of the day. It isn't unusual to see a group of bulk barns with the outdated, humble structures of a former era forming part of the landscape.

None of the "now generation" knows anything about the history of the old barns that stand forlornly as outcasts from society or that there is a story behind them. Cross-country travelers perhaps view them as monstrosities sitting lonely and forgotten, and wonder what purpose they served at some time in history.

Little can they know that there was a certain social status associated with many of those old barns and that a part of life was lived around them; that there were times when romance bloomed under a Southern moon with starlit skies during parties held at tobacco barns during the summer months.

For six or seven weeks every summer, most farm activities centered around the tobacco barns, every day to the week. They were storage places at other seasons, but once the barning season arrived, most everyone in the community was involved in putting in green tobacco.

Even before the barning season began, the area around the

barns and looping shelters was chopped clean of weeds and prepared for barning tobacco.

Once the barning season was under way, the looping area became clogged every day with the yellow leaves of tobacco that were thrown out during the stringing process. Suckers that had been pulled off in the fields along with the tobacco leaves became a part of the refuse at the looping shelters. At the end of the day there was no sign of neatness around the looping horses. But the area was raked and swept clean for the beginning of the next day's work. There was some tidiness at tobacco barns during the curing season — maybe more than in most homes during that particular season.

Then during the several days (and nights) of curing the leaf each week, poking four-foot lengths of wood in the furnaces and keeping the heat in the 180-degree range after the tobacco had yellowed at low heat, someone was on constant duty, and many times there were two or more barns to attend to.

It was almost like an outdoor home during the summer. Bunks, or tobacco trucks were used as sleeping quarters, covered with old quilts for a little comfort. And there were a broom and rake around to keep the premises neat, giving the appearance of being lived in.

Those old tobacco barns served their purpose well. They were gathering places for youth sometimes when teen-age boys were given the chore of curing tobacco. They were ideal places for poker games with flickering lanterns providing the light. They were good places for young fellows who imbibed to get a fifth of moonshine whiskey and tell lies and sing and cut the fool. There was a little bit of "carrying on" too.

But there was more to the tobacco barn story. Chicken fries were popular at tobacco barns during the 1930s and 1940s. Community girls would plan a chicken fry, almost always on a Saturday night, and they would bring the fried chicken, deviled eggs, pickles, cakes and other foods, and sometimes homemade ice cream was turned at the tobacco barns.

Practically every teen-ager in the community would be there and games were played and girls and boys paired off and took strolls down the paths or star-gazed from their perches on tobacco trucks. It was a romantic setting that could be appreciated even by today's youth.

All of you old enough to remember that era, think back to a time when you attended a party at a tobacco barn. There were the cloth-laden tobacco trucks with the lanterns casting shadows over the scene, fireflies lighting up around you, the smell of cured tobacco, wafts of perfume from some flowering plant, pretty girls, yearning boys and a warm night.

And the watermelon parties! Sometimes a farmer had to replace a tobacco truck with a new one — painted bright green — and although it would stand out like a sore thumb it was utilized as often as possible. Picture that splash of color with large watermelons placed on the trucks and ripped open with a long butcher knife, showing deep red melon with rows of black seeds. Plus the sweetness of the melons and everyone biting into the fruit and getting juice all over their faces. Clean clothes and bare feet and summer! What more could life hold?

There were the "rosen ears" thrown in the furnace as they came from the field to cook and the sweet taste of the corn and the juice oozing from the grains when it was eaten. There were the mature ears, shucked and silked and hung on strings over the fire to brown for eating. And apples were hung by their stems attached to a string over the fire until they were brown and juicy.

Those were among the joys of summer and part of the nostalgia associated with a past — gone forever from the face of the earth.

But not every tobacco barn was used for the purposes mentioned. The barns near the homes were those used for parties and barbecues at the end of the curing season. Those far back in the fields and along the marshes stood lonely even then and tobacco curers in the back fields heard owls that hooted and screeched in the night and saw lizards that played around the barns and the lonely howls of dogs somewhere in the darkness to contend with. There were also tales of lights that rose from graveyards to think about.

Like other things from a former era, the old barns are cast-offs, eyesores, detractors from a modern age. But the stories are there, unspoken and unknown by much of the world of today. The barns, too, will succumb and in time be forgotten, as everything is eventually forgotten.

Making Hominy In Washpot

I t was about this time of the year that our mothers of the past out in the sticks used to make wash pots full of hominy. But there had been some advance planning before the fire was built around the pot.

Ma sent us young'uns to the barn when we had caught up from other chores to get the corn she wanted. Every ear had to be almost perfect, with solid grains except for the end that would be shelled off anyway. So we had to shuck a lot of corn to get just what she wanted.

Once in a while we'd find a red ear of corn, and that always pleased us. Somehow, it seemed like it was good luck to find a red ear, and boy! We needed all the good luck we could get. But we didn't put that ear in with the hominy corn, not that it would have mattered, for the lye put into the tub ate off the outer shell anyway. Nevertheless, only white or yellow corn was used.

After we got the amount of corn we thought Ma wanted, we had to shell off the very ends of the grain. We'd take a corn cob to shell off the end grains. Corn can be shelled with the hand, but it sure can hurt if you try to shell it without a cob. We'd take a bucket and place the corn in it and get outside the barn and shell off the grains and all the chickens stood waiting for their morsels. They'd even come up from the rye fields when they realized handouts were in progress.

And about this time of year we were having fits to go barefooted and get out of those long union suits. We'd beg Ma to let us pull off our shoes, knowing full well that mamas in those days had a date set for going barefooted and pulling off long-handles — the tenth of May. They said that was the date leaves on the trees were grown and that we could safely shed those heavy union suits then, and put our bare feet on the ground, and not nary day before.

Truthfully, I don't think there was the extreme temperatures in those days that we find today. In remembering, it seems that there really was a time of spring for us to get acclimated to the changes in seasons. I don't ever remember temperatures in the 90s in April back then, although that is a possibility. Heck, people go barefooted almost any time now, but as has been said many times, things sure have changed since the old days.

We'd get around Ma's coattail and tell her our feet were killing us, that we had blisters and all that mess, and we'd pull our hair up from our foreheads and tell her we were sweating with the heavy union suits on, and she'd finally get tired of all that mess and push us off and give us a slap to boot. But young'uns didn't win in those days.

After we got off the nubbin ends of the corn, we'd start shelling the rest of the ear for hominy. And some folks had corn-shellers and if so, shelling was easy. But if there was no corn-sheller, we utilized the corn cob and shelled all the corn with it. Corn cobs sure came in good in those days!

And just as sure as the world, some young'un had to go to the store for a box of lye. It took so much lye in the wash pots to clean those nasty clothes there was no extra supply around the house. We'd tote water from the well and fill the tub of corn with water, and Ma would sprinkle the amount of lye she wanted over the corn and there was a waiting process of a day or two until all the husk was eaten from the grains of corn, leaving a swollen, white seed.

The corn had to be removed from the tub and placed in more clean water where it sat another day or two to soak out the lye. It required several rinsings before the corn was ready to go to the wash pot. Then we had to rake up chips on the woodpile and get a fire started around the pot.

We'd try to get out of doing whatever we could, but young'uns had to pull their load, too, in those days and if we were rolling wheels or looking for crawfish holes or swinging under the towering oak, Ma would holler and we would come a running.

Ma would stand there with the soap paddle and stir that corn while it was cooking and us young'uns had to rake up more chips as they were needed while the pot was boiling.

There was enough hominy to feed an army, and back then there wasn't a large menu to choose from, and whether you liked hominy or not, it might be the main course (for several days) so you ate hominy (or did without).

And the Lord knows I never really liked hominy. Ma would sort of fry it. She'd put it in a heavy pan, add some fried meat grease and cook it up, and it always seemed like something that had all the taste cooked out of it. It was a filler, and nothing more as far as

I was concerned. It was more edible if there was ham gravy to pour over it.

I was always glad when hominy season came and went, and when it came time to shed those worn-out shoes and those dingy long-handles. We had it made then for several months and felt free to breathe and and be ourselves without the clothing requirements the rest of the year.

Pegging Out Tobacco

A long the path on the edge of the field lush growth has appeared. Wild cherry trees are filled with unripened fruit. Pull a leaf and put it in the mouth and there is a bitter taste when the stem is broken by the tongue.

Miniature peaches hang heavily on a tree a little way in the field. Briers in the thicket are in bloom, with their white blossoms adding a touch of color to the scene, along with wild strawberries that have little berries beginning to turn red.

Poison ivy and poison oak send out their runners across the path, awaiting their victims. A few pines in the thicket whisper their secrets to other species around them. Birds sing in the trees and pitch in the fields to gather insects for their babies. It's the path leading to the tobacco field.

The soil is dry. Tobacco has to be replanted. With some 25 percent of the transplanted plants dead in rows, new plants must replace them. The farmer can't afford a 25 percent loss of his tobacco crop if it can be helped. And even after getting a stand of tobacco, there are blue mold and black shank to contend with.

Nothing is better for replanting tobacco than a wooden peg, usually made from a fat lightwood knot, smoothed down so it fits comfortably in the hand (until the peg is pushed into the soil for a while, after which the entire process becomes uncomfortable).

Barrels of water have been trucked to the field and each person takes a bucket of water and a basket of plants and a hand peg and begins work. And there lies the dead plant that couldn't get a start to form roots and generate new growth. But don't give up just because the plant looks dead from the outside. Sometimes underneath the dead leaves there is a green bud. If that is so, remove the dead part of the plant, scratch around the bud and give it a drink of water, and it will come out.

When the soil is dry, the hole made by the peg often fills with dirt as soon as the peg is removed, and another round of punching is necessary in order to be able to get the plant in the soil.

The back soon becomes tired and workers stand and exercise a little to relieve the strain, and wipe the sweat from their faces. The sun has become hot in the fields and dirt absorbs heat and the waves come up in the face when stooping down.

The throat becomes thirsty and the mouth dry, but the water in the barrels is not fit for drinking. In most cases, it comes from the creek where dead animals are sometimes found, where toad frogs frolic and snakes often slide into the water.

A hill of bear grass stands three or four feet tall with its wiry leaves protecting it from human hands. It has blossomed out with scraggly flowers at the top. Maypops have already come up on the tobacco row and are beginning to run in the middle. Cow witch vines have made their appearance also.

The palm of the hand becomes sore from the peg, and a rag or handkerchief is wrapped around the peg for a cushion. Water is getting low in the barrels and a trip must be made to the creek to replenish the supply. Tobacco plants are also giving out.

There is a return trip to the plant bed to pull more plants (and more stooping). The sun is bearing down and the temperature in the fields feels warmer than the thermometer shows. The stomach begins to growl and there is hunger. But work continues until the neighborhood bell tolls, letting the people know it is time for dinner (as if they didn't know by their own feelings).

There is the respite from work, the food and tea, and a few moments of midday sleep and a soreness in the back from all the bending. The leg muscles also feel sprained.

The wind blows and dust rises in the fields. The task seems interminable and the field seems to grow. There are many more rows to be replanted.

There won't be enough time in one day to put out all the plants. It's hot and dry, but then it's like that every year after tobacco is transplanted. It seems that tobacco-planting time dries up the soil and sends the rain clouds to areas that don't need the moisture.

More water has to be brought and more plants pulled. It's a relief to back the wagon down to the water's edge and dip a bucket into the creek and hand it to the person on the truck, and let a little of the water trickle down the clothing as a coolant. Minnow bugs play on top of the water at the edge of the creek where green scum has accumulated and a frog among the foliage jumps from the bank into the water that creates little ripples on the creek. A fishing line caught in a brush lies on the other side of the creek along with a snuff box in which earthworms were dug and used for bait.

The sun begins to glow red in the west and a day filled with hard work is coming to an end. A lot of hills of tobacco have been transplanted and there is a prayer in the heart that rain will come soon to give life to the fragile plants.

And that's the way we used to do every year about this time, a week or two after tobacco had been set out.

Carts Used To Be Popular

How many of you old codgers that used to walk around those fields a thousand times following an old mule, breaking up the land, running rows, siding cotton, corn and backer, had to mess with an old cart, too? And mention of the word "cart" brings the "U" into play again, just as they used a "U" in garden. The old folks said the word like "cuart" and that's the way I'm going to use it, too.

I'll tell you one thing: If you rode on an old cuart long enough you felt like your goozle had been shook down to where your stomach ought to be. Of all the mess we rode on back there, an old cuart had to be the worst.

A cuart is cumbersome to start with, with nothing movable on the dern thing except the big, heavy wheels. If a mule had to turn around in a close place while hitched to an old cuart, he had to go sideways and that tore up the dirt and anything else that was in its way. I think if I'd a been a mule I'd a bucked when they put me between those two cuart shafts that are an extension of the body.

But just about every farm had a cuart and it was put to use a lot more than you might think. It did have one advantage, or some of them did anyway. They would dump and the tailboard could be pulled out and the dump tripped and whatever the cuart was loaded with could be dumped at one time. It is a one-horse contraption, and it is convenient to use such a vehicle sometimes in place of the two-horse wagon (and there were one-horse wagons, too).

But an old cuart ain't level and the front is hiked up and standing up in one ain't comfortable either. Ever try hauling a barrel of water with a cuart? The barrel is sitting at about a 20-degree angle and you can leave a lot of room at the top of the barrel, but once that old mule gets to pulling the cuart every step he makes jolts the vehicle and water splashes. If you're taking water to the backer patch, or to the field where you're putting out tater slips you ain't got enough to water a row. But I guarantee you that we used to haul water on that old cuart.

You can't put a plank across the cuart body to sit on, for it slides down and you can't make yourself comfortable no way you turn. And if you have to haul corn to the mill to be made into meal, you've got a three or four-mile trip and you're tarder when you git there than if you'd walked. Only good thing about hauling the corn is that there ain't no trouble unloading it. Just slip the tailboard out and the corn rolls out because of the slant of the vehicle.

And if you want to make a woman mad, put her to traveling on an old cuart and she'd git riled up before you had gone a hundred yards. They had to sit down backwards and let their legs go straight in front of them and there was the constant bump when the mule walked. It wouldn't a never done to git a "setting" of eggs from a neighbor and put them in a cuart to haul home. They'd a been shook up so bad everything that was intended to be a biddy would be out of place and there would have been a bunch of rotten eggs at the end of the three-week incubation period.

We used to use the cuart sometimes to haul backer plants from the plant bed to the field. We'd take the big basket that was used in the barn to pack shucks in and load it down with plants and sling that basket and get it on the wagon and high-tail it across the fields and down the paths to the backer patch.

But don't never do one thing with a cuart. Don't never go in a guarden, for if you do, by the time you've turned that thing around there won't be a hill of beans or corn or whatever might be in its path left. It will be squshed into a pulp by those old cuart wheels.

And gitting the hub caps off to grease those rascals is a heck of a job. Somebody's got to back up to the wheel and use all the manpower he's got to git it up off the ground. And who's got a wrench that will fit the hub cap? We shore didn't, so we'd take the hammer and beat the cap loose so we could rub that black axle grease over the end of the axle, then slip the wheel back on and beat the hub cap until it was tight again.

We used to haul up watermelons on the cuart sometimes too, and you had to be careful, for they were at the very back and you had to lift all of them over the tailboard. If it had been lifted they'd have tumbled out and every one busted. Backer trucks were not good for hauling up watermalons and cantaloupes and "mush melons" either unless boards were nailed around the rounds to hold the melons on the truck.

As to convenience, backer trucks were far better than old cuarts. You could git on a truck and let your legs hang off the side and several people could ride the mile or more from the field to the house after a hard day's work so they'd feel a little rested by the time they ate supper and would feel like messing around a little after dark. If you think we let a hard day's work keep us from a little playing at night you've got another thought coming. It is surprising how a young person can recuperate from being tired so quickly and feel like painting the countryside red after the stars come out.

I've ridden on stalk-cutters, disk harrows, hay rakes, log cuarts, wagons, and those old dump cuarts, and I can tell you that the worst of the pack was them old cuarts.

Home Is Where The Heart Is

A catbird sings in the big oak tree that shades the porch and a sparrow disappears in a tiny hole in the eaves of the house with a blade of grass to add to its nest.

When the door is opened, there is a clean smell from scoured floors. The wide boards appear bleached and the nail holes show. Glass-covered pictures of ancient ancestors hang on the hall walls over an old trunk on one side and the sewing machine on the other, along with a calendar.

Winter is past and the feather beds have been taken to the back-room closet for storage until fall. And the mattresses show lumps under the "county pins." Although there are more felt mattresses now than those filled with straw, both are still in evidence. And the straw mattresses may be more comfortable than those filled with felt, for age has worked the material into lumps and they can be uncomfortable until the body works itself into them and sort of gets them out of the way. Straw is less lumpy, but if the ticking is worn or torn and straw sticks through, it sometimes pricks the skin.

The fireplaces have been whitewashed with a lime solution where soot darkened the bricks. Fire screens have also been covered and placed over the fireplace. Colored pages from catalogs and old calendars have been pasted on the screens, using flour as a base, mixed with water. A breeze comes in through the open windows, allowing flies to enter the house and occasionally a wasp or dirt dauber. Curtains push inward from the wind and clothes hanging on nails in the bedrooms show movement.

The baby's cradle is in the path of the breeze, covered with tobacco-cloth netting, where the baby sleeps during a lazy afternoon.

From the back porch, there is an odor of chaney ball blooms wafting in the breeze. It is serene, with the well bucket hovering over the center of of the well and the shaft extending 12 or 15 feet in the yard.

The earth smells sour around the shelf on the back porch, where water is dashed in the yard after faces and hands are washed. The towel shows soil after all the hand-wiping and there are finger marks on the "looking glass" that hangs over the towel. The sun is bright and the crops are green.

Chickens have been on the porch and water must be poured in places to clean up behind them. Clucking hens find insects for their brood and call them up to reap the reward. A hawk flies overhead and the hen sounds an alarm and biddies flock to her for protection.

The cow is staked out behind the barn where the grass has grown rank, and she has wound the chain around the stob and is unable to make the full circle until the chain is untangled.

The dining room table is covered with a white cloth to protect the food from the flies. The mustard and kale left over from dinner has been smoothed over the bowl and the ish taters are lying in their liquor in another bowl. Meat left from dinner is in a plate surrounded by grease and the pieces of fat that were cut off but not eaten. But biscuits and corn bread will have to be cooked for supper. The vinegar cruet and the jar of hot pepper, along with the salt and pepper shakers, make the centerpiece of the table.

The side table in the kitchen has been cleared with all the dinner dishes washed and the table reset for supper, with the plates placed face down. The pot liquor has been poured into the slop bucket, and there are bubbles at the top. The slops will be sour by the time they are taken to the hogs.

The oil cloth looks bad, almost shameful, with several holes cut through and all the corners worn. There is no longer any smell of the cloth that is so strong when a new one is bought and placed on the dining room table. The kitchen table is like a second child: it never gets a new cloth but gets the cut-down version from the dining room table.

The stove-wood box is almost empty and the smallest children will have to fill it when they get home from work. Split wood is beginning to get scarce on the wood pile and the larger boys will have to get out there and split more when they catch up in the fields.

But the kitchen is about the nicest place of all. It is the place where you can go to play after dark with the grown folks out of the kitchen. A lighted lamp on the side table and places to hide make it a child's paradise.

And on rainy days in summer when a coolness lingers in the air and the bones get chilled, to get behind the stove when a fire is going gives warmth and smugness and a haven from the rains. To snuggle up beside the reservoir filled with hot water drives away the chill and makes the children happy. Once they have thawed out, they will go right back to the porch, hold their heads out so the rain from the porch roof will wet their heads and get their clothes soaked again. Then there will be another visit behind the stove.

The kitchen is also the place where they fill tubs with water and bathe and splash water everywhere. But they know before getting their baths that if water is spilled they will have to take rags and get it up.

It's home in the sticks, a haven from the rest of the world, where a family gathers and lives and dreams and hopes, sheltered from all the harshness of life. It's the same as if it were a mansion. There is no difference. It is home in every sense of the word, and a hallowed place in the hearts of people.

A home scene from long ago.

A 30-Minute Time Span

A thirty-minute time span distinguishes this generation from all those that preceded us.

In the days of yore when we were working in the fields, the sun seemed to hang in the skies and we'd plow up and down rows, or chop, or sow soda, and after a few rounds we'd glance at the bright light in the sky and it appeared to be stuck in space.

Younger writers of today say we "scratched" out a living, giving the mental impression of a hen scratching for her biddies in a fresh-plowed field. But we also took pride in our accomplishments. When a field of waist-high corn was plowed and the blades were gourd-green and swaying in the wind, we looked upon our handiwork and felt good about it. The same was true with tobacco lapping in the middles, freshly topped and appearing perfectly smooth over a large field.

There is no way to compare the past with the present. All of us know that today's youth have everything we didn't have. It is amazing how many young people own cars, have their own bank accounts, attend college, entertain, visit the beach on a regular basis, buy expensive clothes and do a thousand things we never thought about, for most were non-existent in those days.

With the exception of farmers, who are growing smaller in number every year, people don't have to work in the fields anymore. And some of those that drive tractors today are in air-conditioned comfort. Some of them help in harvesting tobacco, or maybe I should say all of them, but a lot of hard work is done by aliens who come across the Mexican border and move across the nation doing all manner of menial work that us sharecroppers used to do.

We were exactly what the younger generation would call us — ignorant, poor, uneducated, deprived, completely out of the mainstream of life — trying to cope with an impossible situation. But the redeeming factor with us was that we weren't aware of our plight. What you may consider to be totally abnormal was a way of life with us.

Hard work was no real problem. We were conditioned to our environment, and our free time was spent without worries or cares. If that sounds impossible, it is true. Our minds were at ease and trying to pay out of debt each year and have a few dollars left was our major goal. We could go to bed at night with nothing on our minds. And we slept, despite the lack of air-conditioning in summer and central heat in winter; flies; bedbugs and croaking frogs. We were tough.

Don't worry. You will never have to wear gummy overalls from crapping backer, never have to pull fodder and bale hay and cure tobacco at night. Technology has taken care of those things for the farmer to a great extent, and those ways have faded with time.

The youth of today have reaped the rewards of a computerized world and technological advance. You have inherited the best the world has to offer. But there is a price to pay. Among your other inheritances:

There is enough federal debt hanging over our heads today your grandchildren will be burdened for their lifetimes, and no telling what will be added to that debt.

Your new homes are costing you four or five times more than ours cost (after World War II). Your monthly payments are more than our yearly earnings were in those days in most cases.

The Social Security Act was passed in 1933, when I was 15 years old. And farmers didn't come under the Act for years. In the workplace we paid pennies. And what do you pay? Ha! You're paying through the nose now, and you ain't seen nothing yet. It's all cut out for you, and you're already wondering whether there will be a dime for you when you reach retirement age. You're paying for those who are receiving benefits now and it's enough to make you want to shed your "designer" everything and git a pair of overhalls and go out in the sticks and forget the whole dern thing.

And now to the thirty minutes that separate the generations born since World War II from all those that preceded them.

Thirty minutes was a long time for us farmers when we were plowing in the fields and waiting for the quarter-to-twelve bell to ring for us to go to dinner. It was hot and we were wet with sweat and our guts were growling and we wanted "some'n t'eat." And if we wanted to go some place at night, and the meeting was at 7:30, we had to plan in advance for that. We couldn't go by the sun and make it on time.

But thirty minutes today has a different meaning. If an itchy hand or a wrong signal came through, or an irate leader decided to call the shots, thirty minutes would be all the time required to cause annihilation of the human race.

Just think. In a thirty-minute time span all the manmade advances throughout history could be dissipated in one push of a red button. All the towering structures, all the interstate highways, all the malls and shopping complexes, universities, computers, homes, businesses, art works, farms, dams, parklands, schools, bridges, cathedrals — all of civilization wiped off the map almost — with any remaining alive awaiting a worse death from the effects of radiation.

These are the things you have inherited. They will be with you for as long as you live. There is no escape.

We had the promise of tomorrow. Thirty minutes makes a great difference today.

Remembering Tragedy On Road

U. S. Highway 13 near Snow Hill, N.C. was the scene of a tragic accident in 1985 that resulted in the deaths of six Greene County students and the driver of a truck that struck the school bus. It made national headlines. And it was along the same highway in Wayne County that I grew up.

I remember well when the road was paved from Adamsville, a couple of miles out of Goldsboro, to Snow Hill. Cap'n Hinnant and his crew had a tent city in a field in my neighborhood, from which the paving operation was carried out.

I think the road was paved in 1923 or 1924, and at that time there were no power lines or telephone poles after you turned off at Adamsville down through Greene County. People who needed to use a phone to call a doctor or carry on other business had to go to Adamsville, some five miles away.

There were also a lot of branch roads leading from Highway 13, and it was along many of those roads that I lived my life as a youth in Wayne County.

There was little sign of affluence along the roads, even on the main road that was paved. Of course some homes had been painted, but in most every case the paint was faded. But those homes were the best in the community. One sign of affluence that always got the public's attention were lightning rods. When they were on the roof of a house, you thought in terms of affluence, even though we weren't even aware of the meaning of affluence.

But there were many pleasant surroundings as you traveled along the roads. A house might be sitting a good ways from the road, with a lane leading to the building and rows of trees on each side. There would be a spacious yard and a large barnyard and all manner of farming implements could be seen around the premises with shaded yards, no grass growing, and mules sometimes standing in lots or poking their necks over the boards to nibble at greenery on the outside.

I remember so well how it used to be if a man were working in a field near the road and a woman passed by, he tipped his hat as a gesture of honor to the female of the species. This was a general practice. Does anybody ever see this today?

Then there were the shanty-type houses with their shed rooms with pillows and feather beds out on the porches sunning, flea-hounds lying on guano sack mats on doorsteps and windows plugged with rags or pasteboard where panes were broken out.

When we used to go to town on automobiles we went the "scenic" route, via Adamsville and then to Goldsboro on Highway 70. One of the most picturesque scenes during my boyhood was the Spence dairy between Goldsboro and Adamsville. There was a wooded pasture with a stream and a lot of spotted and black cows lingering among the trees in warm weather with some drinking from the stream. And on the other side was the Orphan Home farm that stretched to the Ball Park Service Station. I thought of this area as being a utopia composed of filthy rich people, and there were handsome homes as you approached the city.

When we went to town on the wagon, we drove over to the Saulston-Goldsboro road and entered Goldsboro from that direction. There was a lot of traffic on the highway between Adamsville and Goldsboro, and driving a wagon on that stretch of road was hazardous. Half-a-century later, travel is more hazardous on the Saulston-Goldsboro highway than from Adamsville to Goldsboro.

But there was one outstanding house on the back road to Goldsboro. It was the home of Mr. Edmund Cox, and it was a fine place even then. It was also snow white and there were large grounds and I thought of it as people would think of Monticello today. Mr. Edmund's home was far ahead of its time and if it still stands would appear modern in today's world.

Mr. Edmund was an influential man in Wayne County, and I believe he served on the Selective Service Board during World War II.

The route along Highway 13 has changed drastically over the years, and it no longer has the typical rural flavor of the past. Homes are everywhere and some are handsome and expensive. It doesn't look like the same highway I remember being paved so many years ago. It was total excitement while Cap'n Hinnant and his crew were living in their tent city nearby. I recall row after row of tents with floors four or five inches off the ground and walkways between the rows of tents. I have no idea what type of labor was used in paving the highway. I don't recall seeing any convicts and certainly none in chains or striped suits worn by convicts in those days. And there was no fence around the encampment.

As to our trips to town along the "scenic" route, we took the old road leading to Goldsboro. Along that road was the pocosin, and the crossing that is New Hope crossing today, where Jennings Restaurant is located. There was Mr. John Worrell's home along the railroad tracks, and at the turnoff to Adamsville Mr. Senas Davis' home. But there were very few residences from the railroad to Adamsville where Berkeley Square Mall is located today. That was open land and the soil had a salt-and-pepper look, with a lot of sand mixed with the darker soil.

To my knowledge there has never been a tragedy comparable to the school bus-truck accident along that segment of Highway 13. People have occasionally been killed on the highway, and two young boys were killed on bicycles on Highway 13 in my area.

There are many remembrances of my life as a youth along the highway leading from Adamsville to Snow Hill.

A long time ago when the summer sun beat down and crops wilted and folks prayed for rain; when young'uns too little to work walked on "tomwalkers" and made themselves six feet tall and mud pies lay drying in the sun, somebody would say something about making ice cream. And they might have said the end of the world was here for all the excitement it created.

Right then a young'un would run to the house and ask Ma if they could make ice cream that night. And Ma would hum and haw and say it was too much trouble and made too big a mess, and naw, there won't going to be no ice cream. Then the young'un would nuzzle up to her, lay his head in her lap and look up with eyes sadder than a Bassett hound's, and she'd say she would see about it.

So Ma would git up and go to the egg basket to see whether there were enough eggs to buy the ice and go in the cream too. Heck, they put six or eight eggs in a six-quart freezer. Then she'd go to the milk safe to see whether there was enough milk and the sugar bucket to check on the sweetener. And if all the ingredients were sufficient, that night after supper they'd make a freezer of ice cream and turn the freezer out on the woodpile so the salty water wouldn't hurt nothing.

A few scraggly plants came up among the chips, but they ought to have been cut down anyway. I think we used to call one of the tall, spreading weeds that grew in such places "gypsum weeds" but I ain't sure that's what they were. We didn't go around labeling plants by their botanical names in those days. We called them whatever we liked. Anyhow, those old plants looked something like a poke berry bush except they had white flowers, kind of long like blooms on cow witch vines.

And you know that everybody that worked in the fields was thrilled at the idea of ice cream, 'specially it being during the week.

And that meant going out to the smokehouse, or the shed and digging out the freezer from the cobwebs and spider webs, and gitting down the turning apparatus and wiping the spider eggs from the shirt and the cobwebs from the mouth.

And they gave that old freezer a washing like you wouldn't believe, with plenty of lye soap suds and a rag. They'd rinse it out (we called it wrench) and turn it bottom upwards on the side table after wiping it out good.

All those eggs were broken and beaten and three cups of sugar added and a tablespoon of vanilla, and it would be brown at the top of the mixture until the flavoring was beaten in. And here somebody comes with the pan of milk with the cream on top, tippy-toeing and trying not to spill it. But look out! There goes a passel of milk on the floor because the pan is tilted. But it's all mixed together and poured in the freezer. And that dasher is washed as much as the freezer, and it is placed in the freezing part and worked around until it fits into the hole and Ma says, "I declare we've forgot the salt." So somebody runs to the smokehouse with a wash pan to scoop up salt. And it works just as well as this ice cream salt you buy at the supermarkets today.

That 15-cent piece of ice is beaten up in a tow sack (and it's melting fast) and they punch that mess down beside the freezer and somebody starts turning. Salt is generously poured over the ice and more added as the ax handle punches the ice down.

'Tain't long til the water begins to rise in the wooden part of the freezer and somebody runs a finger in the hole that turns out the water. And rust is showing at the top where the gears turn the freezer. That thing's getting hard to turn and somebody takes a sack and puts it on top of the freezer and planks down on it and the turner wrestles with the handle and the freezer moves despite the weight.

All the remaining ice is put around the bowl and there ain't none to stack on top of the lid. It wouldn't be left to harden nohow.

And you know as good as me that we didn't have "dishes" as such for ice cream. We had plain old saucers that didn't have much depth to them. And here comes the lid off and uh, oh, there's rust at the top and it has to be dipped off. Then somebody tastes, and durn, they's salt in the mess at the top! All of that good stuff, and some of it wasted. So they start dipping agin. About two good saucerfuls have to be wasted, and they're ready to go. Young'uns eyes look as big as saucers almost, and as soon as they are given the cream they start gobbling it down. It's so good, so delightful, so refreshing it's indescribable. The more you can git in your mouth, the better. But look out!

It hurts some people in the eyes. It hurts others in their foreheads. But wherever, it hurts. And when that coldness gits to you, ain't no way you can eat that ice cream like you want to. And the only consolation you have is that it will hurt the others, too. It used to git me in my eyes. It felt like my eyeballs would kill me.

When the pain struck, you just had to hold off until it went away, and milk was forming in the saucer and there was not time to wait, for everybody wanted all the ice cream they could eat.

The dasher was removed and placed in a bowl and everybody was spooning the ice cream and at the bottom of the freezer where it was harder, and everone wanted some of the hard ice cream.

It was over quickly. A freezer of ice cream among eight or 10 people doesn't last long, especially out in the sticks. Then there's all the mess to clean up. And wouldn't you know, some tow-headed young'un had filled up and gotten off to the side and gone to sleep on the wood pile or in the yard and had to be carried to the house and washed off.

And the skies appeared darker where the trees made their circle around our little world. The stars would be shining and a far-away flash of lightning would lighten the sky for an instant.

It was no big deal. Not even a party. It was just a family making ice cream that might be repeated once or twice during the summer. But it was fun and happened a long time ago.

Hanging Tobacco (Note Turpentine On Tiers)
Courtesy Peggy Dew

Taking Out Cured Tobacco
Courtesy Peggy Dew

Working Green Tobacco At Looping Shelter
Courtesy Peggy Dew

Cropping The Golden Weed In Another Era
Courtesy Peggy Dew

Truck Loaded With Green Tobacco
Courtesy Peggy Dew

Playing On Bales Of Cotton
Courtesy Helen Boykin

Puttin'-In-Backer Time

With blossoms beginning to appear in thigh-high backer, it's time to git the barns ready for another curing season. You can't wait til time to start barning, for a lot has to be done around the backer barns to git them ready for the barning season.

Never knowed how hard weeds could grow so rank around backer barns. Seems like there are more and more of them every year. And them rascals are named right. Even a sharp hoe won't cut them without putting manpower to that hoe handle.

And if you sling the weeds down and leave the stubbles, they'll stick in every foot on the premises before the summer is over. That hurts, too. They make a pure hole in the foot.

And it seems like the looping shelters git more rotten every year. I reckon that's because they're exposed to the elements year round. Even hardwood posts rot off at the ground and have to be replaced, and 1 by 4's that are nailed to the posts to form the looping racks are rotting and have to be replaced, too. The scaffolding that holds the green limbs that are thrown overhead to shade the looping shelters is rotten.

That old barn down by the branch that's sort of tilted is filled with bats, too. They go there every year, and the barn has to be heated for a day or so to git them out. Then some come back after the barn cools off. But when the high heat is put to backer in the barn, that gits rid of them for the year.

Seems like bats are something of the devil the way they look. They don't seem like any kind of animal you ought to come in contact with on earth.

And mortar has fallen off part of the old log barn and it will have to be replaced, for mortar chinks the cracks where heat comes out if left alone. Furnaces have got to be patched, too. There are loose bricks in every one of 'em. If a farmer had the money, he ought to have a brick mason for at least a couple of days to take care of all the things that need doing at backer barns. Instid, he has to do a makeshift job the best he can, for there ain't no money for brick masons.

Cow witch vines have grown completely to the top of the barn nearest the house. They will have to be cut at the roots and pulled off the sides of the barn.

One of the wires holding the smokestack has come loose and more wire will have to be taken to the top of the barn on the outside and fastened to the wood.

Seems like everything has been piled in the backer barns and it will take a day to haul out all the trash so it can be burned.

All this has to be done before you even git into backer barning. Seems like there's just too much to do to backer anyhow. It works you half-to-death almost year round, causes you to lose sleep and your religion too, and apt as not there won't be enough made on it to pay out at the end of the year.

It's too hot to have to go in the loft to find truck curtains, but it has to be done. If they've been used for something else, new curtains will have to be made from guano sacks and sewed together with backer twine. Got to have them curtains to keep the backer on the truck when it's crapped and placed in the truck and while it's being hauled to the looping shelter.

And wouldn't you know the looping horses are shackly, too. Ain't a solid one in the bunch and they'll have to be mended and boards nailed to them to make them solid.

Somebody broke a shade to one of the lanterns, and that will be the hardest thing in the world to remember when you go to town to git twine and a sack or two of lime and cement.

A thermometer has been taken from one of the barns, too. Some young'un has taken it somewhere to check on the temperature during the winter and it's got to be rounded up.

They's a hole in one of the flues at the log barn. Got to check on all the flues anyhow. Shore hope most of them are solid, for them things cost money.

Has the old lady washed out them quilts we use at the backer barns? Couldn't git along without the quilts to place over them hard bunks and backer trucks. Seems like a quilt doubled makes even a hard bunk sort of comfortable.

Got to try to plan puttin' in backer so it will go in the barn the first of the week and killed out by Sad'dy midnight. Don't want to have to be curing backer on God's Day. Sunday is a day of rest, and if you have to poke wood in a furnace on Sunday, you're sinning. Course there are times when it seems to all come off at one time, and you may have to double up and put in more than one time a week, and if that happens you have to try to save the backer and pray that the Heavenly Father will forgive you.

The bedding on one of them backer trucks is pure shackly, and it's got to be worked on. Can't afford to be buying no new backer trucks. Them things would cost $20 or $25 apiece. And that reminds me that there ain't no axle grease and every truck's got to be greased. That's something else that will be hard to remember.

Backer sticks' got to be hauled from the shelter to the backer barns. Might as well git started on that job right away. Put some of the young'uns to hauling sticks and others cutting "swee gum" bushes and hauling them to the looping shelter. Got to patch the scaffolding first, though.

There's so much to do 'fore you start puttin' in backer it's about as bad as when you git out there in them sand lugs. Don't even like to think about that, though. That will separate the men from the boys, and they's too many boys that can't quite be separated into men yit. Just got to do the best we can.

Remembering Childhood

Brighter than moonbeams. Brighter than all the fireflies a child can catch in summer. The brightness emanates from a dull-gray background. It is memories. Memories of childhood.

There is nothing more rewarding than going back in time to the days when we were children, and view it all again. And the gray is more predominant if you grew up far out in the rural area and were very poor.

All the senses are brought into play as scenes are relived. It is like taking a magical journey to a faraway land and recapturing all the beauty lost over the years.

A boy squints his eyes and looks into the distance where the dirt road leads to infinity, and he wonders what is beyond his path of vision. He plays beside the road where sand is plentiful.

A large butterfly glides peacefully around him, getting close enough that he can see the satin-like texture of the wings and the brilliant coloring. He tries to capture the little speck of beauty, but the insect eludes him and flies out of his reach.

Acorns become toys and their symmetry is observed and they become something more than a nut from a tree. They are special for they are a part of his world.

Under his hat, freckles show and perspiration causes dirt to cling to his face, neck and arms.

He watches the cloud formations and marvels as they speed

across the heavens and for a moment he seems to be moving with them.

He is aware of the movement of the air about him. From the tobacco fields comes the odor of green tobacco and his eyes focus on the pink blossoms far in the distance. There is the smell of honeysuckle. Corn silking in the field scatters its odor over the land. He looks across the fields, across the only world he knows, and he is aware even then that a picture has been placed indelibly in his mind that he can recall. He knows the appearance of the sky, the "feeling" of the moment, the beauty of it all seen only in a child's eye.

He walks over to the thicket where a path leads to the garden, and there are wild fern growing, low to the ground and competing with taller growth. Wild flowers shout for recognition among the greenery. A toad frog leaps from the foliage and the boy follows it until it is captured and becomes his plaything.

He hears the wind playing in the pines, whispering to him alone and bringing a soothing sound of the southland.

The wild cherries are calling, small, almost black in their glistening skin. The brierberries are ripe, clustered among the thorns, protecting the fruit that a boy's hand defies.

The shade is inviting under the tall trees. They become a haven from the heat of the sun. And the shadows lengther and the child tries to catch up with his head, but the shadow is always elusive.

There is the call of a bird from afar and vultures soar across the sky and a dog barks and a child cries out in the distance.

The minnows are darting about on the water in the ditch and this invites wading and cupping the bugs in the hand. And there are heavy wild grape vines growing among the trees from which to swing and to pretend you're a Tarzan, even uttering the call as you swing out over the ditch and land up under the trees.

A rabbit darts from the bushes and a young boy begins a chase that is lost before it even begins.

Crawfish holes along the ditch intrigue the boy and he takes a stick and runs it down in the hole, trying to catch the crustacean.

A feeling of great contentment settles over the child. He is in a world he knows something about, a world simple enough to understand, yet mystifying in its bigness.

The day becomes golden with the rays of the sun painting the countryside a different hue as it edges toward the treetops. The boy observes life around the homes as people draw water from the well, women gather clothes from the line and men bring mules home after a day in the fields. The mules linger at the watering trough and swill the cool water and boys head for the barnyard to feed the animals for the night.

The hens with their biddies, the guineas, turkeys, geese and ducks with their goslings edge toward the barnyards and hogs squeal as they await food at the pasture gates. White smoke rises from the kitchen chimneys and hovers over the houses as supper is prepared.

People walk along the roads and become smaller and smaller until they too fade into infinity along a path that appears to lead to nowhere.

There is a hush over the land, except for the songs of the birds that bring a happy conclusion to a pleasant day. Their songs fill the air in the interval between sunset and darkness when the canopy of night hides all the beauty of the day. This sets the scene for nighttime when another beauty takes over.

There are the full moons that show the outline of a sleepy neighborhood in a romantic setting. There are the starless nights when heavy storms shatter the calm for a time, wreaking their vengeance on the area, but providing the rains necessary for fruitful crops.

There are the nights when stars twinkle and cool breezes bring relief to the population and children marvel at the wonders of nature in a simple world uncomplicated by all the problems adults have to contend with. It's childhood, a time to be happy and free without any pretentiousness. It's worth anybody going back in time and remembering.

Canning And Preserving

F ruit's ripening and gardens are coming off. There's a hundred pounds of sugar in the pantry to use for canning and preserving, and it's time to get started on the annual chore. Poor folks depend heavily on canned stuff to tide them over during the winter months.

And even then, it's almost a fight to get that bag of sugar. It's the same story ever year. No money to buy it with. Although the old man and every young'un knows the value of home canning, the old lady has to defend finding the money somewhere to buy sugar for canning and preserving.

The apple tree out in the cotton patch is loaded down and whenever there are a few hours away from the fields, the young'uns tote up tubfuls of apples, old paring knives are sharpened and the old lady and the young'uns get to peeling apples. They just let the peelings drop into the tub, for they will be used to make apple jelly.

Somebody has to go to the smokehouse or the shed room and round up all the jars they can find and wash and rinse them. Lids have to be found and jar rubbers bought. Find all the eggs you can to take to the store to pay for the jar rubbers. No need to put up stuff with old rubbers.

There's another argument about buying peaches. There are peach orchards in the community and canned peaches serve as dessert and everybody loves them. But there's a matter of a few dollars again, and the old lady has to fuss to get somebody to go to the orchard and get a bushel or two of the fruit. Young'uns that might have a dollar or two saved from helping other people put in backer have to dole the money out to Ma so the peaches can be purchased. There is just one time to get them, and that is when they're ripe.

Tomatoes are ripening and corn is coming off as well as butterbeans and peas and everything else in the garden. It's work continually to try to get everything in jars for the winter months.

Bushels of peas and butterbeans are picked in late afternoon and everybody is put to work after supper shelling them. That is, all 'cept them high-and-mighty teen-age boys that high-tail it off somewhere when the first star appears. That makes all the others mad enough to cuss.

The old lady will peel some tomatoes and put them in jars while she is cooking dinner and take them to the backer barn when high heat is running and sit them down on the hot dirt to cook. She might do the same thing to a few jars of peas or butterbeans, too. If not, she places the jars in a big pot of boiling water and lets them cook for an hour or so.

But don't nobody use such canning practices today. I'm talking about half-a-century ago and nothing don't work today like it did then. Such canning would probably kill us now. So go modern if you are canning.

Soup mixture is cut up and placed in the jars and they are either set in the backer barn or boiled in the big pot (in the jars).

The fig bush is checked to see if they are ripening. And since there ain't no grape vine on the premises, there's something else to argue about. But it just won't be right not to have some grape preserves. So when the scuppernongs ripen, there's a trip to a neighbor's house that does have a grape vine and picking the fruit and fighting off the wasps and taking the grapes home and popping the pulps in one pan and putting the hulls in another and cooking the pulps and sifting the juice from the seeds and adding sugar and cooking the preserves.

There's cucumbers to pickle and pepper relish and chow chow to make and there ain't time to eat or sleep hardly.

Was acid put in all the vegetables that were canned? The old lady wonders, for that is something else that has to be bought at the store.

And the space in the dining room where the canned fruit and vegetables and preserves are stacked neatly on the floor is beginning to widen. Despite all the hard work, the old lady looks upon her handiwork with a great deal of pride. She is aware that every person in the house is looking to her to put the vittles on the table three times a day. She has to fuss to get the things necessary to having canned food, and if there isn't plenty of food on the table, they argue at her also. But she has built up a defense against such arguments. She has to do what has to be done, argument or not.

And while all the canning and preserving is going on, she has to prepare meals every day. She is up early, while the dew is still on, gathering vegetables at their very peak to put on the table. She doesn't trust a young'un to pull her corn. They just as soon pull an ear too old as at its peak. She has been warned about pulling field corn to use on the table, but she just laughs at such warnings. She tests each ear, popping a kernel or two to see if it is juicy and milky.

It is the same with all vegetables. She wants them at the peak of their perfection. She scoffs at too-old string beans that have strings on them after they are processed. She wants tender collard leaves and tender squash. Too-old cucumbers are taken to the hog pen.

It ain't easy, planning for a big family, and the first time she hears something funny coming from the dining room and a jar of vegetables is hissing and liquid coming from the jar, she wants to cry. All that work, and then ruined vegetables. Then when she's at some other place in the house and a young'un runs and tells her another jar is working, she does cry. But being the mother, and the one everybody in the house is looking to for food, she can't let it get her down. For every ruined jar of vegetables, she tries to put up another in its place. If everybody else in the house had her fortitude, it would be a lot easier to make ends meet in hard times.

Border Tobacco Markets Open

Once upon a time when the world was younger, but not wiser, people who raised backer as their chief money crop had to do some finaggling to git a little money in their pockets. I tell you, trying to keep a family going and needing a dollar or two as badly as they did, they'd do most anything to git a little pocket change.

One way of doing that was gitting a barn of backer ready and selling it on the N.C. Border or South Carolina markets before the Eastern Belt opened. There was a wider spread between the opening dates between the Border and Eastern Belt in those days.

But gitting that backer ready for market was easier said than done. Oh, there were plenty of hands as far as numbers go. But those old enough to work were at the looping shelter or in the fields crapping the golden weed and gitting it into the barns to be cured.

The old lady was the best bet to git things going (as if she didn't have anything else to do). And Zeb had to handle the situation with kid gloves on.

"Old lady, reckon you could see any way to help git a barn of backer ready to sell on the border market? Looks like we got to do something to git a few dollars," Zeb says.

"Yeah, if I cook nothing but ish taters and fat back and flour-bread, don't do no washing and arning, and let everything in the house go. That means no picking the stuff in the guarden and do-ing nothing else around the house. And you can forgit about cook-ing for hands, too."

"Well, I don't know what we'll do," Zeb says. I 'clare, these girls are lamenting about not having nothing to wear to revival that's coming up soon, and we've got to do everything we can to point them toward the Lord."

"Listen Zeb, I've huern this a hundred times before. And everything you are saying is true, but they's just one of me. And I know the girls could take a piece of cloth and sew up a dress in a little while if they just had the time. And I ain't saying they don't need frocks to wear to church, but they's other things we need just as bad. They ain't no meat in the smokehouse. The flour barrel is near 'bout empty. Sheets are gitting ragged. The boys' drawers look like rags. And one barn of backer wouldn't come close to gitting what we need right now, not after giving Mr. Ed his half."

"I know all of that Mama," Zeb replies. "Still, if we could git that barn of sand lugs graded and tied and git it down to Whitesville or sommers down there, it would help us out of a tight situation."

"Lord, I dread the thought," the old lady replies. "We thought all the sand come off when we was taking the backer out of the barn, but when you set down under a chaney ball tree at a grading bench with a tow sack spread over your lap and it as hot as the devil, you find out that most of the dirt was left to sift through that guano sack and git all over you. Sweating like you was ditching to start with, and all that sand gitting on you, and that trashy backer gitting drier every minute and feeling like shucks, it will drive you crazy."

"We'll sprinkle it down good," Zeb says, trying to console his wife. "And I know what a mess it is. But they ain't nobody else to do it."

"I did see some pretty cloth at the dime store the other Sad'dy," the old lady says. "And it was cheap too. Ten-cent a yard I think, but just 36 inches wide. I thought about the girls and how it would make right pretty dresses. But I'm telling you, Zeb Crebbins, if I'm going to grade and mess with that backer, every one of you have got to tie it and stick it up, and somebody's got to take it off of the sticks, too. They's just too much for me to try to do by myself. And I ain't kidding about som'n t'eat either. You'll just have to do the best you can. And if no washing ain't done everybody will just have to wear nasty clothes. And I ain't taking nothing off of them biggety-acting boys neither. If they start sassing me, I'll put a switch on them just like I did when they was 10 years old, and dare them to even grab at the switch."

So Zeb gets a pail of water and a stumpy broom and saturates the trashy backer with water and packs it down, and the old lady starts grading the mess next day, and it's a time trying to keep it on the grading bench with short leaves and it being trashy and dry. As much goes on the floor as on the grading bench because of the black, worthless leaves.

Everybody pitches in at night and helps git the backer tied and then a lot of bundles become undone because finding tie leaves is a job. There's a lot of complaining about not having clean clothes and young'uns get tired of eating ish taters and sopping the gravy, but some of them doctor the gravy up with hot vinegar or onions. And finally the barn of backer is stuck up and packed down and a neighbor with an old Ford truck is hired to take the backer to the border market. Gas is purchased at the filling station on credit until the backer is sold, and the hauler will get his pay then also.

There's the long drive down Highway 301 and the turnoff that takes you to Whiteville. The backer is sold, if it can be called "sold." An eight or nine-cent average ain't much. But there's a few dollars to use. There'll be a slab of fat back bought, 98 pounds of flour, cloth for the girls' dresses and the old lady says them boys are going to have a new pair of drawers apiece if nothing else ain't bought. "I feel like I'd die if something happened to them with them rags on," she says.

There's a few dollars for the storekeeper. Zeb owes $25 or $30 at the store, and other folks have been charging too. He needs his money. Looking over the list, there's a bottle of Lydia Pinkham's Compound, a bottle of Hadacol, both for the old lady when she felt so down-and-out she couldn't hardly make it; a bottle of chill tonic when one of the young'uns had chills and fevers and they suspected malaria; box after box of lye; kerosens; a can or two of salmon when there didn't seem to be nothing to cook on the place; smoking backer, snuff and other little items.

As for Zeb and the old lady, all they get out of the barn of backer are snuff for her and Golden Grain for the old man. Those are luxuries they have to have to survive.

They long ago stopped thinking about their own welfare. Their hopes were in their children, and they did the best they could for them. What more could be expected of parents?

Bad Months: July, August

When I was a young fellow working in the fields of eastern North Carolina, July and August were the two worst months for me. In the first place, it was as hot as the devil and there was a passel of work to do, all in the name of the mighty weed — tobacco.

It was rush every minute, gitting up early to take out backer, then rush to the fields to crap it, the loopers rushing to git it strung on the sticks and rushing to git it in the barn before pitch dark. It was a time of gummy overalls and gummy shirts. Any of you remember how a chambray shirt felt wih a good coat of backer gum on the sleeve? Suppose you had to use it to wipe the sweat from your face (and we did). Remember how it would feel?

And if a few hours came when you caught up with puttin' in the mess, there was a field full of suckers growing between them backer leaves that had to be pulled off, and that was worse than puttin' in. Ain't many older people but what can remember the sick feeling you got in the pit of your stomach when you were out there in a hot backer patch with your nose close to that rank mess and how you'd almost heave. It was a sickening smell, not at all like cured tobacco smells. Suckering backer was such a slow process and fields were so large, it felt like you had a job that would last you forever and there was no end to it.

Incidentally, just to show how things have changed over the years, there was a headline in our paper in 1985 that read "Wood Used As Fuel For Tobacco Curing." Can you imagine what any farmer that departed this earth 50 years ago would think if it were possible for him to see such a headline in a newspaper? Wood is all that was used in those days.

It was just dismal during that season. Places where a little water stood, it was stagnant and green slime showed and you wondered how tadpoles were able to live in such a mess. We were told not to wade in such water, for we'd be sure to git foot itch.

If you ever got a chance to go swimming in the pond it seemed like even the water was too warm for comfort. That old July and August sun was like a heater and sometimes the water felt like it might have come out of a reservoir to the kitchen stove where water was heated.

And I remember so well how that water smelled and tasted that was toted to the field to us by the young'uns that didnt't have anything else to do (and who didn't want to tote water, either). They'd mess around on their way to the field and break off dog fennel and pull off vines that overhung the ditchbanks along the path, and by the time they got to the field that half-gallon jar of water was about as warm as milk fresh from the cow. There would be little beads in the water, and sometimes we'd just take a mouthful and "wrench" out our mouths and spit the mess out. Even if you're thirsty, hot water ain't refreshing. And we'd cuss too, but that won't nothing new.

Then when it got night and we'd washed off and bedded down, there was still the heat to contend with. We'd pant and fan and blow the sweat off the end of our noses with our breath and hit at skeeters that just loved us. They'd hum right in our ears, and 'fore you could think, one had popped you and got you to itching all over.

Then we'd start roving all over the place. We'd grab quilts and take to the floors and if the skeeters were real bad somebody would light a rag in a bucket and let the smoke fill the air. One thing is for sure, the way that burning rag stank, no skeeter would git in its path, but I've wondered many times whether it was worth it to have that ungodly smell to contend with.

We'd turn and tumble for a while, but sleep soon overtook us, and if we woke from a deep sleep for a monent, our pillows were wet with sweat and it would be running down our necks. But if you work, you sleep. So we slept, despite the discomfort.

And gitting up the next morning and facing the same situation was almost like a death sentence, Man, it could be hot at the breakfast table. You could sweat while eating fat back, scrambled eggs and buttermilk biscuits. By the time the sun rose above the treetops (when we were already on our way to the fields) we knew what was in store for us.

Sure, there were places heavy with shade where the heat from the sun never penetrated in all its fury. Large trees with overhanging branches looked ideal for comfort from the "briling" sun. But do you think we had a chance to go to them? They were forbidden fruit, because there wasn't time to waste under shade trees. That backer had to go in those barns, man. It almost took the place of God during barning season. And some folks who were not religion-oriented did some of that work on Sunday. Everything could be forgiven except to let backer dry up on the stalks or let suckers take over. It was a fight, I tell you.

But do you know what was the saddest part about the whole thing? After all the work, all the worry, all the sleepless nights, we hardly ever got enough out of tobacco in those days to pay out of debt. Many years, we'd end up with a balance due the landlord.

And we had something else to look forward to during the hot month of August, so we weren't all that hepped-up about gitting through puttin' in backer. Fodder pulling time! You might as well have spit in our faces, but that was another reality of life during the days when I was a boy.

But despite the heat and the toil and all the inconveniences, there are at least a million good things that I remember from those days. The good outshines the bad ten to one.

Transplanting Tobacco
Courtesy Mrs. Ed Smith

Old-Fashioned Tater Hill — A Remnant Of The Past
Courtesy Minnie E. Thorne

Friday Was A Good Day

I think Friday used to be about the best day of the week, all things considered. Oh, it was a work day, all right, but in thinking about it it seems that the pace had slackened a bit from what it was at the beginning of the week. To tell you the truth, everybody was getting a little jaded by then, even to the old folks. I think more farmers put in backer on Saturday morning than put in on Friday. Those that barned on Friday would have a barn of yaller backer by Sunday night and had to go up on the heat. There ain't much to do to backer when it's yallering in the barn, 'cept to put in a piece or two of wood every once in a while.

Those clothes that we'd worn all week were smelling pretty high with perspiration also, and we were looking forward to our Sad'dy baths. It made you feel all the cleaner when you had gone for a considerable length of time without bathing.

Everybody knowed that those yards had to be swept before Sunday, and sometimes young'uns got to them Friday afternoon — if the backer had been suckered, all the barning done for the week, the late corn plowed on the hillside — and nothing won't ripening to be picked. There won't no gitting around sweeping the yards. That was a must. Every week.

By August, biddies that had come off in March and April were almost grown. Some of 'em had got their start in the tater hill after all the taters were eaten. And those rascals were Ma's pride and joy. The young roosters she had saved were beginning to crow, with their feathers just a shining. And cocky! They thought they were king of the road. One would fly up on a gate post, or some post, flap his wings and give out a crow that could be heard all over the neighborhood. They were pretty, too. One might be black with red spangles on his breast, and the shining feathers on his back and hackle a red color, or some such combination.

But Ma loved them pullets better'n she did the roosters. She wouldn't kill nary pullet if she didn't have to, and she did it then only in an emergency. She'd watch 'em as their combs began to grow and they'd sing as they meandered over the yard. Ma was always counting the eggs she was going to git from those hens. And if a hungry hog got one of her pullets, she near 'bout had a fit. (But they did get a few of 'em). And I reckon we were more cruel in a way than people are today. I've known us to take a chicken the hogs had killed, and saturate that bird with box lye and throw it back in the pen, and those hogs would eat that mess, chomp their mouths and it apparently didn't even hurt them.

Friday was the day we began to anticipate the weekend. We tried not to give it much thought before then. There was too much to do and it was too long to have to think about it. But by Friday afternoon (evening to us) we were thinking about the picture show. And at our house, we knowed that the fish man was coming on Sad'dy, and that would be a welcome change from butterbeans, summer collards, peas and stuff like that. No matter how much we liked vegetables, there was a saturation point, after all. Rose bushes climbing on fences might have a half-dozen or so blooms as summer reached its mid-point. At the end of some gardens there were sunflowers with blooms as large as the top of a peck bucket. Cannas were bright with their red or yellow blooms. Coxcomb was beginning to show color as a prelude to the deep red it would ac-quire later.

The August sun would beat down in all its fury and the air was stale and sultry. The odor of curing tobacco was everywhere. Cotton had grown tall with mature bolls on the stalks along with profuse blooms. Farmers were beginning to tear open bolls to see how badly they had been damaged by boll weevils. If us boys got the chance, we'd hitch a mule to a backer truck late Friday evening and cut enough green corn to feed over the weekend. The truck would be pushed under a shelter to keep the sun from the corn.

There is no way to associate with those days without a lot of work entering the picture. There was actually more work to be done than ever got done. There were a hundred different things to be done, and nobody to do it except the immediate family. Some things could be put off, like washing out guano sacks, but that eventually had to be done, too. And a few weeks later on, we might have thought there'd be a Friday evening when we could rest. But no, that turnip patch had to be fixed, and the seeds sown. That was something we didn't put off in late August or early September.

Sometime later on in the year, along about November, we'd think we were going to have half a day in which to play around, and that was the very day Ma decided to go git broom straw. So we'd have to hitch up the wagon and go with Ma where the straw grew tall and we'd whack that mess down and tie it in good-sized bundles and Ma would make it into single brooms later on. It was like that about all the time. We finally learned not to anticipate spells of doing nothing on Friday, or any other day.

These are the dog days of summer, the hot, uncomfortable days of July and August. They're called dog days because the Dog Star rises and sets with the sun, and not because dogs pant and carry on during this season, scratch themselves half to death from fleas, and smell like they've never had a bath. But it's a good term, even if the canine world is a consideration. It's a good time to go to the dogs, literally. The beaches and the sand and the sea ain't worth it. Let July, August and September go by, and there are the blue skies of October to look forward to..

Escapades At The Beach

I am recalling a weekend in August in 1985 when, if I had awakened from a long sleep, I'd have sworn it was the fall season. Everything about the weekend spoke of autumn. I have never seen bluer skies, not even in October. There was a coolness in the air that is seldom noted in mid-summer. It was cooler than it was a week before Christmas in 1984.

Autumn is the season I love best. All four seasons have their advantages, but I always considered fall ideal, not only for the crispness in the air and overall quality of life at that particular time, but for the beauty of the world about me as well.

To me, at least, some seasons are to be tolerated, while others are to be enjoyed. October, November and December are my favorite months to be enjoyed. I have always disliked the sweltering summer months more than any season of the year. But that is strictly a matter of opinion.

For those who are beachcombers and who languish by the big waters during the summer months, summer has to be the best season of all. There's plenty of sand to get your feet into, to cradle the large beach towels and get sand all over you, even in your hair, in your sandals, on the beds you sleep in.

There are the beach music, the parties, the bathing and riding the waves on surfboards, and many things to make the beach crowd happy. But as for me, the loneliest place I have ever been in my life is the beach. The setting is so dismal I always want to cry when I am there. And it doesn't matter that there are thousands of condominiums and cottages and hordes of people, to look out on the mighty Atlantic with nothing but waves staring you in the face, and along the sandy beaches the scraggly growth brings a loneliness to the pit of my stomach.

But there is one redeeming factor — the pretty girls that flock there to lie in the sun and grow darker every day as well as to have fun. But ain't they some ugly ones there, too! I tell you, some of them would do well if they never got melted into a bathing suit.

Course we didn't used to git down to Wilmington or Morehead but about once every couple of years. On a sunny Sunday morning somebody with a big-bodied old Chevrolet or Ford truck would lug a bunch of us young folks down there for the day, and under those overalls and dresses we were as white as lilies, and we'd ride back home in the back of that truck burning up. Our hides were as red as a dishwasher's in a hot kitchen. Our backs, faces, arms, hands, legs and feet were blistered and we felt like we couldn't stand it. But we had to. Not only that, we had to work on Monday. If you think being blistered all over would excuse you from work, you have another thought coming, unless somebody actually got sick and had to throw up, and some of 'em did.

There was little mercy for those who got burned from bathing, especially the girls. Most of the old folks frowned on women bathing anyway, and to bare themselves in bathing suits that covered more of their bodies in those days than a lot of the things some women wear today as outer wear, a lot of the old folks said it was good enough for them. My, how we have changed!

I used to look forward to the "September gust" as the old folks called it. That was a storm that usually came at the end of summer to mark a change in seasons. Sometimes the storm was the result of a hurricane messing around in the Atlantic, and it was not always in September. It could come in late August or early October for that matter. And Pa had him a hifalutin name for the storm. He called it the "equinoxical storm." I don't know where on earth he got the "ical" at the end of the word. The equinox storm would have been more appropriate. But then, most of you didn't know Pa.

I wanted the storm to come and wash away the remnants of summer and take us into the new season. I wanted to feel those cool days and see the beauty of the harvest season. I wanted to observe as the trees changed color and smell the sweetness of new-mown hay. And I just loved to stare in the indefinable blueness of the skies above me. Clouds were prettier under an October sky. Even the name October sounds more romantic than the names of the other months to me.

But back to our escapade at the beach. Those blisters all over us would burst in a couple of days, and first thing you knew skin was peeling off the entire body almost, and especially on the nose. We didn't hardly look human and we didn't feel like humans either. Anybody would think we would have had more sense than to jump into the ocean and stay out there for hours with all that sickening white skin and not expect to get burned up. And for the record, there were no sun screens in those days.

To tell the truth, we were not thinking about sunburn at the time. Most of us were too delighted to be at the beach to worry about the consequences. It was a rarity for us to go beyond the swimming hole at home.

But all this helped to break the monotony of summer (and all the hard work we did in those fields). And maybe that is another reason I disliked the summer months so much. I was never the smartest person in the world, although I did a lot of work in my young days. And the hot sun and high humidity didn't do me any good, either. All of you that love the beach, linger on there for as long as you can, and have a barrel of fun. I don't envy you.

These Things Are My Soul

I will always remember, and I will be happier in remembering, for if the soul is that part of man that never dies, it has been nurtured by all those things that contribute to its immortality. Just as a giant tree has a wide root spread, so does the human mind have an even greater spread from which to draw sustenance.

When we are young the five senses — sight, sound, smell, feel, thought — are brought into play as a natural endowment, and they are to us what DNA is to life itself. They make up what we are, our individual uniqueness from all other human beings.

There is nothing else comparable to the human brain. There will never be a computer that can approach man's capacity to think, to comprehend, to know and to reason. Computers can only do what man tells them to do. They can never have an instant recall of a lifetime of memories that lie in the gray matter within the brain.

Could any computer ever recall a threatening sky as daylight begins to end, when just for a moment a part of the clouds reveal a reddening sunset and across the heavens a brilliant rainbow appears?

— A dilapidated step with rotting wood on an unpainted shanty that represents home; a rose on a climbing fence that appears odd in its dull setting; a bumble bee busily gathering nectar from an insignificant flower; a dog having a "running fit;" an outdoor toilet with a tow-sack door; a blinding snowstorm with visibility closing in and isolating the world?

— A total eclipse of the sun or moon; leaves blowing in the wind; golden moons; puppies licking a child's face; a busy street scene; clowns and lions and trapeze artists at a circus; a mother and her baby smiling at each other; the glitter of Christmas decorations on busy city streets?

— A sow nursing her piglets; a cow licking her newborn calf; a baby in its "kiddie coop"; an old man man walking with a cane down a country road; a pretty girl in a flowered dress; a star-filled sky; sharp flashes of lightning when the storms come; a frosty morning when the fields appear to be sifted with snow; dense fog; the gold, yellow, pink, red, purple of the turning leaves merging into a brilliant pattern of color? Sights.

— The call of the wild as migrating geese give their squawks somewhere in the sky; the echoes of a mother calling her children; the sounds of the beautiful melodies of the day; rain on a tin roof; the crackle of fire in the fireplace; sleet hitting windowpanes; the shriek of the wind on a cold night?

— The toll of the bell at dinner time; the conversations around the dining room table; the popping of firecrackers and bands playing; the voice of the teacher in the classroom; trains passing in the night; funeral music; the flow of rushing waters; acorns falling on a housetop? Sounds

— The touch of a baby's skin; a mother's hand on the forehead of her child; snowflakes melting on the face; the pain of arthritis; orgasm; toothache; a firm handshake; the touch of lovers' hands; exhilaration after a happy event; the sting of a cut; warmth following a chill; the feeling in the pit of the stomach while swinging from a tree limb; the firm grasp of a hand, snatching you from danger?

— A fish striking bait; fuzz on peaches and apricots; excruciating pain from nails stuck into the feet; earache; gentle breezes; a heat wave; the comfort of a minister's words; relief after surgery; the hurt of heartbreak; calmness after emotional flareups? Feelings

Roses, honeysuckle, Sweet Betsys and gardenias are fragrances that please. But there is the odor of rotting trash tobacco drenched by rain as it lies beside the packhouse door; country ham cooking in a frying pan and filling the air as far as a mile away; mildew in damp rooms; teacakes baking in an oven; outhouses; face powder and brilliantine and sweet soap; body odor; halitosis; stagnant water; the sweet smell of upturned soil; mule stables and hog pens; clean sheets; vanilla; chocolate boiling in a pot?

— Coal tar poured in cracks on broken pavement; sweating

mules; delicious apples; the aroma of cured tobacco filling the atmosphere; molasses or syrup cooking in the vat; hot dogs; apple blossoms. Smells

And finally, the ability to think, to bring all the senses into play and to know their effects as they are relived through the process of recall.

We accepted all these things, and many more, as part of our environment and they were as natural with us as breathing, just as they are natural for today's generations. They were the roots of our soul and they provided the nutrients from which to grow. They were the foundation and from those experiences we have matured and expanded our horizons beyond the simple things that we learned without effort or design.

What would life be without the simple things in nature that taught us to appreciate all the senses that were given to us by the advent of birth? We are all endowed with the same blessings except for those who were unfortunate and who were denied one or more of the five senses.

For me, at least, these are examples of what have given me whatever values I have in life and all that I can hope to be. They are the simple things that I remember. They are my soul.

Picking Backer Bed
Courtesy Courtesy Sharpe

Clearing New Ground

P eople really did get their money the old-fashioned way in the world of yesterday: They earned it! And money in those days was chicken feed in comparison to what we call money today. But there was a big difference then. Money had a value. The trouble was we didn't have any of it so its value had little meaning for us. Money has little value today, so if we have a few dollars in our pockets, we can't boast of much worldly success.

I'm thinking about how we used to clear new grounds for backer beds, and all the hard work put into it and how little monetary reward we got for it. I'll bet we couldn't even hire migrant labor to clear new grounds today like we used to have to do them.

Forget about tractors or bulldozers or anything modern under the sun. Instid, think about a pair of mules, a bunch of grubbing hoes, a lot of trace chains and a gang of strapping boys and one old man to direct the operation. And somebody at the house better be firing the cookstove and boiling the pot and putting plenty of soul food on the table, for grubbing a new ground will make you "hongrier" than a bitch wolf hunting food for her whelps.

There was just one reason to go out in the piney woods and clear up a new ground, and that was to have a place to plant backer beds where weeds were not already seeded out in the ground. Oh, we could git backer plants in the soil beside ditch banks, or most any place. And with all that guano put down there to grow the plants, we got weeds and grass by the bushel also. That meant no end to picking the grass and weeds from the beds.

But this new-fangled crowd wouldn't know nothing about that, since they have anything you need today to put down in the soil to kill all the weed and grass seed and anything else you don't want growing there. Never mind if the runoff goes into the streams and pollutes our waters or whatever. The main thing is they ain't no weeds to contend with. And we'd a done the same thing if we had a had a choice. We'd a done anything to keep from grubbing a root-filled new ground.

I mean every inch of that new ground held roots, and stumps. And if you couldn't sling an ax, you'd better not git out there among them ax-slingers. You sling an ax and you keep everybody else out of your way. I don't know what would a happened to any-body that didn't sling an ax or use a grubbing hoe on a new ground. It shore wouldn't a been good, I can tell you that.

We'd start grubbing and right off there would be a root six or eight inches thick that we'd have to cut in two. Then a trace chain would be attached to the root and the mules brought up and hitch-ed to the chain to pull up the root. That was just a beginner. And that pile of roots at the edge of the new ground would start to build. And we toted roots and toted roots and toted roots and by then we were gitting sore all over and would have to stop sometimes to catch our breath.

It might a been cool or cold when we started, but the kind of work we were doing got us out of them overall jackets in no time, and when we stopped to rest we'd be hassling and would sit on a pile of stumps and roll us a cigarette and smoke it while we were gitting our second wind. But the old man was just like a time-keeper and had no more mercy on his own young'uns than he'd a had on a pack of hired hands. He got us up off our butts in no time, and we'd start looking to see how high the sun was and listening for the quarter-to-twelve bell for dinner time. Our guts were growling by then.

Ever how much rice was in the pot; ever how much ham was on the bone the rice was cooked in; ever how many collards were boiled; ever how many sweet taters were baked, we et everything on the table and Ma declared she couldn't cook enough at one time to fill us up. But Ma didn't know how many calories we'd used up that morning. It's a pure laugh to see how we count calories today in an effort to keep us from going to pot. In the old days, you couldn't put too many calories in our bellies, leaving them lying around to accumulate fat. Won't nary one left after slinging an ax all day or grubbing in that new ground. Or at any other task for that matter, for it was all manual labor.

We had to cut around every stump and git the roots free so a trace chain could be hooked around a big root and the mules used to pull the stump out of the ground so we could git it up and roll it to the trash pile. Don't it make you tard just to hear about it? But so many of you don't know nothing about what I'm saying nohow. You think the whole thing is a pack of junk. Well, by cracky, if that's the way you feel, it would be all right with me if you had to git out there and help clear a new ground for one half a day. That would teach you the lesson of your life.

Them blisters on your hands are really sore at the end of the day from slinging that ax and grubbing with that hoe. And if they bust and the water runs out of them, you'll have the sorest hand you can imagine the next day. But if you think that excuses you until all that new ground is cleared, you're crazy. Wrap a rag around it or whatever you have to do to try to protect it. Just keep on working.

When the new ground is finally cleared and you're ready to put the finishing touches to the soil, the rakes are put into play, and there are literally thousands of little roots to be raked up and when the bed is prepared to plant the backer seed, it looks like something professionals would do. It's as smooth as a freshly swept yard but by then you're so tard and so disgusted with it all you just want to git the seed sowed, cut pine saplings and place around the beds, drive nails around the poles to hold the backer cloth, git the covers on the beds and git away from that mess. There's a limit even to what country boys used to hard work can put up with. Clearing new grounds was not one of the best aspects of country life.

A Tribute To Zack Coor

Zack Coor was not an ordinary man.
He never learned to read, or write,
Nor did he dream of far horizons.
His domicile was a very small area
    in which he found
    happiness, contentment
    and compassion
    from all who knew him.
He depended upon friends for survival--
    food, outdated clothing;
    for pocket change and odd jobs...
    and for a chance to talk
    and to give the "latest" events
    in the neighborhood.
He walked beside still waters,
And was moved by their calmness.
He observed nature's wonders,
    along roads where huckleberry bushes
    grew beneath the pines;
    where buzzards soared overhead.
His was a world of beauty.
He knew his terrain,
And never strayed to strange grounds.
The forests did not blind him
So that he could not see the trees.
He was a beggar,
    but he didn't beg!
    He didn't need to.
    His needs were met by everyone
    in the community.
He had his mother, Puss--
And his aunt, Bloss,
    who was farther on the edge
    than Zack.
But he chose barns and shelters
    for his sleeping quarters,
And others' tables
    for his sustenance.
Zack had nothing in worldly goods.
Yet he set an example.
  He taught us--
    rather than our teaching him!
All those whose lives Zack touched
Are better people
    for having known him.
His memory has outlived the memories
Of those who ministered to him.
There is a Zack
    in all our lives.

Zack Coor In 1941

Time Changes Everything

W here have all the bluebirds gone? Are they, like so many things we associate with our past, becoming extinct, too? They used to pitch down in the yards with the cardinals, robins sparrows and other species and helped to beautify the premises.

And I hope that somewhere out there is a marshland where corn grows tall and where birds can raise their families in solitude away from man's prying, there is a redheaded woodpecker's nest in an old rotten tree trunk like the one I remember from childhood. The tree stood alone, and was perhaps the victim of a bolt of lightning at some time. The remaining trunk stood about eight feet tall, and it was almost completely rotten.

Only an outer shell stood on one side of the trunk, and where the hollow was left by the decaying wood, this woodpecker had a nest at eye level and there were four babies beginning to feather out in the nest. Just a slight movement would cause them to open their mouths wide in anticipation of food from their mother's mouth.

The mother was a beautiful bird, with a red head, a black back and some white feathering. And the corn is still waving in memory, black-green in the fertile soil, head high and with soda placed beside the roots, had all the nutrients necessary to yield large ears of corn. It was a pleasant setting for a little bird and her babies and a nostalgic thought in remembering. But the red-headed woodpecker is seldom seen, either.

And I often wonder whether there is some place that isn't seen in traveling along country roads where a long lane leads to a house where children still play and where they have to look down the lane to see other neighborhood life. I hope so, and my prayer is that they know all the joys of their surroundings that I remember.

And if there is such a place, let there be June bugs in the trees and as the sun comes over the horizon let them begin their songs that last until the first evening star appears; where mockingbirds sing and children chase butterflies and quench their thirst with cool well water.

And please let there be a scarecrow somewhere on the grounds, complete with an old felt hat, a dark coat and raggedy trousers to give credibility to the surroundings as well as to try to scare away the hawks that prey on the young biddies.

And is there, just maybe, a humble house that has been overlooked by authorities who condemn such buildings for habitation today, where a few open places in the weatherboarding invite moonbeams on light nights, and where dreams reach to the stars in the fantasy world of a child. Where even snowflakes with their icy breath are welcomed in when the snows come. I hope so, and I also hope that there are a few children who can see and know and appreciate such simple things in a complex world.

Is there any place where families gather on the front porch in the evening hours and watch the wonders of nature in the heavens about them; where echoes of the night become a part of their world and where families are all together and where love abounds?

And do the maypops still grow in the fields? Please don't let them disappear. Protect them and bring them to the modern homes if necessary and grow them among the prestigious shrubs, plants and flowers that bear no resemblance to the lowly maypop vine. They gave so much pleasure to children of my time. And they aren't ugly plants. The blooms are rather handsome. If just one child could appreciate them as we did and enjoy the football-shaped fruit they produced, they would be worth saving.

And please, let there be an old pine tree standing by a tobacco barn somewhere with the ground covered in needles and some kind of farming equipment resting under the shelter. It is all right if the door sags or rubber roofing is torn in shreds. The farm implements are no good anyway, and like the very old who are awaiting the ravages of time to claim them, they are spending their time waiting for rust to claim them and return them to the dust of the earth.

And could there still be moonlit paths where boys and girls share their first experience of love and where every tree, every shadow, every building becomes a magical setting because of lovers' dreams? Let there be such a place, I pray.

I hope that somewhere out there there are meadows lush with grass, with gentle slopes that lead down to little streams where the mules and horses and hogs and cows go to drink, surrounded by lots of trees where the fog hangs thick in early morning and as it begins to burn off the fog becomes fleecy white clouds that break apart and float heavenward. I would be happy in knowing that children congregated there to romp over the grass and play baseball and other games played in open places.

Surely there must be places where guineas habitate the growth beside ditch banks and soar into the skies when man encroaches on their domain. And if there are such places, does anybody ever make guinea stew? It used to be considered a delicacy with an original flavor that gave pastry a special taste. And guinea meat is very dark. In fact, it is called black.

I wish for many things for the children of today. They have missed so much in their computerized world. Older citizens who were products of the rural setting know about all these things. And they were beneficial to us. But the young don't know. Indeed, they can't know, for it isn't there unless it is far back from the beaten path. They need to know and it isn't their fault that they don't. They have television and electronic games, but lack the knowledge of nature that we learned as a part of our environment. Let us find them some place and let them see first hand those things that have become a part of our memory bank.

Poor Folks Go Modern

B y the early 1950s a lot of the boys that had followed a mule through the war years or fought on foreign battlefields had married and given up on farming and moved to town. Some took advantage of the GI bill and entered college. Many went into industry — working in factories or plants or becoming clerks in stores. A lot more women were also working. Since many were unqualified for secretarial work or other jobs generally thought of as women's work, working in dime stores was a vocation for some. Others worked at candy counters in the dime stores or sold cloth or slung hash in cafes.

Practically all of this group rented apartments in towns across eastern North Carolina. Buying a home was still a far-fetched dream for many. But they were gitting the grit out of their teeth and becoming "citified." They were shedding the old and taking on the new.

Young married couples were buying refrigerators and (above everything else, washing machines) to take the heavy load of washing with washboards off their shoulders. And don't you think they weren't proud of every one of those electrical appliances to make life easier. Those "fridges" were small with only enough room in the freezer for the ice trays and a few (very small) items. But they loved them. And defrost covered everything so quickly they'd spend hours defrosting them in warm weather, besides making a mess all over the kitchen.

Some still had a single light bulb dangling from the ceiling in the middle of the room, but they were proud to have the electricity.

As soon as they could handle the payments, they bought one of those veneer bedroom suites that came in a variety of colors, all shiny with huge dressers and chests of drawers. And they just loved the new plastic living room suites. Some declared you couldn't tell the fabric from pure leather and just about everybody wanted a plastic couch and a big plastic rocker in their living room. And if they couldn't swing both a couch and chair, they'd opt for a big rocker in a solid color, usually tan or brown.

A lot of bathrooms still had tubs that sat on legs, commodes and lavatories with a mirror that concealed a storage cabinet behind. (They're still around today). Women started buying those shaggy mats to put around the commode and on the seat cover and scattered other thick rugs over the floors. They had quit making towels out of flour sacks and gone to the dime stores and bought those ever-so-soft towels in rainbow colors that felt like goose down after wiping in those hard salt sacks for so many years. But in general, they were not Cannon, the real McCoys. They were thinner and smaller.

The sinks in the kitchens were standing there looking as naked as a picked bird, and there was hardly no cabinet space. A lot of women took heavy twine and placed it around their sinks and made skirts to go around them so they could store taters and other items as well as hiding them from view.

Walls were in bad shape in a lot of cases, and folks flocked to the dime stores to purchase the cheapest paint they could find to splash over the walls and ceilings. DECORATOR colors, too! And a lot of those kitchen cabinets that had been in use in the sticks were still used in the town kitchens.

And Lord, don't you know them women were tickled to death to git a set of Melmac plastic dishes! I mean a whole set — for eight — with every imaginable dish from casseroles to meat platters. Many women even dared to throw those old chipped china dishes away or give them to the young'uns to use in their playhouses.

Plastic shower curtains were the rage, in any color combination anyone could wish, with flowers galore. But some women that felt more sophisticated than the average bought cretonne curtains, thinking them to be a tad above plastic. But it was the age of plastics. Some folks even bought plastic curtains for their windows. So the bathrooms were decorated and having the toilet inside made it such a pleasurable place, the people just loved to go there, whether they had to or not.

Womenfolks got cuttings of wandering dew from their mothers and placed the plants on little tables near sunny windows. Some even placed sweet potatoes in water and they'd sprout and run all the way to the floor.

If they could get them a new linoleum rug, or treat of all treats — a wool rug, 9 x 12 — to go in their living rooms, with that plastic furniture and a bit of the outdoors in their house plants, they were climbing so far up the ladder those old weatherbeaten, shackly houses were like a long-ago dream.

Just about everybody was going to oil heat and there was an oil drum beside every apartment. Wood was so outdated it was pitiful. Everybody longed for a Ziegler heater, but many were not able to afford them. Most bought the cheaper brands, just so they were BIG and looked like furniture.

And television sets were on the scene. Every poor person on earth longed for one and would almost have given their right arm to see the action on the screen. Long before they had sets, they were told about the Ed Sullivan Show and Ted Mack's Amateur Hour, Bishop Fulton J. Sheen's religious program, and other popular shows. A few even got sets before Greenville and Washington became hooked up for network programming and got snowstorms even when the weather was good. Picking up images from Norfolk, 150 miles away, left much to be desired. But when they had that TV set with all their other additions since leaving the sticks, they were beginning to climb high, and you'd better believe it.

And "The Sixty Four Thousand Dollar Question" had everybody in the booth trying to help the contestant until it was learned the show was a phony.

And people who could afford it built fallout shelters. We were so naive as to believe in those days that we could survive a nuclear attack! Whenever people heard of a new shelter it was a diversion on Sunday afternoon for the family to get in their old cars with rebuilt motors and tires with retreads to drive around and observe the shelters even though nothing could be seen except the door leading to the underground shelter. They told about all the packaged foods and supplies placed in the shelters and people thought about all the bad food and being underground and the prospect of nuclear war and that sort of put a damper on their Sunday afternoon excursions.

A Prelude To Autumn

I can see it in the fields, in the forests. I can feel it in the air and in the stirring of the wind. It is a prelude to autumn. Nature is always in preparation for change which gives our world a diversity, a feeling of rebirth.

The corn stalks are brown, the grain ready for picking. Some tobacco fields are looking bare, although much of the crop remains on the stalks in some places. As is always the case in summer, weeds have taken over in many places with their seeds ready to return to the earth to ensure another crop next year. Hurricanes and tropical depressions are busily forming in the Atlantic and threatening coastal areas.

In that long ago that I am always referring to, I can remember the heavy seeds on cane stalks, bending them over with their top-heavy burden. The fodder on cane was still green and at this season of the year we knew the job of harvesting the cane and getting it to the mill was soon at hand.

Potato patches showed large cracks where the tubers had grown to a large size and awaited harvesting. The height of the growing season was past and the foliage was beginning to turn yellow with a hint of brown.

Small white butterflies invaded the collard rows and leaves of the vegetables were dotted with holes from the worms that devoured the plants. The butterflies had deposited the eggs that hatched into worms. It was time to crop off all the leaves except the buds and take them to the hogs. The collard plants had to be poisoned to kill the bugs and allow the buds to develop into large collards for the fall and winter.

It was high time that turnip patches were prepared and the seeds planted.

Nothing but knots were left in the watermelon patches. If a melon were busted in the field, there was a slickness that was unappealing and the sweet taste was gone. They were hauled up to the house and dumped in the hog pasture.

Tobacco patches were forlorn looking and some people took the stalk-cutters and chopped up the stalks to allow them to rot and enrich the soil for the next year.

If peavine hay hadn't already been cut, it was time to take the mowing machine to the fields and mow the hay in order for it to dry and be baled or placed in haystacks for winter use.

A few small, rotten tomatoes still clung to the vines and late blossoming had resulted in a large crop of tiny tomatoes that would grow and ripen if the frosts didn't come too early.

Cotton was beginning to show white in the fields and blossoms were still on the stalks that would result in small bolls that would be food for the boll weevils.

With the foliage dying, those who had pumpkin patches were treated to the brilliant orange color of the pumpkins as they awaited picking.

Scuppernongs were ripening and people were beginning to habitate the vines and reach up through the thick mesh of vine and foliage to pick the fruit.

Children were still in bare feet with sore toes and bruises and proud flesh and savoring the remains of summer. All too soon the school bells would ring and a new season would take over.

The summer sun would beat down and the heat would be oppressive in late afternoon and early evening. Not a leaf would be stirring. But after darkness descended there was coolness in the air and sometimes fog was heavy in early morning.

And yes, the woodpiles were getting bare. What happened to all the wood that was cut in early spring? It was a scramble every day to get wood for the wood ranges for cooking. Women even used the knotty pieces of wood to heat irons from a fire in an open fireplace. Tempers flared, particularly when the wome got ready to cook a meal and there was no wood split. And they could have won the battle in one day. All they needed to do was sit out on the front porch and await dinner time with nothing cooked. But in many cases, they went out and hacked off enough wood from left-over tobacco wood to heat the stoves.

At this time of year people were busy in the packhouses grading and tying tobacco for market. Inside the packhouses it was hot and little air was circulating except through the front door, and this dried out the tobacco. Young'uns were running out to the apple trees and bringing in fruit with small rotten specks and eating around them and the "marshmallow" apples in the bucket by the door smelled like a delicatessen. In a lot of cases, some of them were fried for supper. Everybody would be hungry and beg for chicken, which everyone knew was forbidden except on Sunday. But they'd settle for stewed ish taters, fried side meat, plenty of liquor to sop with a hundred buttermilk biscuits and iced tea.

Old Country Customs

I been thinking about some of the things we used to do, and they seem so far out they're almost funny, even to an old codger like me.

I heard 'em talking on the radio the other night about a "drenching" bottle they used to use to give mules and cows medicine. And I don't remember it being called a drenching bottle back there, but that's as good a name as any. They were any bottle of about a quart size with a long neck. What they failed to tell on the radio was how the job was accomplished. And you might think giving an animal a dose of medicine from a bottle is a cinch. Forget it. Even people don't like to have snything forced down their throats.

It is natural for amimals to hold their heads downward, and they have to be raised in order to get the liquids down their throats.

And why would they be giving them medicine anyway? Well, for one thing, mules and cows got the bloat sometimes, and that means their bellies were swollen and they appeared to be in a lot of pain. And when they got the bloat, won't much good in giving them nothing nohow, for they usually ended up dead and had to be dragged into the woods to feed the buzzards.

We read of horses dying from poisonous grain today, and I reckon that was the case in the old days, too. Or it could have been from moldy fodder, or whatever.

And the way they got them drenched was with the use of a small piece of rope attached to a stick, made for that purpose. They'd take one side of the upper lip of the mule and pull it through the piece of rope and twist it until the mule got your attention. And mules have plenty of lip. They'd hold the stick fairly high so the mule would have to raise its head so that when the liquid went into the mouth it was swallowed by the animal. Ain't no way you could have gotten most old mules to hold their heads high enough to git the liquid down unless that lip was twisted.

I don't know what they used. Maybe it was epsom salts. Maybe it was baking soda (but I shore didn't never hear no old mule with bloat belch). Maybe it was castor oil. I didn't never wait around to see. I just helped to git them drug up in the woods after they kicked the bucket.

And I was thinking the other day how us boys had such a time gitting over fences that had barbed wire at the top. Seems like there were such fences everywhere cause folks wanted to keep their cows and mules in, and sometimes those old animals would cross over barbed wire like it won't even there. I have also seen a cow's teats almost torn off from being scratched by that wire with all them prongs on it.

And us boys would git scratched near 'bout as bad sometimes. We'd start across the fence with those two strands of barbed wire at the top, and it would git caught in our britches somehow or other and we'd land up with our hands all bloody and long scratches on our legs. And talking about sore! Barbed wire scratches could make you so sore you couldn't hardly stand it.

And how 'bout when the road scraper used to come by! You'd a thought it was a circus for all the ruckus it caused. Somebody would see it way up in the pocosin, and long before it passed along the road where I used to run wild, we knew it was on its way, and we stood there just itching for it to come into view.

There were all kinds of soil along the road, from deep sand up near the pocosin to loamy, fertile land in some places, on to red clay hills. And the road was the same as the soil. In some places there was the washboard-effect where traffic had packed the soil. In other places there were deep sand ruts. And in dry weather the red clay hills were almost like cement, and in wet weather like goo, and as slick as ice when winter storms came. You could look out on that clay hill in wet weather, for the back end of the old car would git in the side ditch 'fore it was all over with. And you might git mired up in the sand where it was thick.

But we won't studying none of that. We just wanted to see the man operate the road scraper and turn it so it would go down in the side ditches and drag out the soil that always made its way back there once the V-shaped ditches made by the scraper were cleaned out. Then after the ditches were opened, the scraper spread the dirt over the road and sometimes it seemed worse after the roads were scraped than before.

There was not one thing about the road scraper to cause so much excitement but if you'll show me one young'un that didn't get excited when they saw one, I'll eat your hat. It's a wonder some of us didn't git caught in the scraper and git ourselves dragged a hundred feet. But we were scared of the man running the machine. We knew we'd never get away with it if we tried such a trick.

And picture us, if you will, way out there in the sticks waiting for something exciting to happen, and looking up into the skies and seeing a dirigible up there looking like it was sitting still. Well sir, we almost had fits. We'd shade our eyes and look at that aluminum-looking object in the skies and if there was anybody in the house we got 'em out there, too, for everybody was supposed to see the dirigible. It was something out of this world. Thousands of you out there saw them in those days, and you know what I'm talking about.

Ain't it wonderful, even if you're too old to dream, you ain't too old to remember!

I Just Couldn't Fly High

This old cotton-pickin,' backer-pickin,' pea-pickin' sharecropper was all cut and dried to travel abroad — to Paris, France and Berlin, Germany — when lo and behold, the trip got knocked out of the skies like some of these airplane accidents we been having recently. And maybe that's why it didn't upset me to the extent that I lost any sleep over it. I had also thunk about them rascals that git on planes with guns and cause all kinds of problems.

I was supposed to go over there to attend a world media convention with people from 100 countries in attendance. And can't you just see a former sharecropper among such a conglomeration, looking hither and thither, trying to see everything at once and wanting to communicate with folks that know nothing on earth about my country lingo? And being the ignorant cuss that I am, I can't speak nary word of French with its le's and la's denoting masculinity and femininity.

But I know you'll agree that if just a little bit of culture could have rubbed off on me in a foreign environment it would have been worth all the effort. Maybe it's best that I didn't go, for I'd a taught 'em about inviting country hicks to such high-class shenanigans (I looked that 'un up) so they wouldn't be making no such mistakes again.

Anyway, the French government reneged on its commitment and informed the group planning the conference that there would be no convention space available without giving any reason.

Makes you wonder whether there was some kind of security problem over there. And if there was, you'd better believe I'm glad I
didn't git over there in the midst of some of their notorious (Lord,
Lord) terrorist groups.

I could just see them bringing menus for a country hick like me,
all in French, and me sitting there like a knot on a log and
wondering what in the heck I was going to eat. I just know there
ain't no collards and butterbeans and cornbread on them French
menus, and even if there were, I wouldn't know what on earth they
were talking about.

And I was afraid if I got to using my hands too much in trying to
get my message across I might send out a sign that could have
universal meaning and I'd really have been in a mess then.

I remember my big-shot hotel days fresh from the farm and my
first encounter with menus that didn't sound right to me. I had
seen the word "cuisine" and it said the word was about cooking,
and you know how I pronounced it, don't you? Cu as in cucumber, i
as in I and sine as in the the last syllable of kerosene. Cu'i'sene.
And I still don't know how that "q" got in there.

I looked down the menu and there was roast beef au jus. I
laughed and said to myself, "aw jus what?" They had to be kidding to put such junk on a fancy hotel menu. Even I knowed better
than that.

But that won't the worst embarrassment I suffered. Right away
I spied something on the menu that sounded high-class to me. It
was "hors 'd oeuvres" and I knowed I had come a long way from
the backer patch when I saw that phrase in print. And you know
how I pronounced it, don't you? In public. I pronounced it like it
sounded, which always seemed the best thing to do to me. I believe
in calling a spade a spade. So I said out loud, "hors as in horse except for the "e" sound, 'd as in D and oeuvres as oovers with the
"o" rhyming with the "o"in shoe. "Hors 'd oovers."

After I learned it was supposed to sound like "orderves" I went
upstairs and packed my satchel and tried to find the paper bag I'd
used to bring in some of my junk. I was ready to git out there and
head back to the netherlands, but some of my new-found friends,
after gitting the tears out of their eyes from laughing, persuaded
me to stay on. They said I'd learn all of those little foreign words
they inserted to make menu reading exciting.

This was my initiation (my,my, my, my, my) into the French
language and the extent of my learning. I've huern 'em say "bon
jour" that over the years I learned was good day or good morning
and such mess as that.

And I wouldn't a tackled German with a ten-foot pole. Ain't no way I could ever fix my mouth to say the kind of talk they do when I've huern them on TV.

I was even supposed to wear a tuxedo, including what they call a cummerbund, to one of the shindigs in Paris, and Lord, don't you know I'm better off without gitting into all that mess, being who and what I am? I had done and sent my measurements over to some dood that runs a formal wear shop in Paris. On the form there were two places for marking the sizes — one in inches and one in centimeters — and you'd better believe I marked through that centimeter stuff right quick. I wouldn't a figgered out how many inches to put down in centimeters in a month. But I'll have you know I did don one of them tuxedos when my daughter got married, so I'm not all that far out.

Oh, I had me at least two suits of clothes with vests and all that ready to pack, and I'd a bought me some neckties that didn't have food drippings on them cause I was planning to be one of the boys over there. But no, I'm still trapped in the same old sharecropper image.

The only cost to me was going to be writing a paper of around 20 pages on one of many issues they gave to choose from. And I had wrote 19 pages and had one more to go when I got the message the trip had been canceled. But I tell you, I had wet that pencil eraser so much by the time I got 19 pages wrote down the paper looked like something I'd done in school 55 years ago. I'd a had to do the whole thing over.

So nobody can't say I didn't try being "class" for once in my life, but it just didn't work out. I was planning to give everybody a rundown on my escapades, but I think it must have been predetermined that I was supposed to write about the lowly, the backroads of life and about nothing on earth but poor folks. And you know something: That's all I want to write about, anyhow.

Long Trails Of Summer

The long trails of summer lead to the harvests of October and November, and along those trails are scattered memories of pleasant scenes from a time mellowed by the passing years.

Along those paths gourds hang heavy on wire fences, still clinging to the vines with the large leaves showing signs of age. They grew and fulfilled their mission in a short span of time, completing their life cycle and ensuring fruit for another year.

The popcorn patch is now brown, with the yellow, red, orange and multi-colored ears of miniature corn awaiting picking. The patch is planted a good ways from the field corn to prevent mixing. The husks will be pulled from the ears and tobacco twine looped around the ears and made into strings that will be hung under a shelter for protection.

Every path leads to grapevines where the ripe fruit hangs among the thick foliage, where wasps, yellow jackets and hornets congregate every year for their rituals around the ripening fruit.

The late apples are ripe and the ground under the trees is covered with the half-rotten fruit.

Onions have been pulled from the garden, tied in clusters and hung under the shelter for winter use. And the spider webs are large, extending for several feet sometimes.

Hardweeds have seeded out and only a killing frost will rid the premises of the hardy plants. The grass is tall and brown, bent from its heavy load of seeds.

A solitary tree on a hedgerow glistens in the sun in its solid mass of yellow and in the forests the leaves are changing colors to paint the picture of autumn.

The trails lead to the hog pasture where spring pigs have grown into shoats to be fattened and killed later and the meat used for food. The shoats are lanky, weighing about a hundred pounds, but a floored pen, plenty of shelled corn and water will put weight on

·their thin frames in a short period of time. Only fat hogs are killed (in contrast to the slender, meat-type animals killed today).

Gunsmoke rises in the air and there is a smell of powder as hunters stalk the plump doves that have grown fat from the grain in the fields.

Paths under spreading oak trees are filled with acorns.

A rabbit darts across the path and goes on its way through a whitening cotton field.

There is the show of the goldenrods along country roads. There are thousands of them in their orange color making a flowery pathway for travelers along the roads. They are just weeds during the summer months and go unnoticed, but when we ride on the wagons taking cotton to the gin, every foot of the way is marked with the lowly flowers that do their share to make autumn bright.

That is the same route we walk to and from school. And until cold weather kills the flowers, they greet us morning and afternoon. It is no different if we take the path from the house to the back fields to pick cotton or perform other chores. Goldenrods grow along every path.

Any color is especially appreciated, for ours is a rather dull world with little brightness showing. That makes the magnificence of the fall coloring in the forests all the more appealing.

Wherever there is color, it brings instant attention. That is why the memory of chrysanthemums that bloom late and have colorful flowers has always stood out in my mind. And I never remember seeing the plants in people's yards. They were always at the ends of gardens or standing alone at the edge of yards. Some would be very dark red, others yellow or pink or bronze, but they were never planted en masse and in many cases there was a solitary plant shouting for recognition. And the blooms were always killed by the frosts. I used to wonder how long they would have bloomed if the weather had been warm and I felt they weren't given a fair break, since they bloomed so late.

I remember a few women had straw flowers in their gardens, and they would cut them and take them inside for winter bouquets after they dried.

The corn stalks that were lush green and swayed in the summer breezes during the growing season now stand forlorn and lifeless, holding on to their abundant fruit with heavy ears of corn ready for picking. So much accomplished in such a short time.

It is the beginning of the end of a season, with Mother Nature preparing for the winds and storms of winter, always changing, always coming at an appointed time and ending when the cycle is complete.

Beside a ditch bank thick with summer growth, a snake has shed its skin and the discard has the appearance of the serpent in lifeless form.

So far away. So long ago. So pleasant to remember. A trail of endless memories.

A Barnyard Scene From Long Ago

Sights And Sounds Of Fall

F eathers, feathers everywhere! Roosters with no tail feathers, but they crow just as loud and flap their wings and carry on like you wouldn't believe. Must be mad with the young crop of roosters that can fly and pitch on a fence post and crow and fly down like a bird.

Last year's crop of chickens is shedding, and the whole dern yard is covered with feathers. There's one near 'bout big enough to use for a writing quill. And ain't nary one of the shedding hens laying no eggs, and the pullets ain't got used to it all yit and their eggs ain't half as big as them old hens' when they git down to the business of producing eggs. Oh well, it happens every fall and when they git their feathers back they'll be putting out eggs agin. And them old roosters with no feathers to brag about will git new coats to go along with them one-and-a-half-inch spurs and they'll be the "cocks-of-the-walk" agin.

Them old hickory nuts under the tree on the way to the hog pasture are everywhere, and ain't worth a cuss as far as eating goes. Hardest things to crack you ever seen. And if you do git one cracked ain't enough meat there to mess with. Have to find the littlest nail around to try to pry the meat from the shell. Then there ain't enough to taste. But you know them young'uns. They'll take 'em to the hearth and git a flat arn and hold it up about two feet over the hickory nut and let it come down, and if it cracks it splatters and goes all over the room.

Look at all them cockleburs on my britches legs. And the fields are loaded down with 'em. Shore hope cockleburs don't say nothing 'bout a cold winter. It couldn't be them though, for they's a crop of cockleburs every year, wet or dry or whatever. Hate to even think about the mules' tails when they git in the fields hauling out corn. It'll take til next spring to git all of 'em out of their tails. But at least they ain't so many flies for them to fight this time of the year.

Tell you one thing that's got to be done right quick. Them pigs' done growed into young boars and they got to be trimmed so they can be put in the fattening pen. Dern if that didn't slip up on me. Let me go check on the coal tar.

Gitting a hankering now for the Thanksgiving season to come. Got hunting on my mind and I'm gitting a taste for partridge. It'll take six or eight for the crowd, but old Clyde will see to it that I git at least a dozen if I do half as good a job of shooting them as she does setting them. And when the old lady gits through parboiling them, rolling 'em in flour and frying 'em and then making gravy to go with the birds and a big bowl of rice to pour the gravy over, that'll be something fit for a king to eat.

And old Boots is raring to go in the brier patches and run out all the rabbits anybody could want. But that ain't nothing new with Boots. She does the same thing when hunting season hain't even been thought about.

Uh, oh! I hear a gun going off across the mash. Somebody's already out there looking for game. Tell you what though. Rabbits and doves and partridges come in good to put on the table when meat's all gone from the smokehouse and anything that's left there is so rusty it tastes when it's put in the boiling pot.

Squirrel ain't bad either, 'specially since he's got a furry tail. 'Cept for that, I wouldn't be tasting of no squirrel, cause he looks too much like a rat otherwise. And even then there's a little squeamish feeling in the stomach when I eat squirrel, even if they're about as clean as any animal can be I reckon, with their diets of nuts mostly. Just bring in that furry tail and put it where I can see it and I'll tackle that squirrel meat and even sop the gravy.

But I ain't going to eat no old possum, no matter what anybody says. They can bake 'em any way they want to, have the juiciest sweet taters to go with 'em, or anything else they can concoct, but I don't want to taste of nothing that grins like an old possum grins and that looks like a giant rat, even to its color (and a slick tail like a nasty rat).

Whoo-pee! Look at them purple bullises up there in that "sweegum" tree! The young'uns shore missed 'em when all the leaves hid them from view. Now they're just a shining high up over the ditch and they'll be tree-climbing when I tell 'em the wild grapes are hanging up there in clusters.

I ain't even hardly going to mention all the color I see all around me in the woods. Everybody says I'm a pure nut about the colors that say something to my soul and that everybody can't see what I see and that I carry it too far. Well, all right, I'll just let it rest there. But good Lord, thank You for letting me see it. I 'preciate it and if I've just got to talk about it, I'll say it to You. What I say to You matters more'n everything else I say anyhow, for nobody else cares nohow. Just thank You for the fall season. Thank You, Lord.

Things Almost Forgotten

I am the past.
    I speak of things weathered by time; archaic; yellowed and almost forgotten. I speak of eras as if they came and went without any real impact on their passing.

I speak of times and places and inconsequential events; of a life more beautiful in remembering than when it was a reality; of seasons and trivial everyday activities of people in their walks through life; of events that shaped us and made of us what we are.

I walk down paths, along trails, beside streams that bear no footprints from steps whose imprints were long ago erased by winds and rains and erosion, ensuring there would be no marks left for posterity.

I speak of memories that flood the soul, memories that, unlike footprints, refuse to die. They live and breathe and renew old acquaintances; they erase tears and sorrows and hardships and give a new perspective that enhances every incident, every remembrance, adding a luster that grows more brilliant with age.

I walk again in a world of wonderment, a world so many know nothing about; a world filled with nature; personal and complete with brilliant sunrises, blue skies, gentle winds, painted sunsets, star-filled skies and golden moons. But there are also the storms, the starless nights, sunless days, relentless winds, tin roofs rattling, pails and tubs and other utensils blown about as if they were feathers; of rainy days, lonely landscapes and bitter cold.

My footprints were left where paths existed that are no longer there; where streams ran that are now dry; where happiness reigned in a boy's world, where anything became possible ' because I dared to dream. I lived in a world that is no more, but a world that was real and touchable and that gave me more than I gave the world.

I saw something special in an humble way of life and the beauty of people who made up my world. I failed to recognize it for what it was at that time. But we are all made wiser by the passing years.

I walk through the moth-eaten fabric of yesterday, the mold and the dampness, the dust to which everything returns, uncovering the old and making it new again, recreating a kingdom of the mind in which there is an orderly progression of life, to a time that was a reality, and still lives in the hearts of many from that world.

I hear the songs of an era that must still be echoing somewhere in the vastness of space, songs of a time and a people; songs of love and hope and the plaintive cries of the downtrodden; beautiful melodies and poems that transcend time and still live in the heart.

I see again the scenes of an era that today's generations long to recreate to show quaint life styles that would be treasures for the camera's eye; scenes that live only in the mind. There is no artist's easel to capture them, for memories are intangible.

The seasons come and go, each with its special rewards. The snows of winter change landscapes; tree limbs creak from the winds; fireplaces glow with embers from wood fires; Christmases brighter in memory than all the colorful ornaments of today.

Spring with its rebirth; rushing waters and wildflowers blooming along quaint paths and in back fields, only seen when those places in the heart are visited by the rural people, especially the children who patrol their domain as if it were a military installation.

Summer and swimming holes and growing crops and hard work; parties and chicken fries and watermelon-cuttings; family reunions and church gatherings; storms with thunder and lightning; blue skies and balmy days sometimes and green crops waving in summer breezes.

Births and deaths and romances and marriages; private, insignificant events that make up life and give it reality.

I see lighted windows at the end of long paths, every one leading to home. I see aprons and bonnets, patched clothes and ragged overalls, shackly houses and bare floors, chimneys and washpots, woodpiles and tobacco barns; domestic scenes that spell families and love.

I walk through October, beautiful October, when autumn gives its reward for a year's labor, when birds fly swiftly over corn fields heavy with their yield of grain; where rabbits dart swiftly over the land and seek refuge in brier patches and forests, out of view of the human eye; where squirrels play and store acorns and other nuts for their winter diets; where o'possums roam and raccoons appear beside streams sometimes; where persimmons ripen and walnuts fall and nature heaps its bounty upon the land.

I live again the reality of the simple life, of simple people, of simple life styles and simple pleasures; of scenic scenes that I would impart to the world if that were possible.

I walk in a land where many fear to tread, overgrown with the rubbish of years that has become a heathen environment in which modern man has no place; a way of life many are hesitant to lay claim to in a setting too quaint for many to reminisce about.

I am a sharecropper again, with overalls and straw hat, freckled and with skin reddened by sun and wind; bruised heels and stubbed toes and a simple philosophy. But I am a boy, not wrinkled and aged by time. I am happy in that world.

I am the past.

Not All Was Pretty In Past

S he was young, maybe in her mid-thirties. She held an infant to her blue-veined breast, and the child suckled hungrily for sustenance that wasn't there.

She wore and old dress fashioneed from some discarded material. The hand-sewn stitches were crude and it was evident there was no mastery of the art of sewing. The dress was straight and baggy and her body was thin — very thin.

Hanging on to her skirt were three children — a boy, maybe six, a girl, perhaps four, and another girl, about one-and-one-half years old. The children were whimpering and their teeth were chattering from the cold November winds. Their skin was red from the cold and they were clothed in near-rags that had been gathered from trash piles, or donated by neighbors.

The mother gazed down at her children, and there was a look of total defeat on her face. Her near-black eyes appeared to be staring beyond what she saw and wisps of black hair hung around her face. It was evident that another child was on the way.

The old house was a hovel that had been untenanted for years until they took up residence, allowing the elements to take their toll. A door had fallen when the framing around it rotted. Some of the windows were only gashing holes while a few had a window light or two still intact. Rags were stuffed into the holes in the two inhabited interior rooms.

There was one old iron bedstead and one with a high headboard, with two ragged mattresses filled with pine straw. Ragged quilts in disarry were on the beds. There were no sheets or pillow cases.

Two straight-back chair frames with boards nailed to the top for seats were in the room, and an old trunk with a ragged lid that obviously did not go with the body of the trunk.

A discarded cookstove, pulled from a trash heap, stood in one corner of the kitchen with bricks holding up two missing legs. The top hinge still remained on the fire box. There was a makeshift table, made from rough weatherboarding pulled from an old barn at the back of the premises. But the wood from the barn had long-since been burned. There was a lard can sitting on the stove in which water was boiled, and several smaller cans used for cooking. Chipped saucers were sitting on the table and used as eating utensils. One can was filled with uncooked rice, and there was perhaps a pound of fatback lying on the table. Another bucket was used for water brougt in from the well that was almost filled with debris, leaving only enough room to dip the leaking bucket into the water and pull it back up.

It had been unseasonably warm until an approaching cold front had brought rain, and a shift in the winds to the north after its passage.

He entered from the woods with an armful of dead limbs to light a fire in the fireplace and heat the cookstove. He was bearded and clothed in a ragged denim jacket held together with safety pins, and patched pants that gave the appearance of a patchwork quilt.

Limbs were broken and placed in the fireplace and a search made for a match with which to light the fire. The children waited eagerly for warmth from the fire to ease the cold. When the dead wood ignited, it sent flames up the old chimney and the family gathered in front of the fire and the woman'e eyes looked deeply into the flames.

The baby finally ceased nursing and slept and his mouth slipped from the wrinkled teat and he was placed on the bed and covered with the ragged quilts. The children lay before the fire, savoring the warmth, and the redness left their legs and arms. The one-

and-one-half-year-old girl smiled as she watched the flames rise up the chimney and her face lighted up as if she had been in the company of angels.

A piece of burning limb was taken to the kitchen to light a fire in the cookstove. The family was hungry, for there had been no food during the day.

Rice was put into a lard can and water added and the can placed on the stove. An old griddle that had been found on the edge of the woods was placed on the stove. The fatback was sliced and placed in the pan to fry.

When the rice had boiled a few minutes there were thick bubbles on top, and some of the water was poured into another can to use in making gravy. Starch from the rice would serve as a thickener for the gravy, since there was no flour.

The children gathered around the stove as the meat was fried, their appetites whetted by the aroma of the frying fatback. And when the meat was done, it was placed on a lard stand lid, the grease left in the pan, the rice water added and boiled until there was a slight thickness to the gravy.

They stood around the makeshift table and the parents blew the rice to cool it for the children. They ate the rice and gravy with their hands and crammed their mouths full of the meat. When all the food had been eaten they returned to the fireplace and lay contentedly on the floor.

There was no food for tomorrow. But then, there never was. Somehow, some way, there would be something — a quart of dry peas or butterbeans, a pound of flour and a pound of lard — if anyone could be found that needed work done and had a little pocket change to pay for it, or food.

It was nothing new to them. They had never been in the mainstream of society, although there may have been days when they dared to dream. The reality of life had long-since taken precedence over any other consideration. They struggled just to survive.

It was a classic example of those on the outer fringes of society during the Great Depression. It was the picture too many of later generations think of as being the true picture of the Depression. There was great hunger in many parts of the nation, even in eastern North Carolina, but in the rural areas such cases were few. But it is a picture many from the Depression era still remember — a picture that leaves no radiant afterglow and no fond remembrances.

Cheap Hot Dogs, Ice Cream

T he 1939-1940 era.
Sleepy little towns across eastern North Carolina
weather the summer doldrums and watch as farmers
slave in the tobacco fields to harvest the golden weed. People sit
on their front porches, observing neighborhood life and fanning to
get relief from the heat. Where the sun beats down in the afternoon, many people have planted running beans beside the porches
and run tobacco twine up to the eaves of the porches for the vines
to climb on to provide shade.

The town of Wilson is no exception. Business is at a standstill,
and merchants stand at their doors, pulling anybody inside they
can to show them their merchandise, hoping for a sale, no matter
how small, to put a few pennies in their cash registers.

Wilson boasts the slogan "World's Greatest Tobacco Market,"
and this slogan is not taken lightly. Everyone looks forward to the
opening of the tobacco markets, for it is the rejuvenating process
that brings many people to town.

The warehouse district is spread around the downtown business
district, and when the tobacco starts rolling into the warehouses,
the sweet aroma of the cured leaf settles over the city and
becomes a part of the city smells as long as the market is open. In
the afternoon, haze settles over the city and twilight brings silhouettes of the First Union National Bank Building and the Hotel
Cherry against the darkening sky.

It is the year Adolf Hitler declares war on Poland, precipitating
World War II. It is the era in which Americans cannot foresee de-
velopments that will forever change the face of the nation.

With the tobacco market getting into full swing in September,
Wilson merchants are fully organized and ready for the influx of
customers, particularly its eating establishments.

This is a walk mostly on one side of one block of Barnes Street,
starting at Tarboro Street to Goldsboro Street. The smells of

onions, mustard, chili and roasted peanuts fill the air and there are cries of "hot dogs, five cents, the best in town" and "ice cream, three scoops for a nickel"'and "hot roasted peanuts" from sometimes-embarrassed youngsters of proprietors who are sent ·out to chant the messages to bring in business. There are 11 hot dog stands and restaurants along one side of this block. Count them.

There is Central Lunch, run by Gregory Ladas; Carolina Kitchen, run by George Saleeby; Wilson Lunch whose proprietor is Harry Pappas; Geras' Place, run by Geras Gliarmis; Frozen Delight Ice Cream, run by Eli Abraham (3 dips for a nickel); Dixie Lunch, owned by Harry Sakas; Star Cafe, run by Gus Gliarmis; a place run by Pete Changaris in the basement of Peacock's Grocery; Big Nick's Colony Island; Busy Bee across the street on Goldsboro Street, owned by George Pappas; and Pete and Mike's, corner of Goldsboro and South Streets.

Every owner of the establishments mentioned is an immigrant — mostly Greek, and hardly none even speak English. And there is discrimination against foreigners. It is hard for many of them to find places to live, and most who are able to, build their own homes. But they are happy to be in America, for it was even worse in their mother countries.

The number of employees is to a large extent determined by the number of children in a family. Every child from 10-12 years and up works in the establishment. But in rush seasons, a few extra employees are added.

There is keen competition for the farmers' dollars (or perhaps pocket change would be more appropriate). Hot dogs are a nickel apiece (all the way).

Traffic is slow on the other side of the street. Mr. Gay stands in the doorway of the Gay Company to try to lure customers inside, hoping for a sale of his top-quality merchandise. A few people loiter in front of Heilig & Meyers, looking at furniture displayed in the show windows, comparing it with the "junk" in their homes. And Norman Lewis stands at the back of Bissette's Drug Store No. 2 where the show window displays trusses, bed pans, crutches and such items for the sick.

Nash Street is considered the whites' domain and Barnes Street is the gathering place for colored people. Colored people congregate there by the thousand on Saturday, and a line is drawn in the center of the sidewalk on the side of the street where all the eating establishments are located for people to line up for food, and the outside to traverse Barnes Street.

Capt. H.A. Warren of the police department patrols this one

block every day, from 6 a.m. until noon. This is his only beat.

There are no restroom facilities for blacks along the block, and the alleys are used to relieve themselves. This causes an unpleasant odor in the area. Wine and beer are sold in the eating places, and many people become inebriated and fights are common.

How did they survive? None of those who can remember can answer the question adequately. There is a long season between sales of tobacco when there are not large crowds on the streets every day. It is hard work, beginning long before day — cutting up onions and splitting hot dog rolls — since they don't come already split. It means long hours, lasting into late night and some owners spend the night at their establishments. It is a seven-day-a-week job. It means sacrifice, with only the closeness of families and love for one another to sustain them. The miracle is that they did survive, and their descendants are well-known citizens of Wilson today and as all-American as apple pie and the millions of hot dogs they sold.

For those who will be reminiscing about those days, Vaughan's Jewelers was located between Wilson Lunch and P.L. Woodard Co. Peacock's Grocery was on the corner. There were 15 to 20 eating places around the block that sold hot dogs for five cents and two dips of ice cream for a nickel. But who were the buyers except during the tobacco market seasons during those hard times?

Times sure have changed.

Walking To, From School

When we used to walk two-and-a-half miles to school in the morning and the same distance back home in the afternoon, we had a lot of mess to contend with.

We'd leave home in the morning sometimes when sunlight sparkled on the frost and with not a cloud in the sky. We had to wear our sweaters, caps and toboggans and our long-handles to protect us from the cold, but we carried as little clothing as possible, for there was a booksack slung over our shoulders and a lunch box in one hand, and we didn't want to be burdened with unnecessary clothing.

Well sir, later on in the day a "skirt" of a cloud would cover the sun and rain would come down in sheets for a while, and winds from the north would turn the place into a frigid zone. Somebody would stoke the pot-bellied stove and we young'uns would gather around, trying to thaw out, and time for school to turn out drawing nearer every minute. We had to face that long walk back home.

But bless 'em, somebody in the neighborhood that had an old car would crank it up, stop at people's houses and get heavier coats for us and go to the schoolhouse to pick us up. That tells you something about how people were in those days.

The same thing would happen when an unsuspecting snowfall came during school hours. Sometimes a few flakes might come down and every young'un at school was as excited as he'd be Christmas morning. We'd open up our lunch boxes, wipe off the grease that had solidified on our meats, spoon up mouthfuls of collards and bite off a hunk of peeled baked sweet taters while looking out the window, hoping the snowflakes would thicken and start covering everything in white. And in a lot of cases, that's just what happened.

Meanwhile, folks back home were getting heavy coats to us again to keep us warm, and sure enough, somebody would come and get us.

But getting caught in a spring rainstorm was about the worst thing we had to put up with. We'd high-tail it from school with our burden of clothing and books, carrying on and cutting the fool, and that cloud that had been low on the horizon would suddenly start moving and coming over us. And sometimes we'd get as wet as a "drownded" rat. I've seen every strand of hair on our heads matted from drenching rain. Water would even sqush in our shoes sometimes. But we didn't mind that, cause we won't cold.

They'd stick us in front of the fire when we got home after we took off the wet clothes and shed our shoes. The towel from the back porch would be brought in for us to rub our wet hair in, but being hard material made from salt sacks, it didn't absorb any of the wetness. Besides, the towel had already been used for hand-wiping anyway.

We'd turn our shoes sideways and put them as close to the fire as we could and pull off our socks and lay them close to the fire also. Our feet would be wrinkled from all the water in our shoes, and we'd watch as the steam rose from the smelly socks and we dreaded what was coming.

And you know our noses were getting stopped up by then, so after supper Ma would come by with the blue bottle of Vicks "pneumonia cure" and run her finger down in the greasy mess, come up with a little lump and run it into our nostrils. And she always did the dipping and running the salve up our noses. She never let us doctor ourselves.

And of course, before bedtime, there was the rubbing ritual. And what was rubbed on us depended on what was around the house. "Pneumonia cure" was one good bet, saturated all over our chests. Camphorated oil was another, but at any given time any one of several remedies might be out. They'd rub Sloan's Liniment over a chest in a hot minute if there wasn't something else around that might have done better. If medicines were scarce enough, each young'un might git a different remedy. And it's amazing how much salve can be retrieved from a seemingly empty container. Ma could take that index finger and run it around a Cloverine Salve can that looked completely empty and come up with enough to spread over a young'uns chest 'fore you could count to 10.

There might even be 10 drops of kerosene over a teaspoon of sugar for us to swallow, or turpentine if they thought about it. And just for good measure, they might bring out the bottle of castor oil and dangle that in front of us. They were going to git a jump on the colds by working them out of us before they had a chance to git us all full of phlegm.

I don't reckon there was anything in the animal line of medicines around the place to use for colds, but for some ailments, they'd resort to salves used on a mule, or a cow's teats for cuts and bruises, and think nothing about it. This young crowd just don't know nothing about the old folks in those days. As far as I know they never used creosote dip or Paris Green on us young'uns, but excluding those, just about anything else was for human treatment as well as lower animals.

I been thinking about it, and it's a wonder to me that didn't more of us fail to git past the stage of saying "ain't, shant, airy, nary, nuther, druther" and such words than did. I tell you, we had something to put up with in trying to learn the ABC's and geography and all that. We sacrificed to git our educations.

Fat Hogs From A Nostalgic Era
Courtesy Joyce Proctor Beaman

Hogs Were Turned Out

Y ou've got to be old, outdated and a country hick by
birth to remember the days when farmers turned out
their hogs after the corn was housed. But they did turn
them out, and I mean to tell you those rootin'-tootin' hogs cut them
a shine.

They had fields to roam in all over the neighborhood. There
were nubbins of corn left in the fields, and no matter how hard you
tried to git up all the taters, plenty of them were left in the fields,
and the hogs had their chance at them, too. But hogs is just like
everything else. They want to git into whatever they ain't supposed to. And there was nothing they loved better than to git in people's yards and root up everything around. And there shore won't
nothing in a yard for a hog to eat, 'less it was acorns that fell under
them big oaks. And they rooted just as bad in yards that didn't
have no oak trees.

Them rascals roamed in herds, and I ain't never known how
they'd stray like they did and come home at night. No more sense
than most hogs showed, you'd a thought they'd stray away and
just keep on going.

Womenfolks used to git so mad at hogs rooting they couldn't

hardly stand it. They'd look outside and see a gang of hogs tearing up everything in the yard and they'd go outside, shaking their aprons and hollering, "git." Sometimes the aprons fanning in the breeze would git their attention and they might go into a field, but in too many cases they just kept on rooting unless she picked up a stick and beat them on their fattening behinds.

I've known them to turn over washpots while munching through the ashes and chewing little bits of partially-burned wood around the washpots.

And some of the holes they rooted didn't git filled in all winter, and the result was a lot of mudholes in yards. But some folks made them young'uns git out there and shovel the dirt back in the holes, 'specially if the yard was all tore up where the path led to the clothesline. Take a woman with a heavy tub of wet clothes to be hung out and having her jumping over holes and gitting over-balanced and having pieces of clothing fall in the dirt made some of the maddest women you ever seen.

And everybody knows that hogs were of a general mixture in most cases, for people weren't raising no show prospects. Oh, there were Poland China, Duroc Jersey, Spotted Poland China, Hampshire and breeds like that back then, but in most cases a sow was bred to the nearest boar and the pigs were of all colors. But you know another person's hogs looked pure "quare" when you'd see them in the yard. Anybody can put up with his own mess better'n somebody else's. It's like having somebody else's dog come in your yard and do you-know-what. It's a lot worse than if it's your own flea-hound. Same way with hogs.

We'd look at them and Pa would try to figger out whose they were, knowing no more about it than I did. The only way we could spot whose they might be was if it was a whole pack or Poland Chinas or solid reds that we knew one or two people in the community raised.

And hogs and fall always remind me of pine straw. Every hog shelter had to have a plentiful supply of pine straw, 'specially if a sow was going to have pigs. Every shelter had a top and pine straw for a bed. We'd haul straw from the woods in big wagon loads and toss it in the hog shelters.

To show you the sense of a hog, there ain't nothing on earth for a hog to root or eat on a paved road unless somebody has lost corn out of a wagon, and that didn't happen much. But I guarantee you that every herd of hogs that was turned out took them a walk down the highway while they were on the loose. They were just like a pack of rowdy boys — willing to try anything on God's earth just for the heck of it. And they was traffic on the highways in them days, too. But if it was today wouldn't a one of them simple swine survive. They'd be hit 'fore they even got used to the solid pavement under their feet.

Anybody that saw them on the highway would go out and run them off and try to direct them back to the fields. But sometimes it was too late. Ever so often, some shoat or hog would git knocked off, and if the owner could be found they'd take the carcass and try to save it. They'd dress the hog, and if it won't too bruised and beat up, they'd either eat it right then, or if the weather was cold they'd salt it down. But I didn't never like the looks of momicked up hog, and I don't never remember eating any of it. But Lord, I might have. Some things just don't stay in the mind.

But them hogs would start fattening while running in the fields (and in yards and on highways) and by the time they were put in floored pens they were easily fattened with plenty of shelled corn and water. During the summer months they had survived with Red Dog wheat chops that we'd stir up for them in five-gallon cans (and always having some of the chops ending up on our overhall legs). I thought several times during those years that our hogs would starve to death, from the way they acted. I never thought wheat chops had much strength in it nohow, but it must of been stronger than I thought. Anyhow, every time anything was bought in town, a sack of wheat chops was bought too. And they could of eaten three times as much as they were given, plus the slops from the table and a few ears of corn at night.

The best thing I can say about the hogs in those days is that they gave us those hams I've raved about, the luscious sausages, the good old chitlins, the cracklings, the boiling meat that seasoned vegetables, including those pots of collards, ham hocks and sides and shoulders and livers and feet — in fact — everything 'cept the hair.

Moving Was A Common Sight

I t could have been a scene from an Erskine Caldwell novel. There they were, old shackly wagons moving at a snail's pace along dusty roads, some with wobbly wheels where the boxing that held the axles had busted, drawn by raw-bony mules with the driver sitting high above the wagon atop a conglomeration of "junk" furniture and other household items being moved from one farm to another. It was a common sight 50 years ago.

There were bedstids placed at the front end of the wagon body, separated by quilts, bureaus and washstands, ladder-back chairs placed upside down around the body of the wagon with feather beds, pillows and bolsters piled high above the furniture. Where the bed ticking had been pierced, goose down escaped and appeared as snowflakes surrounding the wagons.

On some wagons would be barrels with broom sage or cooking utensils piled full along with other items of furniture. There was no end to the accumulation of articles with large families of the day. And neighbors would help in the moving process.

Some tenants and sharecroppers lived at the same place for many years and raised their families. And when that was the case, the tenant usually made small repairs without bothering the landlord, such as replacing a rotten piece of weatherboarding or patching porch floors rotted by time and water. But for a number of reasons, there was an appreciable amount of moving every year. A tenant or a sharecropper might feel he had been cheated by the landlord, or those tending the land might be careless farmers and unacceptable to the landlord. And some people simply liked the idea of moving, always searching for greener pastures.

It was a mess from beginning to end. Everything had to be packed up before the moving could progress, and boxes were full of shoes and clothing and things from the kitchen. All the jars of fruit had to be wrapped with mewspaper and placed in boxes to try to keep them from breakage. Ths strings of pepper had to be placed in the box, the dried sage leaves in the small sugar sack, the dried apples and peaches, the coffee grinder, the plates and cups and saucers and dishes. It seemed endless.

Sometimes it looked like a small caravan traveling down the road. A cow might be hitched to the end of a wagon, or a goat. But the household furnishings were moved first.

There was a problem with moving sometimes. If a tenant or sharecropper had been told to move by a certain date and the house he was moving into was still occupied, there were occasions when "moving in" was a necessity. That was when one family would move in on another, resulting in two families occupying one house at the same time, and talking about a mess! That was about the worst you could git into. I know, 'cause a family moved in on us one time. The party that "moved in" on the other had to do this or have his furniture set in the yard.

It was a matter of courtesy for most movers to clean out the house they were moving from. That entailed getting out all the trash and sweeping the floors, but not scouring them. If the old rug in the kitchesn was too rotten to be moved (they usually were) the women would pull up the pieces and throw them onto a trash pile and burn them. But this was not a requirement, and occasionally people moved into houses that were filthy and had to be cleaned out before the furniture could be placed in the rooms.

The women used to say they were swapping chinches with the people they were replacing and those that were moving where they had lived. Nothing could be truer, for those old houses were literally filled with bedbugs.

It took some doing to get all the beds up and the kitchen stove in place and wood to burn in the fireplace and the stove, find bed clothing and make the beds, get the wash basins out on the porch shelf and a towel hung for drying hands. Pots and pans had to be found and put to use in getting something to eat prepared.

Some tenants owned farm machinery and implements, and the moving process extended over a week or more. Wire fencing had to be taken down and rolled up and hauled by wagon to the new residence, as did tobacco sticks. Chickens had to be cooped up, guineas caught at their roosting places in the trees, geese penned up, and the wooden crates hauled over the dirt roads.

Clothesline posts and the metal line were taken down to be repositioned at the new residence. Sometimes the cats were just left at the old place for they wandered off many times anyway when taken to a strange place. There were no doubt some left by the people moving out. And there were plenty to go around anyway.

It seemed strange at a new place for a while and there was a period of orientation. The sun didn't seem in the right orbit and the landscape was different. There were new neighbors and new children and a general feeling of isolation until the family became a part of the neighborhood.

If a house was open, some families would move before Christmas so they would be settled down for the new year. But a lot of people moved around the first of the year.

Moving always messed up the hens' laying cycle, and there was a week or two with no eggs. Women would try to save up enough eggs to tide them over after moving until the hens went back to laying again.

And of course the well water tasted different and everybody complained about it. They longed for water from the well at the other house. Things just weren't right for a few weeks after people moved, and there was a lot of adjusting to do. But in general, every place was about the same except for the location and that foul-tasting water. But people did adjust, and things went on at a normal pace.

The Day I Was Born

T he old house was hardly noticed from the road. It fitted into the color scheme of the soil and the surroundings — dull gray.

Only the shackly mailbox at the edge of the road told who the inhabitants were. The post holding up the mailbox fit loosely in the ground and the box was slanted. Tire tracks made by the old Overland automobile stopping at the mailbox cut deeply and spewed mud on the outer rims of the tracks.

The path leading to the house was filled with mudholes and the tater patch beside the road was torn up by the hogs that were running out. Corn stalks were brown with many pushed over by the hogs that hunted for nubbin ears, and the September gust that had blown down many stalks as the winds roared over the fields from the equinox storm that separated the summer and fall seasons.

The old flea-hound, whatever his name, lay on the guano-sack mat at the bottom porch step, scratching his life away (from mange, not fleas). An old yaller tabby cat with thin sides watched carefully from her ground position for a rat or mouse to come from under the barn to furnish a morsel of food for her kittens that were sucking her half to death.

Oats were hanging from the loft door where they had been pulled down to throw into the mule stables. A hinge was broken on the loft door, and it sagged inward, taking up part of the door space.

The large oaks in the yards were shorn of their leaves and the thousands of branches poked themselves toward the sky. From a ground view, the limbs were knotted and gave the appearance of being afflicted with rheumatism. Remaining leaves were lying around the smokehouse and any other place they could be blown by the wind.

It was a dismal setting, with the woods brown in the edges and a background of green where the tall pines grew and whispered their secrets to other inhabitants of the forest. The ground was black, made more obvious by dead foliage and bare places where greenery had changed the landscape in summer.

Some half-a-mile from the house was a cotton field where specks of white glistened in the Saturday morning sunshine, and where members of the family were "scrapping" cotton. It was a yearly ritual. The first picking always left unopened bolls of cotton in the fields, and when they finally matured and the lint was there to pick, the cotton was picked and taken to the gin and sold for buying Christmas supplies. And Christmas was only two-and-a-half weeks away.

Pots of boiling water were on the stove and preparations were under way for the big event. Another baby! The ninth! After over five years! Aunt Emma Bryant, the midwife, was there. Ragged sheets were torn for use during the birth and things were going on normal-like.

Aunt Emma was in there tending to the boiling pots and gumming a baked sweet tater and licking her fingers where the juice oozed out after the yam was taken from its jacket.

Then she went to the back bedroom where the old brown cradle had been for some four years and where junk could be dumped easily. There were the rag bag and a bunch of socks that needed darning and ragged clothes that needed patching and an old corset or two — things like that. All of that had to be cleared away to make room for the NEW arrival. I reckon Ma just got too loaded down and let getting the cradle ready slip up on her.

When Aunt Emma went back to the bedroom there was travail, and a wail, and there I was! And I think that's the way it was, although I'll admit I can't readily recall that day.

I can just see the pack as they came home for lunch and my

sisters warmed up the collards and made a hoecake of cornbread and patted it out on the griddle on top of the stove. I expect there were some cracklings around to go with the juicy sweet taters and I can just see 'em as they peeped under the crib sheet and saw the little monstrosity. I'll bet one of them young'uns said, "What's wrong with his ears"? (except they said 'yuers'. "They stick out like a bat's."

And I know there was some giggling going on as the whole brood came up to git their peek. There shore won't nothing new about another baby in the house.

And to tell the truth, if it was today they would go and do an amniocentesis long before the baby was due, or whatever it is when they take a needle and draw some amniotic fluid from the uterus and check to see if a normal baby is growing in there. You see, Ma was 44 and Pa 45 when I "happened" for it shore won't planned. And they say babies from such matings in the older years hain't got quite all they're supposed to have up there. They'd a sure found something wrong with that fluid (as if you didn't already know).

But I need to clue you in on a few details about that old house. There was an L-shaped porch and doorsteps going up each L. One set of steps led to the front room and the other the kitchen.

There were all of four rooms for the 10 of us and wherever there was room, a bedstid was put up. And you can forgit about brothers and sisters not sharing the same rooms. Heck, we had to share the same bed sometimes, and I never heard no tell of nobody thinking anything about it nor of anybody being raped or abused or whatever they say is wrong with a sick society of today. Our sickness was poorness, and we didn't have no fever with that.

There won't nary drop of paint put on that old house, inside or outside, and the windows were little and it looked dreary inside. But you know that with a pack of young'uns, it was not dreary around that place.

So I got my start in life only a month after the Armistice was signed ending World War I, and of all the things they could have done better for me, the Japs decided to bomb Pearl Harbor on my birthday, too! What a winner!

That's me folks, and it happened in 1918.

A Hog-Killing From The Past

Courtesy Minnie E. Thorne

Hog-Killing, Round Two

T he old man sat up close to the fireplace on a Sunday afternoon in December. In fact, his brogans were on the hearth. He was sharpening knives. He had bought a new file and rammed half a corncob on the spindly end of the file in order to have a better hand grip. And he had the old gray whetstone beside him. He'd file a while, then spit on the stone and sharpen a knife so it would cut paper upon touch. He got too warm and pushed his old chair back and got tangled up under the bureau and he jumped up and stomped.

The old lady looked at him like she could have killed him because he was working on the sabbath. But the old man paid her no attention. Instead, he told her them shoats had to be killed; that they were lard fat and the old sow too and they were eating him out of corn 'fore Christmas. But he was worried about the weather. It won't cold enough to kill hogs, but something had to be done. They'd always trusted God to provide weather for saving meat and they'd have to trust Him again. If push came to shove, and the weather was too warm he could git a block of ice, place old oilcloth over the meat and crack the ice and place it on top of the meat.

He said he'd told them boys on Sad'dy that a hole had to be dug on the edge of the cotton patch for ridding the chitlins and that the barrel had to be put in the ground and Jiley's vat hauled to the woodpile to use with the old sow that would weigh 500 pounds if she weighed a pound. But no, they had something to do Sad'dy night, Sunday evening and Sunday night, too. Well, they could git up at 4 o'clock Monday morning 'stid of 5, and do all them things.

Night came and he went out and scanned the skies and "felt out" the weather, but there was nothing to go by. Plenty of stars were in the heavens but they were muted and didn't shine very brightly. He figgered there were high clouds up there that hid the stars from full view.

The old man didn't sleep good that night. He tossed and turned, and sometime after midnight got chilly and hunted for more "kivver" and finally dozed off. But being a man in command of himself, he could will himself to awaken whenever he wanted to. So as the clock was striking 4 he got up and built a fire. Then he called them deep-sleeping boys and listened to their groans as they eased out of bed and ran into the room where the fire was, in their long drawers, dragging their overalls and shoes with them.

Shine went to the window and said he be durned if it won't snowing out there and the old man said naw, it couldn't be snowing. But sure enough, it was, and the menfolks got things going while snowflakes pelted down.

The old man told Hank he was 18 years old and it was time for him to knock them hogs in the head and stick 'em, too. There was a knife with a long, narrow blade for sticking the hogs. So Hank took the ax in hand and the younger boys climbed in the pen with him so they could turn the hogs on their backs after they were felled.

Luby and Dora and Jiley and Lizzie came to help with the hog-killing, and as the hogs were scalded and the hair scraped off and some of them hung up, the old man took Hank to the gallows and said he was going to gut them hogs, too. No sense in raising a boy to be grown and not teach him everything about farm life. He showed Hank where to begin cutting and as soon as there was room for two fingers to get inside, he told Hank to be careful and not cut a gut or there would be a mess. So Hank cut all the way down the hog and its guts hung out and a tub was placed under the carcass to catch them.

Snow was falling fast and patches of white began to show on grass in the fields and the inside of the hog was steaming while Hank was doing his work. He took out the haslet and hung it on the gallows and the old man told Little Bud to carry it to his mammy so she could make some liver hash for dinner. She'd need to git it in the pot as soon as she could.

A gilt was next to be dressd out, and Hank was taking pride in his work. She had run out after the corn was housed with other gilts and young boars. She was carrying pigs and the old man pointed and told Hank "that" was not part of the chitlins — to cut it out and throw it in the hole where the chitlins were being worked on.

That old sow was near 'bout more than they could handle. They had to put a trace chain around her and it took all the men to git her on the scales. And she did weigh right at 500 pounds. She was so big the old man took pity on Hank and dressed her out. And wouldn't you know, he was the one that cut a slit in a gut. This made the old man cuss and he told Fuzz to run and git a piece of backer twine so they could tie up the hole or there'd be a mess to beat the band.

It looked like a slaughter house by the time all 12 shoats and the sow were dressed, and the snow had ceased and the sun was trying to come out, but the wind was colder. The Good Lord had looked down on the old man agin, and he said out loud, "Thank You, God." The old lady was standing at the back door inspecting collard leaves as he spoke. She didn't say a word, just shook her head.

They had a time gitting all them hogs cut out and sausage ground and stuffed, and the old man told the old lady to be sure and save a right smart of them big chitlins for sausage, and be sure to stuff a few Tom Thumbs, too, 'cause he loved big sausage when it cured out good, and the young'uns did, too.

And there won't half as much corn-shucking going on when it was time to feed up that night. Them boys had shucked and shelled so much corn for that pack of hogs their hands were pure sore.

After all them freshes at dinner, everybody was puny at the supper table. It was just a little too much greasy stuff at one time, and they said they shore didn't want no brains and eggs for breakfast, either. But they liked the idea of sausage patted out and fried to a golden brown with flecks of red pepper showing when it was broken open, and the taste of sage to add to the flavor. They were also thinking how nice it would have been if the snow could have fallen on Christmas morning.

Thanksgiving: Cotton Patches

W ith Thanksgiving behind us and reminders of sour stomach and burping and belching grease after feasting on "the bird" and all the trimmings plus pumpkin pie and all that stuff, we're headed for the biggest day of all now — Christmas.

But I am eternally talking about change and its impact on our lives. And I can tell you one thing right now. If we'd a seen an old white turkey strutting around in the barnyard in the old days, we'd a thought it was an old turkey "haint." Out there behind the pines we'd never seen the likes of a white turkey. Now there may have been some somewhere, but we shore hadn't seen none of them.

There were white rabbits in those days, and white mice that some crazy young'uns kept as pets. But I hated a white mouse as bad as I did a gray one even then. In other words, I ain't never had nothing in common with no kind of rodent, and I think of a mouse in the same sense I think of a nasty rat.

But back to the white turkey. Before Thanksgiving they had the white gobblers strutting around on their way to the White House and they looked just like turkeys, but I didn't see the beauty in them I see in the bronze birds that show some color in their feathering.

Course I know the advantages in having a white-feathered bird. It makes for a cleaner carcass and if a few feathers are left on they don't show up against the light skin. Those dark-colored turkeys and chickens don't dress out as well and on their backs the pin feathers are dark and hard to get out sometimes. So I reckon it's all right that they developed the colorless birds for us Americans that don't want to take the time to clean them like we had to do in the old days. We need all the help we can get to be able to do whatever has to be done with the very least inconvenience possible. We're on the go all the time now whereas when I was a young'un there was nowhere to go and plenty to do, just to keep us out of trouble if nothing else.

Somehow or other I got off on the wrong foot about Thanksgiving. Oh, we read the poem...

Over the river and through the woods, to grandfather's house we go.

The horse knows the way to carry the sleigh o'er the white and drifted snow...and all that, and it seemed wonderful to be anticipating such a delightful day. But the truth of the matter is that we knew that instid of that we'd be out there with cotton sacks on our backs picking those scraggly bolls of cotton that had popped open since the first picking. And nothing's uglier than a field of cotton with just enough white to make it boring to look at.

But the cotton scrappings had their advantages, too. They gave us what spending money we had for Christmas. Most years we didn't pay out nohow, and the cotton that we picked Thanksgiving Day and Friday, and maybe even Saturday, we took to the gin and sold and that provided fruits and nuts and other items we didn't grow to feast on during Christmas.

I tell you I was ready to go back to school on Monday morning and would rather have been there Thanksgiving Day for that matter. It just ain't no fun scrapping cotton. And when I used to pretend to pick cotton, I'd resort to homemade knee pads so I could get down and try to pull the lint from the burs. But whatever I didn't accomplish in picking cotton, I certainly managed to get hangnails on my fingers where the sharp ends of the cotton burs picked away at the skin. And when I was wearing knee pads and a cocklebur got on the under side and my knee mashed down on the pad, those spikes would dig into the knee and I'd have a fit. I could do any other kind of farm work with speed, but I simply could not pick cotton.

Even that far back in history, I dreamed about a machine that would pull cotton from the burs, but I was born a little too soon for the invention to be of any value to me. In fact, I was born too soon for any of the modern-day inventions that make farming easier to be of any value to me.

'Stid of turkey and dressing and cranberry sauce and all that stuff we associate with Thanksgiving today, Ma just might bake a fat hen and make chicken pastry so that when we came home for a little while we could feel like there was something special about the holiday. But it might be a pot of collards and sweet taters instead. We always thought of baked hen as being pretty high on the chicken, if we can call ham pretty high on the hog.

I love the story of Thanksgiving and how the Pilgrims celebrated at Plymouth Rock by giving thanks and serving wild turkey and venison and all such delicacies. But I just couldn't associate that with what I knew about Thanksgiving as a boy.

The best recollections I have about Thanksgiving in those days were the turkey gobbler cutouts stuck on the blackboard on the schoolhouse windows. Those old birds were really doing the "turkey strut" for every one of their tail feathers was spread in a perfect half-circle and I'd look at them and think about the cotton patch and that ruined the whole picture of Thanksgiving for me.

A Ride On A Tobacco Truck
Courtesy Lynwood Sharpe

Two Men Plowing With One Plow
Courtesy Lynwood Sharpe

Children Drinking Pop At Tobacco Market
Courtesy Jimmy Ellis

A Walk Down City Streets

I guess it is a natural instinct to view about everything in retrospect as we grow older. Maybe we are trying to recapture a feeling of what life was like as we look backward to former days. But when we get to thinking about it, we have to pinch ourselves sometimes to realize we are still in the 20th Century.

And there are many things that I miss about the past, and about Wilson, the city of beautiful trees.

I miss the old Imperial Hotel on Nash Street across from the Hotel Cherry, although it was a very plain building that catered to the poorer class people. Even the front porch was slanted, but it was a part of the Wilson scene that is no more.

I miss the beautiful old white house that was Thomas Yelverton Funeral Home. The front porch was so inviting it looked like anybody could while away the day happily and watch the Nash Street traffic go by.

I miss the Briggs Hotel and the good food served in its cafeteria. I remember how many people used to go there for lunch (and other meals).

I miss the J.C. Penney Store across the street, and Efird's as well. And there was also Charles Stores.

Bruce Lamm was a popular men's store located in the old Planters Bank Building on Nash Street and he managed to have the latest styles and fabrics, even during the war years, although they were in a limited number. And Howard Adkins, across the street, was also patronized by men in the area who could expect to find reliable merchandise there.

Then there were the Mother and Daughter Store and Oettinger's Department Store that were prominent on the Wilson scene.

But Bissette's Drug Store No. 1 on Nash Street was a very special place in those days. It was convenient and there were always icy drinks — Coca-Colas, Pepsis, lemonades, orangeades, limeades, and booths to sit in and rest and pass the time of day. But those delicious pies were the greatest calling card in the store. They were homemade, using Mrs. Bissette's recipes, and those cocoanut, chocolate, lemon and other fillings topped with thick meringue for 15 cents a slice were out of this world.

And there was the Wilson Theatre that spoke of dignity and prestige in those days, and Mr. Stallings was manager of the theater for years and the general public flocked to Wilson to see the best the movie world had to offer.

One block off Nash, on Tarboro, was Moss & Co. Department Store, where most area people went to shop. There was Mr. Cobb in the women's department, tall and distinguished looking, and Mr. Vernon in the men's department, equally as impressive, who possessed the greatest sales ability it has ever been my privilege to witness. I once worked at Moss & Co., and they always had a policy of satisfying the customer, or your money back. And I've seen customers lugging the box in which a suit Mr. Vernon had sold returned, and I've heard a few of his many customers say, "Mr. Moss, you sold me this suit so fast I didn't even know what color I was buying," and Mr. Vernon would sell him another suit, and in many cases double the sale. Then later on when the returned suit was hung up, a church program could be found in an inside pocket.

And I miss seeing Mr. Silas Lucas in about any section of Wilson one might be traveling, often on the very outskirts of the city, on his daily walks before walking and jogging became a routine part of life.

In memory, I can still see the Woodard-Herring Hospital at the corner of Douglas and Green Streets, and the Carolina General Hospital on Pine Street.

I also miss Dr. Robert Goudy, the county coroner and chiropractor who was prominent on the Wilson scene. And I miss Dr. Ralph Fike, Dr. M.A. Pittman and Dr. Erick Bell.

I remember old George that used to push his cart around town, selling fat lightwood. George was dirty and appeared to be out of touch with the times even in those days, but he was a part of the Wilson scene that I miss.

Then there was George Courie with his Liberty Bell cab that many people depended on for transportation. To my knowledge, George never became a part of the large cab companies in town and he was a talkative, likable person and I recall that he had a family rather late in life and was very proud of them.

I miss Southern Dairies that had a plant just across the railroad for many years and employed a lot of people. And I miss all the excitement and the crowds that hung around the train station during the days when train travel was about the only way to go.

I also miss Elizabeth's on Nash Street, for that was another popular place for women shoppers. During those days, Elizabeth's and Barshay's were the two best-known women's stores downtown.

And let us never forget Miss Mollie and the Paris Hat Shoppe. That is where the ladies at the top level went to have their individual hats designed, during the days when hats were considered essential to the well-dressed woman.

And all of us old enough remember the ohs and ahs about Madam Barnes and her stitching witchery. About the best compliment a woman could receive in those days was to be dressed in a gown made by Madam Barnes.

And just think. Everything I have mentioned is a part of a past that holds no reminders of that era today. But in another 25 years, the change will be as evident on the local scene of today. It's sure a changing world.

Memories That Live Forever
Courtesy Hugh B. Johnston

Filling Up The Old-Fashioned Way
Courtesy Ina Fulghum

Mules Hitched to Cultivator In 1940
Courtesy Gladys E. Evans

A Man Takes Pride In His Horse And Buggy
Courtesy Peggy Dew

An Old Milk House Under The Tree
Courtesy Russell and Bethena Kennedy

Digging A Ditch In Olden Days
Courtesy Peggy Dew

An Old House Becomes A Barn
Courtesy Hugh B. Johnston

Top left, a sand-lot ball game in the 1940s; top right, a pile of stove wood; bottom left, cutting out fresh meat; bottom right, gutting a hog.

A Beautiful Scene From The Past
Courtesy Hugh B. Johnston

Cotton Blossoms, Green Tobacco And Music, Too
Courtesy Helen Boykin

1918 Model T Ford
Courtesy Nellie E. Thorne

Unloading Corn From Old Wagon
Courtesy Horace Raper

Tranquility At Its Best In The Good Old Days
Courtesy Helen Boykin

Memories Of A Past Wilson

I'm going to meander around Wilson again today just to see what's going on around town. Not too many people on the streets but I reckon the weather's got something to do with that. A cup of hot coffee would be just the thing to get the chill out of the bones. I'll step into the M&J and speak to Jack Hadge and Mr. Novas, sip that coffee and catch up on the news by glancing at the morning paper to see just what's going on in the middle of the 1950s.

It's cozy inside, and as always, Jack is jovial and smiling and talking about topics of the day and greeting diners as they come in. Sure would be nice to order bacon and eggs, but with 35 cents in my pocket, forget it.

Can't hang around the M&J all day though, so might as well mosey on down the Street and see what's in the windows. Don't go far though before there's Mrs. Margoulis motioning for me to come in. Everybody with young'uns knows Mrs. Margoulis, and Mrs. Margoulis knows everybody with young'uns, cause she and Mr. Margoulis own the Stork's Nest, and they cater to the small fry.

Now Mrs. Margoulis is a real salesperson if there ever was one. She knows how to git right to the heart of the matter. And I know that the higher-ups trade there, too. But heck, some of us $50-a-week poor folks buy a piece from there every once-in-a-while, too. Just because you're poor, by golly, ain't no reason you don't want your young'un dressed as well as them that live in the big houses.

Mrs. Margoulis will git you inside and dangle a dress before you that has just come in and you look at it and it looks like it ought to be on some kind of little-girl beauty queen. It might be velvet or all flowered up or plain-colored, but with something fancy about it that makes little girls look all dressed up.

You tell her how pretty it is and that you'd like to have it for your little girl, but you just ain't got the money, and she gives you a little lesson in life right quick. She reminds you that men are judged by how their wives and children are dressed and that if you want to be regarded in high standing in the community, you've got to keep your family looking good and then you git a guilty feeling and tell Mrs. Margoulis when you git paid you'll bring a dollar by and put that dress on lay-away for that little girl of yourn. It just don't pay to be poor.

Everything looks quiet at Wilson Drug and I just wave my hand and pass on, and there's Leon Leder heading for the bank with his bag of money and Mr. Vernon's headed up towards Nash also. I reckon he's going to a Savings and Loan board meeting or something else important, for there'd be no other reason he'd leave that store. But if he meets somebody hunting backer cloth he'll take them back to the store and sell it to 'em in a hot minute. Don't see Mr. Roma Grice nowhere around Grice's Seed Store.

It's dull on the women' side of Moss & Co., too. All them smiling women with scissors on their waists ready to cut that cloth for those wanting to make dresses and things and nobody to sell it to. But I can at least greet Miss Annie, Miss Martha, Miss Ophelia, Belva, Hazel, Nannie, Celia Mae, Elise, Dora and Red Hawley that I see at the time, and here comes a clerk from the men's department with a pair of britches to send up to Miss Effie and her crew to be hemmed, and they're pulling them up by hand in the basket that is attached to a rope.

I need a paint brush but just ain't got the money, so I'll just stop by Bridgers Paint & Wallpaper and speak to Buck, Mildred, Mary Ella and Mr. Rountree just to pass the time of day. They give me a paint-stirrer although I ain't even got no paint.

I can't afford another cup of coffee, but if I could I'd stop at the Red Apple Cafe and swill down a cup and just watch traffic on the eastern end of town. (I can just see that big red apple on the glass panel).

Lord, I'm hungry. And one of these days when I can save up enough money we're going down to the Hotel Cherry on a Sunday after church and we're going to dine like a king in that big dining room there by the railroad tracks with those yellow-clad waitresses with their uniforms starched stiff and hair all done up in hair nets. We'll order bowls of their delicious soup for starters and munch on crackers and hope we don't spill that soup on those spotlessly white tablecloths.

And we'll git some kind of fancy salad or something — pineapple with grated cheese or something congealed and dilly-dally with that while waiting for that good roast turkey and dressing and I'll ask for a double-dip of gravy and there just has to be some parsley-buttered potatoes, not that it makes them taste any better, but because those green flecks of parsley just look good (upper class,man). And we'll top it off with some of Les' good apple or peach cobbler and it'll be a pretty day and folks will be milling about the station across the way, waiting to board them trains going somewhere I hain't never been and we'll feel like SOMEBODY for an hour or so at least.

Just because you're poor ain't no reason you shouldn't go out on the town at least once or twice a year. But I tell you with 63 cents a week for insurance, 30 cents for the paper, a dollar for the milk man, and another dollar here and there, you're dollared to death and fifty dollars just ain't enough to go around. Ain't no difference now and the way it was when I was an old sharecropper as fer as money goes. It's scace.

Ah, what the heck. We didn't come here with anything and we ain't taking nothing with us when we leave. We'll have that special Sunday, come spring.

A Special Room And Place

I t was Christmas Eve and the skies were threatening. The air was chilly, but not cold. Hope was gone for a white Christmas. But the streets were bustling with people.

It was hard getting through the crowds, particularly on street corners and in front of the 10-cent stores. The Salvation Army bell was ringing and there was a live Santa Claus in front of a little red house with a line of children waiting to give him their wish list.

At the end of the street was a lean-to and before it a man posing as a shepherd, dressed in a long robe, and there were live sheep. The year was 1930 or 1931.

On the sidewalks at Pender's and A&P, fruits and nuts in crates and boxes were stacked up against the store fronts, and on the sides of the building attendants were busy pulling live chickens, turkeys, geese and ducks from piled-high crates, tying twine around their legs and collecting the money. The Christmas feast would soon begin.

Even on Christmas Eve, hot dog stands were busy and the scent of onions wafted into the streets, and in the restaurants there were small plates of barbecue available for a quarter, with larger helpings for thirty-five cents.

Out in the country, the yards were swept clean, with smoke still rising from piles of leaves being burned. Children played in yards and men went about the premises attending to small chores. The kitchens were the busiest places with ovens going full blast and the smells of cooking meats and cakes and pies combining to whet the appetite.

The front room was empty and the fire had died to embers. The clock ticked away the seconds, the sound magnified by the quietness. Looking from the front window, naked limbs stood stark as they stretched skyward. There was a loneliness about the scene.

Quilts were piled high over the feather bed and the figures of the quilt formed a geometric pattern with the fine stitching showing.

Everything in the room was familiar — the bed, wardrobe, bureau, sewing machine, trunk, even the fern that sat on the little center table in front of a window. The old andirons in the fireplace had always been there, although the backs had been burned out with time and bricks provided for them to sit on. The unevenness of the bricks on the hearth stood out and the skillet was in the place it always sat, on the left side of the hearth. It had never been on the right side, and the fire poker was on the right side, nearest to Pa's old chair so he could punch the burning wood and send sparks flying up the chimney.

Even the burned places in the flooring on the edge of the hearth were familiar. At some time coals had fallen from the fireplace and landed on the floor for a little while, giving a permanent marking to the wood. The mantle piece was nothing but a planed piece of wood extending over the hearth, held up by homemade braces nailed into the wall. In front of the clock was a shoe tack nailed into the wood to hold the doily that Ma always kept there, embroidered in several colors and washed, starched and ironed periodically.

The chairs had always been there, never varying in the position in which they were placed. Rounds wore down and rockers on the rocking chairs became thin and there was broken straw in the bottoms, but they remained a large part of the room.

I observed the scene I have described, and I knew even then that what I was observing would remain alive in my heart for as long as I lived. Realizing that memories are preserved in such a manner they are not affected by the ravages of time, I knew that I could bring them back in all their clarity, without losing any of the color or substance. But at that time I never realized how much they would come to mean to me as everything else from that world faded except what was preserved in my mind.

So when Christmas comes during these years, I often find myself relaxing and letting the memories of long-lost youth brighten my leisure hours. I take it all apart and put it back together again, trying to focus on what was the most important thing that has lived through the years.

I had to discard the grounds — the trees where the birds sang for countless hours, where we swung from the limbs and were shaded from summer's hot sun; the buldings, every one of which was dear to me; the barnyard and its animal life; the kitchen where good food was prepared every day of the year; even the dining area with the long table and the homemade bench on which we sat and the bedrooms where we lived out our fantasies in dreams sometimes.

And in the final analysis, I chose the front room where Ma and Pa slept; where the fire burned brightly in winter; where we sat and studied and joked and did all the things children do. I think of it in all seasons, but when Christmas arrives it is with a very special feeling that I go back in memory and make it a reality in my own heart again. The setting was so simple it spoke of elegance.

That scene spoke a message we didn't have hanging on our walls in those days. Today there are "Home Sweet Home" panels in elaborate frames, done in needlepoint. Our walls were bare except for the few calendars Pa was able to find in stores in town. But that front room expressed the message without any pronouncements. It was truly "Home Sweet Home," and the "sweet" was emphasized every day of the year.

I give most of the credit for the atmosphere that prevailed at the old home of my dreams to the two great people who guided us and made a palace for us in its humble setting. They gave us leeway to find our own way in life, but they didn't crowd us in and try to dominate our lives. They were there when they were needed, and it seems they were always needed, just to give our lives a sense of direction.

It has been many years since those days, and although I tried very hard to make my home what I remember my boyhood home as being, it never turned out as well as I had hoped. But then, I always knew I would never be worthy of touching the garments of the two who guided us. Their hands were calloused and wrinkled and they thought simply and lived simple lives, and hard work had been their lot, but they were special hands and special hearts. They represented the best in mankind. I always love the memories I have of them and all the other members of my family, but when Christmas carols are sung, the logs burn brightly, the lights

on the tree twinkle and families gather, I love them best of all.
Merry Christmas.

Stories Behind Old Houses

A heavy growth of bushes that had grown into trees surrounded the old building and century-old oaks that bore
the scars of age surrounded the place. Briers and other
climbing vines covered the sagging top and part of the roof had
fallen in. Growth was so thick around the old house it was almost
impossible to get to the sagging door.

A few boards were still intact on the porch, but many had rotted
away completely. The two-by-fours that held up the roof of the
porch were almost rotted away.

An old man and a young boy observed the scene.

"I want to go inside," the boy told his grandfather.

"It looks too dangerous, son," the old man replied. "It's about
rotten down. I don't know if it would be safe to go inside."

"We can be careful," the boy said. "You said you were born
here and grew up in this old house. I want to see what it was like."

"Well, let's see if we can get through these bushes and briers,"
the old man said. "But you be careful and don't touch anything
overhead. We don't want this old house to fall on us."

They inched their way through the bushes and stood on the
boards of the porch that were still relatively solid. The old door
creaked but pushed open with ease and they were inside where
cobwebs were thick and debris scattered over the floors.

"This was Pap's and Mammy's room," the old man said as he
went up to the fireplace, running his hand on the inside of the
chimney to see if the old hook was still there. "Feel this," he said
to the boy. "That's where Mammy said her mother used to hang
heavy pots that sat in the coals and where food was cooked in the
fireplace."

"How many rooms are there?" the boy asked.

"Five including the shed room," the old man said.

"And how many children were there?" the boy asked.

"Ten."

"Ten children in a house this little!"

"Yep."

"How did you manage?"

"Fine."

"How did youall sleep in such a little space?"

"Come on," the old man said as he felt the flooring to see whether it would hold him up. "There were two beds in this room, so four boys slept here. And there were two beds in the other room over there, and four children slept there. And two slept in the shed room."

"Were you happy?" the boy asked.

"As happy as a dead pig in the sunshine," the old man replied. A smile came over his face as he recalled events from so many yesterdays. "We used to play in front of the fireplace in winter and scrape sweet potatoes with our knives and eat them raw. We'd pop popcorn over the coals and Pap would tell us stories about his school days and the old Blue Back Speller and the one-room schoolhouse.

"And in summer we'd play under those old oak trees that are half-rotten now with all the dead limbs on the ground. We'd run races down the path and swim naked in the sand pit a ways down the road.

"We always had to look after the younger children and we'd take them with us while we were playing. Of course there was sadness too. One little sister died with colitus and a little brother had pneumonia and died.

"But I remember my oldest sister was married before the fireplace and people from all around came that Sunday, and the house and yard were overflowing.

"And we boys would go to bed and talk about everything in the world. We'd tell jokes and carry on and sometimes Pap would have to call us down."

"How in the world did all of you eat at the same time? the boy asked.

"Nothing to it," the old man said. He pointed to the area in the kitchen where the table had sat. "Pap built a table the length of this space. He allowed for two chairs at the end, and built benches for both sides of the table. Twelve peope could get around that table without any trouble.

"What kind of games did you play?" the boy asked.

"Oh, there were horseshoes, hide-and-seek, baseball and at night we'd play blindfold and tell "haint" stories."

"Why did you let it go down like this?" the boy asked. "If it had been my home I would have wanted to keep it."

"Time takes care of all that," the grandfather replied. "Times change and people move on to other things. At the time such things are happening you lose sight of what is going on. People move away sometimes and just leave the very old places for time and the elements to take their toll. It's like old, forgotten graveyards where people were buried a century ago. The old finally passes from the scene and the new takes over. That's just the way of life.''

"But don't you like to think about those days?'' the boy asked.

"Sure,'' the old man said, "And I do think about them. I think about this old place often, and if I could do it all over, I would preserve it and keep it up for you and generations to follow. But it's too late now. It's just a dream that lives on. We never know until it's too late what simple things like this old house that I grew up in means to us.

"This old house has a story all its own, and hundreds of other dilapidated old houses strewn around the countryside have their own tales also. But they are buried with the past. There was plenty of loving and living in those old houses and if they could only speak, they could tell us some of the most remarkable stories of all.''

Horse-Shoer Makes Rounds

W e used to love to see the horse-shoer make his rounds. It seems like he came twice a year — in the spring and on in the fall — but I ain't sure about that. I do know that when we used to drive mules to town a right smart on them hard surfaced roads, it would wear down their hooves in no time if they didn't have on shoes. And it seems like our old mules would lose their shoes after a time.

Anyhow, you didn't know nothing about when the horse-shoer was coming until he drove his old truck in the yard. He'd git out, and it was pure pitiful to see him gitting about. That poor man — I think his name was Carter — was so stooped in the back he looked like it was torture for him to walk. He had stooped so much with a mule's hoof on his knee and worked on them he was near 'bout shaped that a way.

Of course, if the mules were in the field plowing, won't nothing he could do, so he'd go on up the road and tell us he'd be back on a certain day, and we were ready for him then. Besides, the old man could have time to try to fork up enough money to pay him.

Now Zeb, our old black mule, had fine feet and he was more or less a gentle mule as I said in the "SHARECROPPERS,'' and the horse-shoer could trim off his hooves and put shoes on him and they looked fine. But it was a different story with old Gray. She was the only gray mule I ever had any dealings with, but I concluded as a young'un that gray mules were different than other colors. Were they really? I'm asking the question at this late date, cause I want to know.

Well, Gray's feet were about like the rest of her — a mess. I don't know if she had soft hooves, or what, but shoes just wouldn't stay on her feet long. And in a matter of time, those hooves were cracking, 'specially the front ones, and gitting out of shape. They put you in mind of a woman's shoe that turned on the side, making her walk sort of splay-footed. And if Gray was foolish about everthing else, you can imagine how she was about those feet.

The horse-shoer (he may have been a blacksmith for all I know but I'll call him what I know he was) had an easy time with Gray's front feet. He'd side up to her and she might nudge him a little with her mouth, but he'd reach down and git a foot and turn it under and git his legs positioned like he wanted them and cut off that old hoof with ease. He'd have a pure pile of dead hoof at his feet by the time he got through. And it won't no trouble nailing the shoes on.

And the first time he tackled Gray's hind feet he tried the same thing. He took hold of her on the hip and reached down to pick up the hind foot (and he was standing behind her with us hollering and telling him to be careful, and old gray pulled that leg away and gave a good solid kick and old Carter was far enough on the side he just got a glancing blow, but it set him on his butt and we ran to help him git up and he was glad for our hands too, for I tell you, that man had hard enough time gitting around at best.

But we found a way to git to them hind feet anyhow. Carter made a lasso out of a rope and opened it wide, then backed Gray up until a hind foot was within the circle, and pulled the rope gently until it slid up above her hoof, and we pulled the hind leg out behind her and he worked on her that way. Old Gray would lay her ears back, but there won't nary thing she could do about that stuck-out foot. And Carter cut off all the dead hoof, put a shoe on and nailed it good, then did the other one the same way, and we had new-shod mules. And that made us feel good. We really cared about them old mules and we wanted the best for them we could git. But old Gray just made it hard for us to do by her like we wanted to. She was a kicker too, as I also noted in "SHARECROPPERS," and tore her stable all to pieces several times during her tirades.

Ma came to the door 'bout that time and said dinner was ready, and we could invite the horse-shoer if he could go cabbage that had been in the garden so long they had done turned pink, boiled with fat back, boiled ish taters, a few string beans and nothing sweet. But there was plenty of pot liquor and cornbread. And Carter took her up on it.

He went to the wash basin and scrubbed his hands a good five minutes, rubbing lye soap all over them and working up a lather, but when he got through there won't much difference. In his line of work, his hands stayed chapped and wrinkled and it seemed like the dirt seeped under his skin. But he didn't git no dirt on the towel hanging on the back porch, and that's more than we could say for ourselves.

Being of short stature to start with, and with his bent back, he didn't go much higher than the table top. But that man et him one more dinner and acted like that pot liquor from the cabbage was better than cake. It seems like he didn't have any teeth either, and I believe it caused him to open his mouth wider than he would have, for I seem to remember a lot of pink gum and jaws coming mighty close together when he et. But you already know how a pack of young'uns is. They watch everything anybody does that ain't a part of their everyday world. We didn't say nary thing about how much Carter et that day, nor about the funny way he sat when he et that cornbread and spooned out the pot liquor. But we mocked that man for months after he left and were threatened with whuppings if we didn't stop that messing. But I don't believe we ever were run from the table on account of the horse-shoer. There were plenty of other things that we were run out of the dining room over though. Memories are so real!

Hand-Carved Model Of Old-Timey Log Cart
Courtesy Bruce R. Owens

Visiting Sawmills

A sawmill was a youngun's delight when I was growing up. And every one that I knew visited them whenever they could. Of course, we had to go on Sad'dy evening or Sunday evening when they won't running, unless once in a great while we'd git to go with a grown-up to haul lumber, and that won't often. They'd usually look at a young'un like they could kill him when he asked to go to such a place and gitting in the way and wanting to git up close to them big saws with wide teeth that would a cut us into little bits 'fore we could have got tangled up.

Sawmills were lonesome-looking places back then. They were always in the edge of a woods that had been cleared of most of its trees, leaving a barelooking background and muddy ruts where log carts hauled the logs from the woods.

There was a long, covered shelter where the wood was sawed and the carriage that rolled the log as it was being sawed. And it was like a dream to actually see the logs being sawed. The outer edges of the wood that held the bark were put in a pile to be cut for burning, and the saws would cut some of the wood in different widths, depending on its use. It seems like a lot of it came out rough.

And man that sawdust was flying when they went to town with them saws. And the sawdust pile is what attracted us most. Any young'un that ain't never played in a sawdust pile has missed a lot, let me tell you. And I mean them piles of sawdust were big, and high.

On the outside the sawdust looked like it was perfectly dry, but when you wade into it, it's wet underneath. And you know that we would run to the top and down the sides and dig into it and almost bury ourselves, and by then our shoes were filled with the mess and it was down our necks and into our clothes and we were beginning to itch. But that didn't faze us one bit.

When our shoes got too full, we'd pull them off if we could git the strings untied. Our shoestrings were always tied together. I don't never remember gitting a new pair of shoestrings that stayed in two pieces more than a week or so. They'd break and we'd tie them in a hard knot, and the hard ends would come off and we'd put them in our mouths to wet them, twist them around and try to git them through the eye of the shoe, and that was like gitting the camel through the eye of a needle to us.

When shoestrings are tied in a hard knot they won't go through the eye of the shoe, and we had to do some finaggling to git them to work. We'd lace the shoes as far as we could, and when we got to the knot we might have to skip a lace or two. I've seen many a boy's shoes half-laced. We even had to use half a shoestring sometimes. That thread they were made out of shore must not a been no count, or we were mighty rough on them.

But we'd work on them shoes, for I tell you that sawdust had filled 'em up, and it seems like we always visited the sawmills when it was shoe-wearing weather. If it won't time to go barefooted, we didn't take the chance of somebody telling Ma and Pa and gitting our hind ends tore down. In them days, you went barefooted when the old folks said go barefooted.

When we got so much sawdust in our clothes we couldn't stand it no more, we'd git out and shake as hard as we could, but there won't no way we could git it all out. It got into our sweaters, in our hair and overalls pockets, and it's easy to imagine how it felt. But the main thing was that it was fun and it actually seemed good to git in a washtub and wash that mess off after we got home and were scolded by Ma about gitting ourselves in such a mess and daring us to git sawdust on her floors. That was sort of strange too, for we usually hated to take a bath. We turned our overall pockets inside out 'fore we ever got to the house, and dumped our shoes agin too.

Then sometimes on our way from school we'd see log carts hauling the logs to the sawmill, and that was exciting too. The logs were big and long, and the carts that hauled them were heavy, with big hind wheels and smaller front wheels with wide rims. It made us want to climb up on top of the log being hauled, but we knowed better than to ask.

But we'd linger on the edge of the road and watch the activities for a long time. We'd even see them pen up the lumber sometimes. They did this to make it dry out sooner from the air and wind.

I reckon that's how they learned how to pen up stove wood after it was split on the woodpile. I know after the menfolks got a lot of wood split, Ma would send us to the woodpile to pen up the wood so it would dry out in a hurry. She needed dried-out, seasoned wood to make hot fires in the cookstove. We'd see how high we could make the pens, and sometimes we got them higher than our heads, and they'd come tumbling down and we had to do the whole thing over agin.

I used to dream about working at a sawmill. I thought that would be about the most exciting job in the world. And there won't so much manual labor to it. The carts unloaded the logs close to the carriage so they could be rolled on with ease, and pulling the levers that made the big saws cut the wood was too exciting to imagine.

But every once in a while we'd hear of somebody losing a finger or a hand at a sawmill, and once in a great while somebody would slip and fall into a saw and git ground up like sausage meat. When I heard them stories, I decided I wouldn't go for work at a sawmill, after all. I figgered it was better to keep on putting in backer, chopping and plowing cotton, sowing soda and gitting up fodder and cleaning out the privy if I had to instid of taking on work at a sawmill. It might be harder work, but it was safer. Besides, they had to tote all them two by fours and all that other lumber out on the yard and pen it up too. That's the part about sawmills I had forgotten until it come to mind while I was penning up stove wood.

A 51-Year-Old Diary

I t has been buried for the most part, like other rubble from the past — at the bottom of dresser drawers or old trunks or packed away in pasteboard boxes on closet shelves and forgotten. Yet it has survived all the years with me. And on the occasions when it has surfaced I have shied away from looking at it closely. It was too simple, too dreary, too dull to merit my interest again... until now.

It is a diary, 51 years old, that was given to me as a Christmas present in 1934. And I haven't the faintest idea why I was given a diary, for I had never heard of one before. Anyway, I began keeping the diary in 1935 and for the first year I kept it religiously. And there were parts of several other years, but no other full year.

Those were the days when I was the sharecropper in every sense of the word. Pages from history — personal, inconsequential — yet reflecting on the simplicity of life and youth during the days of the Great Depression.

I will reflect on one week in history and since that week is January 12-19 at this writing, I will give an account of that week for the years 1935, 1936, 1937, 1938 and 1940. I did not record events in 1939.

Saturday, Jan. 12, 1935: I saw Bob Steele and Clyde Beatty. A group of young people gathered that night at a neighborhood home.

Sunday, Jan. 13: I went to church in the morning. Was with a neighborhood girl in the afternoon. And I went to see her that night, too! I wrote that I got her ring and pocket handkerchief! Lord have mercy, have mercy, have mercy. All of 16. Oh, the innocence and naivete of youth.

Monday, Jan. 14: I cut corn stalks in the morning and of all things, I went to see this young thing again that night. And after 51 years, I'm still not calling her name. But she acted mad and I didn't make another date! I showed her something, I reckon.

Tuesday, Jan. 15: I bruised my leg when I slipped off the fender of my brother's automobile. How tragic. But I shrubbed that morning (shrubbing is cutting the growth from ditchbanks). And I was nice and stayed home that night.   Wednesday, Jan. 16: I went to the show that night and saw "The Family That Traveled 3,000 Miles." Where did I get the 15 cents to go to the show twice in one week? It was cold and raining that night.

Thursday, Jan. 17: We got a new disk harrow, and I can't imagine how we wrangled that one. I shrubbed ditch banks that morning.

Friday, Jan. 18: I shrubbed in the morning, and you wouldn't believe it, but I went to a movie again! Saw Tom Tyler and Clyde Beatty.

Saturday, Jan. 19: I shrubbed ditch banks again. And I was actually at home that Saturday night. And I said it was the first Saturday afternoon I'd been home in a long time. It was cold and cloudy and looked like snow.

Sunday, Jan. 12, 1936: Went to church in the morning and to those naughty neighborhood stores in the afternoon, mixing the good with the bad.

Monday: Jan. 13: I shrubbed that morning and my brother and I got "lidard" from the woods that afternoon. It was partly cloudy that day.

Tuesday, Jan. 14: I didn't do anything that day. The weather was fair.

Wednesday, Jan. 15: It was rainy that day and I didn't do anything.

Thursday, Jan. 16: My brother and I split stove wood in the morning and shrubbed in the afternoon. Boy, we really had the ditch banks to shrub!

Friday, Jan. 17: We shrubbed that day. A lady in the neighborhood died and I was at the "sitting up" all night.

Saturday, Jan. 18: I slept in the morning after my all-night vigil. But I saw Buck Jones that night.

Sunday: Jan. 19: I spent about all my time that day at the stores.

Tuesday, Jan. 12, 1937: I helped my brother move corn. It was cloudy and rather warm that day.

Wednesday Jan. 13: My brother moved that day (he and his wife had lived with us for three years). A hearing was held that day concerning a young man that got a neighborhood girl pregnant.

Thursday, Jan. 14: I went to another neighborhood girl's house that night. It was partly cloudy and warm that day.

Friday, Jan. 15: I helped Raymond, my brother, move hogs and corn that day. It was rainy and very warm.

Saturday, Jan. 16: Saw Johnny Weissmuller in "Tarzan Escapes." You can't say I didn't go to the picture shows in those days. It was fair and much cooler.

Sunday, Jan. 17: It was very rainy and foggy. Didn't go anywhere except to the store.

Monday, Jan. 18: It was a routine day and the weather was fair and warm.

Tuesday, Jan. 19: I didn't do anything. It rained and turned cooler.

Wednesday, Jan. 12, 1938: My mother suffered a stroke on the night of Jan. 10, and I wrote that she couldn't talk and on Jan. 12 thought she was going to die. She motioned to a neighbor and to the wardrobe where she let her know that was where her burying clothes were located. Then I wrote that for the next two weeks she was in a coma but that in about four weeks she began sitting up. She did live for seven years, but her sickness ended the diary for the year.

Friday, Jan. 13, 1940: It was warm and rainy and I didn't do any work.

Saturday, Jan. 13: I was home all day and the weather was foggy and misty. I went to Cleo's that night.

Sunday, Jan. 14: I stayed home all day and that night, too. It was rainy and a lot warmer.

Monday, Jan. 15: Did nothing again and the weather was warmer.

Tuesday, Jan. 16: It was fair and colder and I loafed again.

Wednesday, Jan. 17: It was mostly fair and cool and I was still loafing.

Thursday, Jan. 18, It was warmer and fair but I was still lying around doing nothing.

Friday, Jan. 19: It snowed pretty in the morning, about an inch deep, and was cold. What did I do? Nothing.

There you have it folks, five weeks from my youth. And it happened so long ago!

Events From Old Diary

Some things in that "100 percent pure leather"-bound diary that shows its age are some insights into the days of my youth and events that transpired when we were at our poorest as well as reflections on who and what I was as a young person.

On Jan. 28, 1937 Ohio and Kentucky were experiencing their worst floods in history.

On Jan. 29 we we cut logs to go around the tobacco bed.

In memoranda for 1936 I wrote that I bought shoes for $4.50 and "slippers" for $2.04.

On Feb. 1, 1936 I wrote that the temperature fell below zero.

Sunday, Feb 5, 1939 was "the dullest day I ever saw."

A tornado struck Calhoun, Ga. on Feb. 10, 1940, killing 22 people.

Evidence in the Bruno Hauptmann trial ended on Monday, Feb. 11, 1935.

On Feb. 20, 1935 I was shrubbing again, and upon becoming thirsty I lay down, head first, on the ground and lowered myself into a ditch with crystal-clear water to take a drink, and lo and behold, I slipped all the way in and got wet to my skin. And it was cold, man. I burned one of those piles of brush and stood as close to the fire as I could, then skeedaddled the mile home to change clothes. I remember that day as clearly as if it had been yesterday.

And don't you know that on Feb. 28, 1935 I was listening to Little Jimmy Dickens play on the "reddy-o."

And on Sunday, Feb. 28, 1937 snow was on the ground and I wrote it was the largest snow since the one on March 2, 1927.

On the memoranda page for February, 1936 I wrote that people hadn't hardly done any work in the fields; that snow had been on the ground most all the time since Christmas. I surmised that work would be piled up later.

I bought drawers for $1 in February, 1935.

On March 5, 1935 our black sow "found" nine pigs. I distributed stable manure that day. On the same day in 1937 I slabbed stove wood.

On Friday, March 27, 1935 I really pulled a dilly. I wrote that for the first time ever, I smoked a cigarette. It has followed me through the years.

And on Wednesday, April 1, 1936, six pigs were born to the "red sow."

They started putting up the "light line" in my area on Thursday, April 8, 1937.

I played my guitar for a dance on Thursday, April 9, 1937. Made $2.

We boys broadcast from WFTC, Kinston, on Friday, April 30, 1937 for the first time. Lord have mercy, twice. No practice, no nothing. Ignorance was bliss in those days, and I suppose it still applies today.

Under memoranda for April, 1935 I recorded that Boots (the best rabbit dog it was ever my pleasure to be associated with), had five puppies, and I'll bet every one of 'em was knocked in the head.

Also in April 1935, I purchased a pair of pants and a shirt for $5; overalls for $1.14; belt, 20 cents and approximately 40 cents for socks.

On April 3, 1936, Bruno Richard Hauptmann paid with his life in the electric chair in the Lindbergh kidnapping case.

On May 12, 1937 the coronation of King George of England was held.

On May 25 I wrote that John D. Rockefeller and George Isaac Hughes "died sometime along now."

The entry for June 7, 1937 said Jean Harlow, famous movie star, "died today of uremic poisoning." I replanted tobacco that day and the weather was hot.

On June 19, 1935 a popular girl in the neighborhood who was engaged to be married had a tonsillectomy at a local doctor's office, and strangled to death from her own blood before she came out of the anesthetic.

On June 21, 1941 I was classified 3-A by the local draft board.

I worked by the day in 1937 (when there was work available). And on July 1 that year I recorded that "I figure I've worked out $31.06 this year so far." Could there be a better insight into a period in time and what the economy was like?

But despite the hard times, we had a chicken fry at the tobacco barn on the night of Aug. 9, 1935.

On Sunday, Aug. 11, 1935 "I went to Carolina Beach with George Peele and a gang of young people."

Aug. 18, 1935 was the first time I remember us curing tobacco on Sunday.

On Aug. 22, 1935 I recorded that "Will Rogers was buried today. Killed several days ago in an airplane accident. We've worked in dry tobacco today. Raymond and I played the guitars at Walter Williams' store tonight."

The tobacco market opened on Aug. 26, 1935 "lower than last year."

On Sept. 4, 1940 "Gone With the Wind" came back for the second showing. "Was a grand picture, four hours long. Technicolor. One of the best I've seen."

I recorded on Sept. 5, 1935 that the equinox storm had done much damage in N.C. "for the last few days."

I also got my driver's license on the same date in 1940.

On Sept, 19, 1941 I listed some of the year's song hits. They included "Elmer's Tune," "The Hut Sut Song," "Chattanooga Choo Choo," " My Sister and I," "Goodbye Dear, I'll Be Back in A Year," (I don't even remember that one), "So You're the One," and "Shepherd Serenade" (that I don't remember either).

Memoranda for September, 1935: On Sunday, Sept. 8, Senator Huey P. Long of Louisiana was killed by a Dr. Weiss. England and

Italy are talking about war.

October 3, 1935: 1700 people were killed in Ethiopia today.

Sunday, Oct. 13, 1935 was Rev. Cornelius Jackson's last day at our church. (He had been there during most of my lifetime).

All men between the ages of 21-35 registered for the first peace-time draft in history on Oct. 16, 1940.

Memoranda for October, 1935: "Gray's foot (our mule) has been 'bad off' all this month."

Memoranda for October, 1936: "This year's tobacco crop has been very short with us. If we pay out we'll do well. With us it is so much different from what it was last year." And on Nov. 1, 1936 I noted that "we have managed to pay our debts, which has left us almost penniless. I've never remembered a fall as dull as this one is, not only for us but most everybody. Today is election day."

In ending this segment, allow me to say I removed my rose-tinted glasses in the face of reality, for this wasn't the wanderings of the mind, but rather pages from history without any adornments and without the benefits of a halo. The unpleasantness had not sifted through the sieve of time.

Smile, Don't Laugh At Me

I ask for your sympathy, but please don't laugh openly, for I am writing about personal things during the days when I was still wet behind the ears. And when it was recorded 50 years ago, I wouldn't have made it public for any amount of money. It is laughable now as the old man looks back upon his early manhood, but even from this great distance I remember the pain and anguish of the moment.

On Nov. 9, 1936, when I was 18 years old I will quote from that old diary the exact words I wrote:

"What might have been now never will be. One hope I had cherished is gone. I shall try to forget that part of it though, but always, always will I have a feeling for (no name, please), which I shall never have for any other girl. Even if she doesn't care, that hasn't caused me to forget.

"I hope she's happy if I'm not. Since childhood, the day we first met, I've liked her as I've never liked any other girl. She hasn't ever cared anything about me, but still I remember her with a feeling which I shall never express to anyone."

"I hope for her all the happiness life can give her. If we never speak again I shall always wish her success and if things happen that I may talk with her again I shall be happy. I hope I shall be able to forget her and to forget my dreams of us together which now are shattered and forever gone."

That is an indication of how young love can be so blind. It seemed like the end of the world at that time, but it was only puppy love at a period in our lives when it is the dominating force.

I noted that on May 13, 1937, Hood Swamp School closed. That meant the end for the six-room structure where the children in the area got their primary education. A new high school has been built for the area. And while I am writing about schools, allow me to explain that I did not attend school in 1935 because of our circumstances, but went back to school in 1936. I had made the first and second grades my first year anyway, so I wasn't behind my age group by being out of school for a year.

On May 22, 1936 I wrote that I made the best grade in my math class; made a 1 in English; 1 in science and 3+ in manual training. I was on the honor roll for the last month of school (Braggart).

In 1941 I wrote that it was a Saturday in May and had been dry for several weeks. People had set out tobacco and it was dying for lack of water. Corn was up. That morning an airplane came over writing "Pepsi Cola" in the air. It was warm.

On Saturday afternoon people had gone to town "as usual." Just before sunset a black cloud made up in the west. We thought we were going to get some rain. The cloud looked very peculiar. It would be black, then white. It moved fast.

We could hear it roaring as it came closer and closer. We were in the hallway of the house. The storm broke in all its fury. Everything turned as black as midnight. But no harm was done to the people. We were badly afraid. Dust was thick on everything and crops were badly damaged.

It was a dust storm, the likes of which I've never seen before or since. But I can tell you that that was the day I thought I was going to meet my maker at the tender age of 18. It lives in my memory.

I noted that on Jan. 2, 1939 the Duke Blue Devils played the Trojans of Southern California in the Rose Bowl. "They held the Trojans out til the last 40 seconds of the game. Then Duke was defeated 7-3."

I wrote that the Rose Bowl game was moved to Duke University at Durham Jan. 1, 1942 because of the war. Oregon State beat the Duke Blue Devils 20-16.

In 1940 I wrote — Some of the best pictures I've seen: "Gone With the Wind," "Citizen Kane," "Virginia," "One Foot in

Heaven," "Honky Tonk," "Boom Town," "Moon Over Miami,"
"Saratoga," "Hell's Angels," "The End of the Trail," "Scatter
Brain," "Jungle Princess," and "Kiss the Boys Goodbye."

In 1941 farmers got higher prices for their crops "than I ever
remember. Tobacco sold high. I think it exceeded 1934 prices.
Cotton has been 16-17 cents."

I noted Japan's attack on Pearl Harbor on Sunday, Dec. 7, 1941
and that on Monday, Dec. 8, the U.S. declared war on Japan. On
Dec. 9, I wrote that Germany declared war on the U.S. and the
U.S. declared war on Germany.

On Dec. 10, 1936 I recorded King Edward's abdication of his
throne in England to marry Mrs. Wallis Warfield Simpson and
must leave England.

And on Dec. 16, 1935 I ordered firecrackers for Christmas.

On Dec. 22, 1935 it began snowing in the afternoon and there was
a pretty snow on the ground next morning. There was a shooting
match at the store that day. And on Christmas Eve, despite the
snow, I said it was dull, although we boys shot fireworks in the
nieghborhood. And I made no big deal about Christmas either.
And snow was on the ground Christmas Day, 1935.

I was upbeat about the year 1935. I wrote that it was cold on the
last day of the year and the ground was covered with ice and snow.
At the last of that entry I wrote "A very successful year."

From the things I recorded so many years ago, I have been back
and picked out those that are of some possible interest. For the
most part, what was written was too trivial to even mention. It
took fine-tooth combing to find the morsels I have recorded here.
It has allowed me to look at myself again, from a different
perspective. But I know that in many respects, I am still the same
person today I was in the days of my youth.

On Jan. 9, 1940 I wrote: "looking back through the years, I can
see a lot of things written here that are silly and foolish, that don't
make sense. At least one-fourth of what's written in this diary is
worthless and has no value whatsoever, so far as records are
concerned." (How right you were, Leroy).

I even made me up a code, and man, I wrote like crazy in that
mess that is totally unrecognizable to me now. I had the code in
the diary, and I erased it many years ago. But you can be sure of
one thing: It wasn't worth a dime and held no deep dark secrets
that would be of interest to the general public. In retrospect, I
think it would be sort of nice to have something to brag about.

Memories Of A Young Boy

During the summer months when I was from about five until I was eight or so, there was so much exploring to do it took all day to git going good.

We were into wheel rolling by then, and I can see those old wheels today as clearly in my mind as I saw them in reality way back there. I hain't never seen one that won't rusty, and I'll bet you hain't neither. Time had eaten away at the iron and the outer surface was not smooth. They had pock marks in them, and they were of several sizes, for you found a wheel wherever you could. And we rolled 'em and rolled 'em and rolled 'em. That nail driven into the backer stick worked just right to keep the wheel rolling just by holding the stick and nail to it.

And sometimes boys and girls played together. Tiring of the wheels, somebody would stake off a playhouse with sticks and backer twine and make several rooms and leave doorways and all that mess. Somebody would bring in a fish box or something for a table while others would comb the premises for broken pieces of glass and old bottles and mess like that to use for kitchen utensils.

Somebody would go to the chaney ball tree and pull off the green balls and they'd be used for garden peas. And wild cherries, as green as grass, were collected and used for some kind of food that we didn't really eat. But we did put a few green cherries and chaney balls in our mouths and once in a while our teeth would crack the skin and we'd get such a bitter taste in our mouths we'd push our arms up to our mouths and run our tongues over our nasty shirt or dress sleeves and try to rub off the taste. And you know that every young'un in this neck of the woods that ever made a playhouse had poke berries in it when they were ripe. That was because they were red and you could add water and paint the countryside with it as well as getting the juice on the clothing that wouldn't come off.

And if maypops weren't a toy for young'uns I don't know what was. We'd go in the field and find them, for they grew wild and ran like watermelon vines and there'd be the purple flowers and grown maypops on the vines and we'd harvest us a handful and go up under the shade trees and cut them up into furniture and all kinds of things. You could take a pocket knife and cut them into baskets, chairs, beds, and most anything you wanted to. You could even take the blooms and pull off part of the petals and make dolls out of them. It's enlightening to learn 60 years later they're sold in florists as "passion flowers."

There was a grass that grew in moist places that had a thousand roots to each hill that were long and red-looking. You could clean them off good and the roots looked like hair. I've seen young'uns tie a string not too far from the roots and make dolls out of them. They'd even plait their hair.

And wild strawberries were popular in playhouses. They were edible, although very small, and red, they had all the taste of cultivated strawberries.

Young'uns would take cherry leaves or peach leaves or poke berry leaves and bruise them up and pour water over them and serve them at their make-believe meals.

We hadn't never had no telephones, but we knew what they were, and we'd take cans that salmon or something like that came in, make a hole in the center of the bottom with a nail, string backer twine through the hole, add another can where another playhouse was located, or maybe two if three playhouses were habitated. And we'd talk through those cans and the sound carried! Alexander Graham Bell had little on us.

But that would become old hat too, and we'd play hiding and there was running and carrying on and hollering and trying to dodge the one designated to tag the hiders before they got home (usually a tree).

We played Doctor and had something for a satchel, and I guarantee you we did "thorough" examinations way back there. God, we were mean! But we got in all the fun we could. Eight and nine-year-old young'uns had to work at the backer shelter in summer, help sucker backer and things like that, and take off cured backer after school. So there won't much time for doing nothing in God's world but playing.

But we were learning about life. We were observing, not missing a trick, even if we were hidden from view of the masses.

If our ma's would let us, we'd roam down to the mill pond and play on the banks, but we didn't get to go unless an older young'un was along. We'd sit on the bank and observe the "skeeter hawks" just above the water and there was a fishy smell and sometimes we'd throw out our reed poles with a hunk of worm on them and it seemed like they always ate the worm and seldom got caught in the hook. And if we did get a bite we'd jerk the pole so fast it would send the string and hook into a bush beside the bank.

And when they'd let us go in the pond, we wore overalls cut off above the knees (we'd never owned a bathing suit, and wouldn't for years and years). Course it wouldn't a made no difference if we'd gone in naked, but that was a no-no. The grown boys went swimming in those cut-off overalls too, unless there won't nobody at the pond but "he's". Sometimes they'd slip out of those overalls and skeedaddle around as naked as they came into the world and if somebody said a girl was coming, they'd skeedaddle agin and git them overalls on. But sometimes one would git bold and say, "Let'em come on up. I don't give a damn." It was a time, let me tell you.

Remembering Age 10

W hen I was a young'un, age 10 or 11, I was really ready for something to eat by the time the sun was setting, and as nasty as a pig. And today you see young'uns that turn up their noses at vegetables. We wanted to stick our noses in 'em. Course they didn't spoil you at the table in those days. You could go without if you wanted to, or you could eat what was on the table. Take your choice. We "et" it all up!

I always loved meat skins, and Ma's teeth were bad by then and she couldn't chew the fried skin, so she'd cut them off and put them in my plate. They were as good then as these processed pork skins are now, or maybe even better.

And I loved to gnaw fish bones. Some of the crowd would leave the tails and a little meat around the backbone, and man, I jumped on that like a hungry hound would do. I ain't never loved soft white fish meat. I want that fish fried brown, split half in two if it ain't too big, and I always want the piece with the backbone in it. But I always loved to chew any kind of bone. I'd gnaw the head of a frying-size chicken, crush the skull and git out the brains and they were really good. I'd take a thigh bone and crush it and eat the marrow out.

I'd a got by without washing if I could when it got time to go to bed. But no, I had to take a rag and git off the dirt around my neck, my arms, legs, and ever where else. I even had to wash my nasty feet. Then it was good and dark and I was gitting that funny feeling in my stomach agin. Haints! Bad dreams. Fear of the darkness. Afraid to open my eyes for fear of seeing "Raw Head and Bloody Bones." Skeered that judgment day would come before morning, and I hadn't had a Chinaman's chance at life.

But as soon as the sun rose I was ready to git out there agin and see what I could find out. I was still watching the roosters running the hens and all such mess.

And I had been looking in stump holes to see if I could find babies, and other young'uns had too. When we used to ask where babies came from they'd say, "An old stump hole." They didn't even know anything about the stork. And that's how your curiosity was treated in the 1920s and 1930s.

There was a 'simmon tree close to the window in the front room of our house and it didn't never have no 'simmons on it. I heard some of the grown-ups say it was a male tree, and I couldn't believe my ears. Male trees? How could there be such things? Well sir, I set out to find what made the difference, and I raise my right hand to heaven and hope to die if I didn't try to find out. And I looked all over that 'simmon tree and I never did find out any physical difference in that old tree and any other. That will give you a general idea of the extent of my curiosity before I was knee-high to a grasshopper.

And do you know what they called pregnant women in those days? You wouldn't believe it, but it's the truth so help me God. Now I didn't hear women call it anything. They just showed it, but men and them smart boys used to say a woman was "bigged" and the Lord knows there's no better way of expressing it. But it shore sounded funny to me, even then.

But I was running every which-a-way, learning about my world. I'd sit in the sun on the porch steps and squint my eyes and look at the horizon and the trees that surrounded me and the panorama of life in that round circle. And I fantasized about a world beyond the little domain that I knew.

I loved nature and animals and trees and the sky and the shimmering waters and I was curious about bugs and turtles and crawfish and eels and just about everything. It was all a world of wonderment for me and a challenge every day to learn something new.

I heard the bells toll for dinner and watched the mules as they flexed their muscles while pulling a plow that was buried deep in the soil. I was keen to the smell of the country and there were as many pleasant odors as there were unpleasant ones and they all merged to give a distinct smell to the area.

I heard the thunder, saw the flashes of lightning, became afraid and wondered what caused such turbulence in a usually-placid world. I thought about the wind and where it came from. I was bothered because I couldn't see what was having such a profound effect on my environment. And I wondered where the winds went after they spent their fury on my area.

It was a beautiful landscape. From the time the sun rose until darkness settled over the land, change was evident throughout the day. The sun climbed in the sky, changing the shade pattern. The heavy dew of morning was erased by the heat from the sun. The spider webs that had been outlined with dewdrops became indistinguishable after the sun dried out the surroundings and the morning glories folded their petals and slept until the night came when they would again open to beautify the morning in the fields about me.

I watched the stars twinkle after day had ended and observed the Milky Way and the Big Dipper and how they twinkled and sparkled in the darkness.

The fall coloring intrigued me and I learned early to appreciate the autumn season more than any other throughout the year, even surpassing spring. I loved the crispness of October and the blueness of the sky and the fleecy white clouds that floated overhead without any threat of harm to me or the area.

Winter was also a beautiful season to me, with frosty mornings and cold temperatures. Like all children, I always wanted it to snow and an open fireplace was a picturesque sight before I was old enough to go to school.

I was glad I was born and happy to be a part of the human experience. I was content in my world.

And about school. That was something else. Every boy that ever entered the first grade knows that some smart-aleck wises him up by the time he's been in class two days. And Lord, it hurts to learn that the whole mess about Santa Claus is a lie. That'll put you down in the dumps about as far as you can go.

And the next thing you learn is what male and female are all about, and why. This is always from some bigger boy that would have you think he is an "experienced" male. He takes a great delight in telling you what will happen to you a few years hence that seems like an eternity, and he gits you all confused and wondering about a million things. It ain't never the same no more. The innocent boy has been stripped of that innocence and he's left to wonder about all the hanky-panky he's being fed.

But that little bit of offhanded information sets up a curiosity that is insatiable. And you got to be a boy to understand. But I know that girls are also told about those things by other "knowing" girls, but it ain't the same. You got to know a boy's mind to know what I'm talking about.

The Awkward Years

Y ears 13 and 14 are something else for a boy. All of you men know what that stage is like and the thousands of different feelings you have at such an awkward age. You're a pure young'un in mentality and thinking, while your body is changing from a boy to a man. You're trying to go through the transition period from childhood to manhood, trying to put it all together and grow out of that morbid period and settle down to a stable pattern. It ain't easy.

And that ain't the only problem you have to wrestle with. Us young'uns back in the sticks were brought up by Biblical principles, and religion was a part of our heritage. They intended for us to become decent men and women and their way of showing it was to take us to church and Sunday school to hear the Word. And while you are in the innocence of childhood there ain't no great squabble with the mind about obeying God and becoming a genuine Christian, but I tell you after that strapping boy gits a man's body on him, he's thinking about carnal things the whole livelong day.

I can remember times at the annual revivals when the evangelists would have altar call after the scorching sermons, and I've been scared half to death at what they said.

"I ask you to come to Christ before it is too late. God's spirit does not always strive with man. This may be the last time some person in this congregation will have a chance to come to Christ. Tomorrow may be too late. You would not want to go to a sinner's grave and be cast into hell on judgment day where the fire is not quenched and the soul dieth not," was the typical message at altar calls.

With such a prospect, I went to the altar a few times for fear of being the victim of a "last chance," but I never felt right at altar service either. I guess I felt that if I would at least go to the altar God would have mercy on me.

But that didn't stop those lustful thoughts that dominated my mind. I was right back at the same old tricks the next day. However, let me say that I had a sense of the presence of God in my life from my earliest recollection. He has been the guiding force in my life, no matter how evil my thoughts, or deeds have been, and I am glad He knows all the imperfections and can sort them out of any good that may be in my heart. At least He understands, and no human ever does.

And you know, many of us go through life and never know whether our experiences and the emotions we felt as youngsters were the same as others, too. And I can speak only for myself, but I've heard enough stories from other people that I know all the mess I tell about is typical of what other boys were experiencing too.

If we only stopped to think for a minute, human nature is the same everywhere. We are human beings and we have to think and do like human beings. All of us more or less fit into a general pattern. But many of our emotions remain sealed in our hearts. So I know I ain't so fer off the beaten path.

And family is so important. It is our heritage, and in the modern world we have somehow become less concerned about our roots, although in recent years there has been a revival of looking back on our ancestry.

When I was a young'un, family was all-important. We knew our close-up kindred but even back there it went no further than first cousins. Pa must have had a hundred first cousins, but I never heard him mention but one or two, and I was fool enough not to even ask him whether he knew any of them. As a matter of fact, I wasn't aware of such a long lineage of kindred until the book "The Descendants of Elijah Smith" was published. Then I found out I was kin to a whole bunch of folks that weren't named Taylor.

But we shore learned about our first cousins, cause Ma and Pa saw to it that we visited them and learned a little something about their lives. It was always a once-a-year visit, but you could mark it down that we visited their brothers and sisters every year, and they visited us.

We learned a lot on those visits. It wasn't worth five cents as far as history is concerned, but it helped to educate us about life.

We observed family life among our kindred and any deviation from the patterns of our everyday living. We learned how their outhouses smelled (just like ourn) and what kind of chickens they had running over the yard. And we weren't surprised if we'd see one with necks as clean as a picked bird. They's that kind you know, where their necks are red with those pin-prick places where feathers would be if there hadn't been something wrong in their chromosomal makeup that prevented the formation of feathers on the neck..

We might have poland china or red-spotted shoats and theirs might be white or white and black spotted. And all cows don't look alike. All of them have sad faces, but sometimes there were horn deformities that would set one old cow apart from another.

We might have a hound and they might have a fice. Some had grapevines, where we didn't, and we'd git to eat grapes when they were ripe (and wasp stings too). Some made cider. Others didn't. Some asked the blessing. Some didn't. And you know what we had to eat when we visited on Sunday. We never let them know in advance, for there were no telephones and sending a 2-cent postcard took half a week to arrive. It was chicken stew every time we visited along with the other things they had prepared for the family without any company.

And we learned the moods of our cousins and what they thought about and how they did things.

We'd ramble all over the place and explore every building and roam down to the hog pasture with our string balls and something for a bat and the hogs would be running everywhere while we were chunking that ball and running bases. If we got in hog manure, won't no worse than them chicken droppings in the yard, and we shore got into them, all right.

It was all part of the learning experience.

Beauty, Innocence of 16

I was just starting to go to parties at age 16 or so, and that's one thing that we believed in in the old days. That was the best way to get a bunch of young people together and it was always an enjoyable occasion.

Kissing games were the most popular form of entertainment, and you were going a pretty fer ways when you really kissed a girl. And go ahead and laugh. I don't blame you, 'specially in thinking about how things are today. And yeah, all of us oldsters know we were born generations too early.

Anyhow, we'd git hot and bothered and slobbery-mouthed with the "closeness" of the situation. And some of those girls were responsive, too!

And don't you think for one minute there was no sex outside of marriage way back there. Every once in a while a girl became pregnant and a lot of times the old man arranged for a quick wedding. And sometimes the girl went away to have the baby. Some kept the babies. But it was a different story back then. And a family was disgraced when a baby was born out of wedlock.

They kept us working our butts off, but they couldn't find enough work to keep us busy every single minute. So there were half-days occasionally when we could wash all over in the washtub, put on a pair of clean overalls, git in the shade or on a backer truck pulled up under an oak or chaney ball tree, and watch the clouds floating across the sky and take advantage of what breeze there was. Blades of corn moving with the breeze were a pretty sight, with cotton blossoms shining in cotton fields. Hens were scratching for worms and catching insects and calling their biddies to fight over them. Cows were grazing under poplar or sweet gum or oak trees, or lying in the shade chewing their cuds. Pigs were squealing in the pasture and crows and hawks and buzzards were soaring overhead.

Children were making mud pies or rolling wheels or swinging under the trees and people traveling up and down the road.

Those were the years of youth; beautiful in every sense of the word. Just to be innocent and without full responsibility was beautiful. Whatever was not at the present, there was always tomorrow — always hope for everything the young can yearn for. It wasn't necessary to chart your goals at that stage in life. Live in a fairyland. Have a make-believe world. Laugh at hardship. Live the good life in dreams.

The purple martins tended their nests in gourds high above the ground. Mockingbirds sang their songs and bluejays squawked and cats toted kittens everywhere around the place and dirty wash water in tubs showed specks of black where flies drowned. Sows had their pigs and lay on half of them and those that lived squealed and the sow talked sow talk to them when she was letting her milk down. Goats bleated somewhere in the distance and sassy roosters crowed and ran down more hens.

The "reddy-o" was on in the front room with the volume turned up and Ernest Tubb was singing "Born to Lose" and you were thinking about some little old gal and gitting all walleyed, knowing old Ernest was telling it like it was, and that you didn't stand no more chance than a rat with that little beauty . It was enough to make you chaw your fingernails. That got you out of a daydream right quick.

And the creek was calling. There was a hankering to take a fishing pole and throw it in the water and catch a 3-inch perch. But that would disturb the rest, and rest didn't come easy. You had to take advantage of every minute of it.

Knock that old fly away and lie still when a yaller jacket comes by. Don't think about a nickel Pepsi and quarter-pound Power House. That would be 15 cents, and you hain't got 15 cents. Don't think about nothing. Just lie there and turn over ever once in a while to rest the back and the butt. Close your eyes and dream the sweet dreams.

And just look at Miss Priss promenading up the road looking like her hips' been knocked out of joint the way she's wobbling. She's done changed her walk since she growed out of that bean-pole of a waif with stringy hair and got that teasing look in them big eyes. Whoo-ee! Don't you start that messing, Miss Priss. You shore can swing them hips and you done got right purty and all that. But I done done some growing too. You and me's about the same age, don't you know? School and all that and little boy-little girl carryings-on — it's over, Miss Priss. Uhm! Uhm! Look at her pass. You better quit teasing, little old purty girl.

Don't think about the backer patch or the soda bucket or that sickly Paris Green and 'lasses that you've got to put on cotton tomorrow with a mop and the nauseating odor that makes you want to spew and the syrupy mess that gits on your overalls and goms you up. Don't think about the boll weevils that are gitting down in cotton bolls trying to ruin a crop.

Listen for the sounds. Somebody's hollering way over yander, and a mule is neighing in a nearby field. A young'un laughs down the road and somebody's heading to the store with eggs to git ice for tea. Somebody's pulling up a bucket of water and you can hear the chain rolling over the wheel.

Is that Lube hollering to them hogs to git back in the pasture? It ain't even Sunday and the hogs are gitting out. Something's wrong.

Remembrances of those days shine like emeralds as inconsequential events are relived, and the way things seemed. A country store was the most idyllic place in all the world, where worldly ways were at their peak and where youth gained more experience by observing the adult population than at any other place. In summer an electric fan would make its half-turns, cooling a very small part of the store. Men would sit on the counters or on drink crates turned on edge, scratch themselves, cuss and tell lies and smoke and chew and sweat. But it seemed like heaven.

I can remember how the sky looked on some of those occasions; how the air felt circulating about me; how the wind would pick up an odor and carry it swiftly by and the feeling of being enveloped in total security without a care in the world. I want to pinch myself sometimes to see if I'm the same person I was back in that paradise of memories.

Scene From Big Snow March 2, 1927
Courtesy Hugh B. Johnston

Big Snow Of March 2, 1927

So, where were you on March 2, 1927? That was the night of the "big" snow. I know that many of you had never been thought about on God's green earth that long ago.

To be perfectly truthful, I don't remember much about that day either. It was one of the many times when that long trail of memory ran off the edge and got lost in the mist for the most part. And except for other events it would have been like 99 percent of my past — forgotten.

I know I went to Hood Swamp School that day, but I have no idea what we studied. After all, I was only nine years old. But knowing us as we were in those days, I can just about give you an accurate description of what I was like that day.

It had been six months since they bought me my two pairs of

overhalls, so they were well above my brogan tops. The bib was as low as I could get it and they were tight in the straddle and kept me trying to yank them lower. And I was unbuttoning the cuffs of my shirt for they were three inches above my wrists at least. The soles of my shoes were coming loose, also.

I expect the sweater I was wearing that day was blue, or maybe maroon, depending on the color they bought for me back in the fall. And it was time for the wind to be stirring so I know my lips were chapped and there was a dark streak around my mouth where I licked them for the cooling effect.

There is no doubt but that I had a cold, for children in those days seemed to carry around colds through most of the winter and on into spring. Ma put a handkerchief in the hind pockets of our overhalls, but we'd fill them up before you could turn around. Then we'd resort to our sweater sleeves for nose-wipers.

And you know as good as me that there was a stiff, gray, glazy-looking streak on the top of my sweater sleeves. The only things I remember as being worse than those sweater sleeves were the snotty noses when someone would say, "Wipe your nose," and the young'un would instead suck the stuff back up his nostrils. Lordy! Lordy!

We walked in droves on the way to and from school, and on that day I remember that Gertrude Gurganus walked with us. Gertrude lived the opposite way from Hood Swamp school than us, but she was spending the night with Margaret Peele. Even back there schoolmates would spend the night with each other once or twice during the school term. So I remember that part of March 2, 1927 well enough.

And I know that all five of us boys were at home then and that one of my sisters, her husband and a baby, or maybe two babies, were also staying at our house because they were building a house and it wasn't ready to move into.

And remembering how the eating situation was in those days, I know that Ma was having a time feeding that crowd. All the ish taters were gone. All the sweet taters were gone. The collard stalks had run up to flowers. But since we threshed peas every fall and picked dry butterbeans, I just know that one of the two was on the table for supper. There was no doubt some fried pork shoulder also, for Ma wouldn't have cut a ham no longer than the meat had been killed. It hadn't had time to get that cured taste. And I suspect there were canned peaches or canned apples on the table also, for that was the time of year women were emptying those half-gallon jars pretty regularly to add to the diets.

There had to be at least a hundred buttermilk biscuits cooked, and there had to be 'lasses or syrup or preserves on the table. And that's about the way it was that night, folks.

I haven't mentioned the fact that a few snowflakes fell while we were on our way from school. That must have been about four o'clock. Of course we were excited and hollering and carrying on. But it was getting late for snow. We were waiting for the robins. Ma had even had a hen to set and come off and the hen and biddies were in the empty tater hill, and thriving. So we didn't think very much about snow, and it was not very cold, either.

Well sir, after supper one of the boys went to the door and looked out and hollered for the rest of us to go and look. And we did. And man, you ain't never seen snow falling so fast, or as big a flakes. I mean it was piling up.

Somebody rounded up the shovel and the spade and the pitchfork and another boy went to the woodpile and dug the ax out of the snow and brought the tools to the back porch. And we just stood and watched as the world turned white. There was little sleeping at our house that night.

It snowed all night long, hard, and was still coming down next morning, and I'm here to tell you that was the daggumedst snowfall we ever saw in eastern North Carolina. There's never been another one even approaching it in my lifetime.

And on March 3, it looked as isolated as the TV pictures of the moon's surface looked when our astronauts walked up there. Nobody was stirring for the snow was deeper than men's straddles. The wind had drifted the snow up to the window sills at our house, and there were drifts 10 to 15 feet deep in some places.

I've been told snow was around 27 inches deep out in the fields, and I don't doubt it one bit. The grown boys at our house got out and shoveled a path to the barn so the mules could be fed. I don't know what in the heck the chickens did unless they did without, for no path was shoveled out to the chicken house. And what they did with any hogs left after hog-killing, God only knows. I shore don't.

It was three or four days before the snow was gone and we got maneuvering again. And Gertrude Gurganus got snowed in at Miss Eva's, and the only clothing she took with her except for what she was wearing, was her night gown. And I'd never have thought about Gertrude going home with Margaret if it hadn't been for that humongous snowfall. In fact, I wouldn't have thought about that day in history again.

And in thinking about Miss Eva's, it brought to mind the cuckoo clock she had on her mantlepiece. It was the only cuckoo clock I had ever seen and it fascinated me. Every hour that door would fly open and that little bird would cuckoo whatever hour it was, then retreat in a flash and the door would close. I hope Gertrude enjoyed that little bird as much as I did whenever I was at Miss Eva's.

Ain't it something, the workings of the mind?

Beautiful Days Of Past

The years of my youth were fun times ... great, beautiful days filled with golden hues. Some folks would have you believe that there was no fun, no joy in living, nothing to look forward to during the days when the good old US of A was at its poorest.

Some folks would have you believe it was all gloom and doom and nothing on earth but back-breaking work, and I can't deny that we worked our share. But when you're young and filled with the zest for life, work is good exercise and you recuperate quickly after 10 or more hours in the fields.

In retrospect, it was the inconveniences that made our lives unpleasant, but since we had never had conveniences, they were of no concern at that time. We don't feel like we could bear the heat today without air conditioners and ceiling fans and refrigerators to supply us with ice and cool our soft drinks. It's the same way about cold. We'd literally freeze today in the houses many of us grew up in. We don't have the stamina and we haven't been conditioned for the kind of life we knew then. But except for the coolness in summer and the warmth in winter, and an inside toilet and bathroom, other parts of country living were a breeze.

These young codgers today haven't the faintest idea how exciting it was back then to be looking forward to going to the show on Saturday and then attending a party that night and smooching and singing and hollering. It was almost like heaven.

And what were our chores in those days? Ha!

They included cleaning off new grounds for backer beds; sawing wood for curing backer and to burn in the cookstove, shrubbing ditchbanks, piling and burning brush, cutting stalks, disking land, running rows, breaking up land with one-horse or two-horse plows, one furrow at a time; sowing backer beds, hauling and sowing guano, planting crops, transplanting backer, plowing and chopping crops, ditching, putting in backer, curing backer, suckering backer, grading and tying backer, cleaning out stables, milking cows, shucking corn;

Picking cotton, getting up corn, cutting and baling hay, pulling fodder, sowing soda, splitting wood, feeding up (every day of the year); and this don't count the odd jobs.

We'd sweat our overhalls and chambray shirts down in hot weather, git rank under the arms and smell like polecats. We tried not to raise our arms too high or draw in our breath while they were up. If we were wearing shoes, sweat would run down our legs and pond in them and our feet would actually slosh about in the shoes sometimes. We'd go without socks in the summer for the kind we wore were them heavy cotton knits and they rumpled up in our shoes and caused our feet to sweat.

No tub of water feels better than to draw it from the well in hot weather and sink your butt down in it. It causes you to draw in your breath for a minute, but then it soothes the galded legs and you wish it were only possible to git all parts of your body saturated. Since that was impossible in a washtub, we'd take that old hard rag torn from some old shirt or sheet or something too far gone to do anybody any good, scrub ourselves down with plenty of soap (usually the home-made kind) and then stand in the water and wash off our feet. I tell you, it felt refreshing after you wiped off good and got on some clean clothes. When we worked in the fields in hot weather won't no way we could go for a full week without taking a bath.

After we got "cleaned up" we'd hold up our arms and test them agin for them scents that had made us half sick. Won't no way we were going to no girl's house like we were when we came in from the fields.

But let me tell you something that will bring down your ego to zero in one minute. You think you're something when you go to a girl's house with your Sunday slippers on and a white shirt, a pair of pants 'stid of overhalls, and as soon as you're seated you start smelling something peculiar. The first time your girl's eyes are turned you look down at them slippers, and one is "plastered" with a mushy chicken dropping, bottom and side too. You want to faint but you know you've got to git out of there and clean off that shoe. So you make an excuse to go outside, and in the darkness have to find a stick and do a lot of scraping and then finding a leaf or something to try to rub the scent away. But it's almost impossible to do. But thank God, girls know about all that mess too; country girls, that is.

Take a growing young'un that does all them things and put him down to a laden table and I guarantee he will eat 10 or 15 biscuits, sop all the gravy, all the'lasses, all the "zerves" he can git and chaw on the leg of the table. You can't hardly fill him up and if he's got a dime when he goes to the store he's going to git him a pop and a bag of ground peas and put them in the bottle and eat them as he guzzles the drink, belch a time or two and he's ready to go to the safe when he gits home and fork him out a cold tater.

That's adolescence for you. That's a growing boy and a world filled with work. That's a time for exploring, for learning about the world and about yourself and your relationship to others in life. It's a gangly time when you ain't boy nor man; when you can't quite fit yourself comfortably into society' when you ain't sure about yourself, or others. That was me for a fare-you-well.

But time was passing. Fifteen, 16, 17 what's the difference? Gitting taller and hitting six feet and toned down a little bit but with far too much belly and hips, and much too bunglesome and hating it with a passion.

But I'm savoring all that boyhood has to offer. It's soon going to be "goodbye youth, goodbye yesterday, goodbye everything" it seems like. Ain't but one time around, buddy. Youth is reserved for a few short years, and after that the fireworks!

Things Now Extinct

I n the romantic language of the Indians, it was called maize. They cleared the land and planted the grain and valued it as a food before the white man came.

Before my time, the grain was widely used as a source of food for the animal world as well as for man. The value of corn is now known worldwide and is a major contributor to the breadbasket of the world.

Warm sunshine caused the kernels to germinate and peep from the earth and brought crows on the scene as they vied with nature for their share of the spoils. Thunderstorms brought showers that nurtured the plants while they were stretching upward for their place in the sun.

We used corn as food for our mules, hogs, and poultry. We used it equally as much for our own nutrition. And because we were very poor people lacking the money with which to purchase many appetizing products that were on the market even then, we extended its use in ways that appealed to our tastes. From the time the tender kernels were filled with milk, we gathered the corn and cooked it as "rosen ears" cut off the cob, boiled on the pot as corn on the cob, and in other ways.

And when ears were too old to be used in the usual manner, they were baked to a golden brown in the oven and provided real treats for the young folks. Sometimes, when there were not more appetizing treats around, kernels of dry corn would be parched and eaten by the younger population. After the corn was ground into meal, children would often parch the meal in heavy skillets, add salt and eat it as a delicacy.

Sweet potatoes were prized by the people as a pleasant addition to their diets. From late summer when they were placed on shelters to sweeten through a good part of the winter, baked yams were always on the table. They were used in other ways also — for pies and jacks, fried and souffled and even in "tater" bisucits. But because we were poor and unable to have all the delicacies we desired, we found pleasure in "raw taters." We remembered all the work in getting the slips into the ground and hoeing them high on their ridges and turning vines in order to plow them and then criss-crossing the vines so they would grow on both sides of the row.

So when the tubers were sweet and we were hungry after our walks from school, it was a special delight to go out to the hill, find a fairly good-sized potato, peel it and eat it raw. They were delicious. We even scraped potatoes sometimes, added milk and flavoring along with sugar and had a dessert as good as ice cream.

Recognizing the need for a winter vegetable at a time when little could be grown in the garden to provide food for the table for large families, turnip patches were always sown in late summer. The seeds were sown on top of the ground, and in few days they sprouted and showed green over the beds.

The plants grew rapidly and within a few weeks turnip salet was ready to be picked, But the plants were not pulled up, and new leaves soon appeared. All the while the roots were beginning to grow into turnips that were also prized for their sweetness. In a few more weeks the turnips were ready to be pulled and boiled to add food for the table. Sometimes they were boiled separately and at other times the leaves and the turnips were cooked together, or added together after they were cooked. When the turnips were cooked alone they left pot liquor with a sweet flavor that the people savored.

And because we were poor and lacking the money with which to buy the delicacies offered at the stores, we often pulled up turnip roots, peeled them and ate of their sweetness. They were delicious.

The honeysuckles were as welcome as the springtime. From the men plowing the land to the women slaving away in the homes, to children playing in yards, honeysuckle blooms brought pleasant odors and spoke something romantic to the soul. They spoke of warm days and star-filled nights and the summer season when the world was reborn.

Honeysuckles had their fruit also, although it was not very sweet. It was different, to say the least. And the fruit was scattered eratically among the blossoms. It was like a tropical fruit, semi transparent with a whitish-green tint. It was not very sweet nor very tasty, but we ate it because it was there to gather at will.

And on the hillsides and out-of-the-way places the wild plums grew in abundance. They were the only kind of plums we ever learned to love. In their red and yellow skins, they were filled with sweet juice and when the morning dew was thick on the fruit, we ate to our stomachs' delight. We preferred the ripe plums to the delicacies at the store.

Likewise, we ran our hands among the briers to retrieve the blue-black berries. Even if they turned our hands and lips purple, they were a rare delicacy that was a part of our world every summer. The briers pierced our hands and became tangled in our clothing and left their marks on our bodies, but we were the conquerors.

All of us ate the wild strawberries that grew in out-of-way places. We waited for frost to ripen the persimmons, and when they were at their peak we congregated at the trees and ate of the mealy, sweet fruit. Sometimes on the way to the persimmon trees we would find ripe maypops that had shriveled up with maturity that were now a golden yellow. The ripe maypops held sweet-as-sugar jucies that we would swallow, leaving the seeds for next year's crop.

Bullises grew heavenward in the tall trees along the ditch banks, and the brave Tarzans and Janes climbed the trees to eat of the wild grapes high above the streams of water.

If we had been affluent like the children of the 1980s we would never have indulged in such practices. We were explorers, which is not a part of the make-up of today's generations. Even if we had had the resources to indulge in the delicacies available in those days, it was our nature to try anything once. It was not because of ignorance that we did those things. It was because we wanted to know first-hand what life was all about.

We learned so much as children; many things that the world of today can never be a part of. As a matter of fact, they won't even know about them unless we tell them.

Aunt Bet

Aunt Bet's Life Colorful

Where in the heck do you begin with a character like Aunt Bet, Pa's sister? I reckon the proper name is as good a way as any. Her last name was Killette, but in the olden days we called names the old-fashioned way. Then it was pronounced "Killit" like you would say to a young'un after catching a chicken, "kill it." But no, that won't good enough after this sinful world turned modern. The pronunciation was changed to "Kill ette" with the "ette" pronounced like we used to say "et" instead of ate.

Well, let's name the young'uns first, in order. There were Gilbert, Lala, Simon (they called him "Slick") and I know his proper name was Simeon, but that ain't what they said when they called him anything besides "Slick."

Next was Jake, then Sophie, Teena and Josh. And of course Josh is really Joshua.

Aunt Bet was married to Uncle Jim, but I don't remember nothing about him except many stories that were told about his escapades. Something happened to uncle Jim's mind after some of the young'uns were born, and they had to eventually confine him to the 'sylum in Raleigh. They called it "Dix Hill" at that time. And I was told about Uncle Jim escaping and having to swim a river to git back home (and I hain't got no idea how long he stayed at home). I know after his trips home, another young'un was on the way.

Anyhow, they said that Uncle Jim rigged up pieces of iron (like plow sweeps and things like that) and hung them in the doorway and made Aunt Bet walk into them when she entered the other room. And he had been good to her when he had his right mind.

Pa told me that Uncle Jim was as strong as a bull yearling. Uncle Jim was not tall, but very muscular, and Pa said he could back up to a 500-pound bale of cotton, stoop over and balance the cotton on his back and walk with it. Is that as strong as a bull yearling?

And one time while he was out of the 'sylum, Uncle Jim built him a coffin and put rockers on it and had it in the front yard. Lord! Lord! I reckon he was going to rock all the way to heaven, and I hope he did.

I have been told that he got bit by a snake while he was gathering corn, and that the snake clung to his hand when he pulled it up from the ground.

Well, Jake got into the lye box when he was a baby and I reckon it "et" the palate of his mouth out or got the rough part that you can feel if you run your tongue up there. Anyhow, Aunt Bet always cooked "Jake biscuits" for Jake. They were flat and harder than the average biscuit. I reckon the dough in the biscuit stuck to the top of his mouth.

Gilbert got married young and had a whole pack of young'uns, and today they're the finest bunch of folks you ever saw — handsome and modern and community leaders — six boys and two girls.

"Slick" finally got married, but he was gitting on up there and gray-headed before he tied the knot, so he was with Aunt Bet for a long time. And he didn't stay married too long, for I think Clyde couldn't take "Slick's" drinking. He didn't stay drunk all the time, but he pulled stinkos when he did git on a drunk.

"Slick" was a good farmer, and a fool about bird hunting. And he had the best-trained bird dogs when I was a young'un that I ever saw. He meant business with his bird dogs, and he had mostly setters over the years. And those dogs minded "slick" too. He'd holler their names and they'd come and do "exactly" what he told them. He didn't mind beating the mess out of one if he had to to make it mind.

I remember one time "Slick" had sold backer, and his wallet was either in the bib pocket of his overalls or in the hip pocket of his britches, and he lost it jumping over rank soybean vines and corn stalks while hunting his dog. And I mean there were rank vines everywhere. Ditchbanks were six-feet wide over the edges from summer growth. And what did "Slick" do?

He called his dog and sent her out to find his wallet. She knew his scent anyway, and he knew the dog would be searching for that scent, and yep, she brought the pocket book back with every cent of money in it!

Aunt Bet had erysipelas in one of her legs, and it plagued her over much of her lifetime. You could see that leg sometimes and it looked like it was going to rot off. But Dr. Heck went by ever so often and left her salve to smear on it and she'd wear a white rag on it. It would cure up for a while, then flare up again.

Jake lived with Aunt Bet for a long time too, although he eventually married and moved to town. Jake came to our house one time and he had the "monkeys" and he was seeing the devil on the walls of the room. What a time that was!

Josh got married early, to Irene, and in a year or two they started having young'uns and ended up with five I think. Their young'uns turned out good, too. But Josh had diabetes and I reckon it done him in. After he got so he couldn't work he and Irene separated and went their own ways. Josh lived in town, and he died, no doubt from a diabetic coma, and it was several days before they found him. Josh was about my age, and he used to come and spend the night with me, and I'd go there sometimes.

Sophie married O'Neal after his first wife died, leaving him with two fine boys. O'Neal was a good bit older than Sophie. Sophie helped to finish raising them and had five handsome children of her own, three girls and two boys. Four of the five were college graduates.

Sophie worked hard and her health failed fairly early. But she was the backbone of the family. Aunt Bet died there. Slick died there, and Lala died there.

And Lala won't no baby when she married Bert, her first cousin (Aunt Mariah's and Uncle Branch's boy). I think she had four young'uns, and I don't know if it was after the first one or the next, she had milk leg and that leg was as stiff as a board til the day she died. She was bad off a long time and went and stayed with

Aunt Bet and Aunt Bet managed to cook and wash and iron and the boys tended the crops. After a long period of time, Lala was finally able to go back home and keep house. but she had a time of it. And Lala was a hundred years behind the times, even then, so you can imagine how outdated she was.

I can't tell you anything about Lala's children.

Then there was Teena. And I don't remember her, but I was told that she was the prettiest girl in the community with a different color red hair than the Taylor crowd in general. Her hair was a deep auburn, and her eyes must have been green, according to the description I was given when I was a young'un. She was only 17, and she was bitten by a snake that resulted in her death. So snakes played major roles in the lives of two of Aunt Bet's folks.

But I tell you, there were a lot of thickets and branches and places where briers grew, where poison ivy climbed up in the trees and grew rank on the ground close to the houses that Aunt Bet and her family habitated. So it was one thing after the other with Aunt Bet's folks, and much of it tragic. But at least her life was colorful, whereas for most of us it was a hum-drum existence with nothing happening.

Aunt Bet Of Old School

I t's hard to define Aunt Bet. She was a good woman and loved all her people with a passion. But she had a mind of her own and you didn't change how she felt. And although the boys did the farm work, Aunt Bet was the leader and she was the one that went to town when they had to have a few dollars or when guano was bought, or when they had to stock up on staples.

I can see Aunt Bet today as she made her way to town, on a two-horse wagon if somebody would drive the mules, or in somebody's Model T Ford with her Sunday hat made of black straw with a little faded ribbon and some kind of artificial fruit on it, in her Sunday frock with a brooch on the collar. She wore faded out clothes around home and an apron. She might go to town when tobacco was sold also. I reckon she felt like if she left the check in "Slick" or Jake's hands, they might git into a little booze and upset the apple cart.

And in the modern generations, the young crowd thinks that

any new fad is something that was never tried before. Remember how a lot of people felt when some liberated women became braless? Well, back then the older women didn't wear bras either. And that ain't all. It just goes to show there ain't nothing new under the sun.

Aunt Bet was one of many older women way back yander that just stepped behind the smokehouse or the barn or a shelter and wet standing up. If you doubt older women did that, ask some of the old-timers. If you'd a said "panties" to them they'd a thought you were trying to talk biggety about a man's britches, and they didn't wear a man's pants, nor no underpants for that matter.

They'd a known about bloomers, but they were something new-fangled to them. They didn't want to feel that elastic around their legs and waists and the ballooning material under their clothes. Bloomers were young folks'es mess. Yet, they'd put them tight corsets on and wear them. But not Aunt Bet. She didn't need one.

Aunt Bet could live in some of the most God-awful places you ever seen. I mean away from civilization! I know when she lived beyond Coker Town her house was the only one you could see in that big field and that one little shanty-like place on the edge. After you turned off the road at Coker Town you passed Mr. Henry Worrell's and Miss Jackie Matthews' places and headed on back through a patch of woods and then there were only wagon tracks and a path leading to Aunt Bet's.

I think Aunt Bet liked the out-of-the-way places better than those more thickly settled. I think that lifestyle suited her and some of her children and they would have chosen no other places to live.

There weren't a lot of stables and outbuildings around the places Aunt Bet lived. There was a look of desolation about the premises. There were mule stables, a scant woodpile and a saw bench, a wash pot and clothesline. There weren't a lot of chickens running over the yard. Aunt Bet liked game chickens, for they foraged for themselves and didn't have to be fed and catered to like those old lazy domesticated chickens. If she wanted a hen for chicken stew or corn meal broth to ease queamy stomachs after drunks, one of the boys would take the shotgun and blow the old hen's head off. You didn't run down games among the bushes. They could duck into the woods before you could turn around, or soar like a bird.

Aunt Bet didn't go in for knitting and crocheting and things like that. She won't made that way. She was practical, and when she mended the boys' britches she just as soon use white thread on blue overalls as not. And she made wide stitches, too. She'd can grape preserves and leave all the seeds in the grapes, but let me tell you those preserves were good, and the seeds tasted like some rare nut. And there were a lot of 'em.

Aunt Bet didn't care about fine furniture or totally uncluttered surroundings. Oh, she was clean, but it didn't bother her if a chair was filled with roughdried clothes and another was loaded down with quilts. She had a couple of chairs around the fireplace and an oil lamp on a table. She decorated with nails, driven into the studs that held the weatherboarding to the house. In the kitchen there were nails for pots and dippers and skillets and griddles and strings of pepper and sage and like most people, she had a mixture of beds with high head boards and metal steads with chipped-off paint. She was happy with her accommodations.

In the summer when the porch was shaded, she would take a straight chair and sit and shell beans or peas and fight off the flies and fan herself with an old funeral home fan. She wore a slatted bonnet until it got too hot. Then she'd lay it aside for comfort's sake.

"Slick" had an old banjo, and he'd play it on the porch sometimes, sitting flat on the floor, or with his legs hanging down on the edge of the porch. He went barefooted in summer with his overalls legs turned up a couple of notches.

There would be the tall corn dominating the scene and cutting off the summer breezes, and beyound the corn the backer patch and the cotton patch, and the horizon.

It was lonely at Aunt Bet's. It was far enough away from the railroad there wasn't even the sound of the train passing through, only quietness except for the singing of birds or the bark of a dog or the cries of animals during the night. The fields loomed large and a haze was over the crops during the heat of the day. Heat waves were detectable over the fields and crops wilted in the hot sun. It was almost total isolation, away from the mainstream of life.

But when winter came it could have been an ideal subject for a professional photograper. There was a serenity there and a quaintness so unique it made you feel you were in another world. To be there as the sun began to set on a cold, cloudy day was a treat, indeed. There were golden rays peeping through the clouds low on the horizon and darkening skies. Coveys of birds would fly over the fields and the little house was warm with heat from an open fireplace sending white smoke up the chimney that curved northward from the wind and dissipated in the atmosphere.

Tiny specks of precipitation would strike the face and the feeling in the air gave forebodings of snow. And I never saw a snowfall at Aunt Bet's house, but it is easy to imagine that in its setting, the beauty would be almost sublime, with white covering the fields except for bits of stalks that protruded through the snow and birds hopping around the premises for handouts.

And Aunt Bet visited her folks, too. She'd go to a brother's or a sister's and stay three or four days at the time. But that was after all the boys had left home. I know she used to visit us a couple of times a year at least, and her and Pa could git into some of the biggest arguments you ever saw — over nothing. Pa might say something about the sun setting in a certain place, and Aunt Bet would take him up on it in a hot minute. "Now the sun sets yander, Gaston," she'd say, pointing to some other place at the treetops. And it was like that about anything. And Pa liked to argue too. He thought he was right and Aunt Bet thought she was right, and it made for a lively time with nobody paying them any attention.

A Salute To Aunt Bet

A unt Bet didn't laugh a lot. She'd get a broad smile on her face sometimes, but for the most part, she was serious. And it wasn't that she felt dejected or deprived. Aunt Bet was perhaps happier than most of her people. The life she lived was the only life she knew.

Aunt Bet was typical of the entire Taylor clan. She had a head full of hair and when she, Aunt Cass, Aunt Lora, Aunt Laura or Aunt Mariah would let down that ball of hair, it fell almost to the hips. It took some real pinning to keep that hair up.

Every one of the Taylors, including Pa, Uncle Craven, Uncle John and Uncle Ben, had that ugly color red hair. It was a yellowish red, light and sort of colorless, especially after it became tinged with white, to go with gander-gray eyes. I mean every one of 'em, including Grandma and Grandpa Taylor. They were like peas in a pod and anybody would have known they were Taylors a mile away.

Pa had more hair on his red head the day he died than I had when I was eighteen years old, so when the genes for hair were dished out, I didn't git nary one from Pa, although some of the young'uns did, thank God.

All the Taylors had fair skins and sort of purplish lips, but most of their offspring were dark-haired. Unless they were exposed to the sun a lot, they looked a little pale. But that ain't saying they won't fine folks.

And as I said, Aunt Bet was downright silly about her folks — brothers, sisters, young'uns, grandyoung'uns, and anybody else in the family. She set them up a little higher than other people. But Aunt Bet had a way of wanting all of them to sort of do like she said.

All of her motherly instincts would come to the surface when "Slick" or Jake would git on binges. They were the only two of her youn'uns that ever gave her any trouble about drinking, or anything else much. When "Slick" or Jake were drunk she'd try to git them settled down and they'd brush her off, saying, "Ah, Ma, go on about your business," and Aunt Bet would whine and half cry and pull at them, but they didn't pay her no more mind than if she hadn't been there.

Aunt Bet did her share of worrying, 'specially about the crops if the boys were hitting the bottle. If the backer or corn or cotton needed plowing, she was in a tizzy to git them out there behind a plow to try to git rid of grass that was trying to take over.

She attended preaching when she could, but she won't one of these "hell-and-damnation" Christians. I believe she was a member of Bethel Church and I'm sure she was buried there. She believed in God but she didn't do much talking about religion.

I'm sure that if there are isolated places in heaven, Aunt Bet will be happiest behind some heavenly thicket with a rural scene to view as she shouts all over God's heaven. She would never be her happiest in marble mansions or on streets of gold. They were not her thing in life. And I believe that she will be accommodated in heaven with surroundings that will appeal to her.

But just suppose I git up there by the grace of God one of these days, and find a new Aunt Bet, diked out in finery and enjoying a special mansion. And to tell you the truth, I might be happier with something of the lifestyle I've known on earth, minus all the earthly worries. But I can tell you one thing: I ain't going to worry one minute about what accommodations I will receive in heaven. I'm just praying and hoping I git there, no matter how.

I think about all the people on both sides of my family, and we are as non-descript as they come, with the exception of Aunt Bet. She may have lived a harder life than any of the others. She may have had less than some of them. All were very poor people with little in worldly goods to lay claim to. But there was excitement in Aunt Bet's life. All the circumstances surrounding her life contributed to that color.

She didn't bear ill will toward Uncle Jim because of his actions after he lost his mind. She tried to protect him and loved him. She held no remorse in her heart toward "Slick" and Jake after their bouts with the bottle. She was happy in knowing they decided to sober up and took pride in them when they were going straight.

Aunt Bet was at home under the great expanse of sky about her and among the tall trees and bushy areas where she lived. She was in tune with nature and birds and small animals were a part of her world. She believed in the signs and looked to the heavens for guidance — watching for different phases of the moon to guide her in planting and making soap. I am convinced that she was about as happy as the average person can be in her environment. I never heard her covet anything anybody else had or wish for things she knew were beyond her reach. She made mansions out of her humble abodes and asked nothing special from life. That can't be said for many people.

I take my hat off to a great woman and consider it a special privilege to have known her during the days when she was at her best.

But tragedy has followed Aunt Bet's family, through Sophie. Sophie's oldest daughter has two sons and both were born with eye defects. Everything possible was done to restore sight to their eyes, but the oldest is totally blind. The youngest has some vision, but is declared legally blind. Both are fine young men and highly educated.

Sophie's second daughter married a man from Indiana when he was in service in North Carolina and moved out there to live. She had several children, and two were killed in a church bus accident on its way to some church activity.

Sophie's second son was a major in the Air Force, and upon retirement returned to N.C. to live. He had flown countless thousands of miles as an Air Force pilot. But he crawled under his car without adequate protection and lost his life when the vehicle fell on him. But the tragedies in Sophie's family occurred after Aunt Bet was laid to rest in a cemetery in Greene County.

And that's the story of Aunt Bet.

All The Things We Used To Do

H ow busy were people out in the country 50 or more years ago? How long have you got to listen?

Start with January. The old lady's busy sewing cloth to cover the backer beds, either with thread and needle or on the sewing machine. On a warm day the men are shrubbing ditch banks. Young'uns getting home from school are rushed out to the woodpile to get in stove wood and wood for the fireplace.

"Run and git up the eggs, Sis. And you be careful and don't break them eggs."

"Go git the basket of shucks in the barn and dump'em in the cow stable, Little Bud. And you start shucking corn, Shine."

"Run and make a fire in the cook stove," Lizzie Mae. Cut up some of that fresh side and put it in the skillet too. Your daddy wants to git the backer cloth on the bed tomorrow and I like a lot having it put together."

February: "Less go up in the woods boys and git them trees cut down. Moon's right and we can saw wood when we git the chance. Fuzz, you git out there and start disking land. Shine's done finished cutting stalks, and we got to git started on breaking land right away. They's 60 acres to be broke, one 'fur' at a time, you know."

March: "Lord, that wind's blowing. Look at that whirlwind out there in the field. My eyes are plumb full of grit, seems like. Just look at the dust flying where Shine is breaking up land. Time to start running rows, too. Planting time's just around the corner. All that guano's got to be put out, too. And weeds are growing like wildfire on them backer beds. Time to git the "guarden" started, too."

April: "Every hen on the yard is trying to set. Ain't gitting no eggs. Sis, run out to the privy and throw that old hen off the nest in that pasteboard box. Find some sticks to fill up the nest. Then I reckon she'll git on top of the sticks and just sit there. Crazy old hen. When you want them to set all they study is laying, and when you set all the hens you need to, all the rest want to set too."

"We got to bear down, boys. Tote that guano out in the fields and git it in them rows and ridge 'em up. Cotton's got to be planted and the backer rows ridged up. Thank God, corn rows ain't got to be ridged up. Got to git that corn in the ground so the crows can start feasting."

May: "Don't start this "aching back" mess to me. This backer's got to be set out. Got to strain the back in the daytime to git the plants in the ground and let it rest at night. This is just the beginning with backer, you know. We'll be hurting all over 'fore it's all over with.''

June: "Ain't the crops pretty shining in the fields? Corn's green and growing. Cotton's beginning to show up down the rows. Looks like a right good stand of backer. Soda's got to be put to corn when it starts to silking. Backer's got to be side-dressed. Them beans' got to be picked right away. Lord, I hope they will bring a little better price than last year. Got to git some baskets too and see about gitting somebody to help pick'em. That cotton's got to be chopped, too. Look at that coat of grass showing up everywhere. Watermelons will soon have to be laid by, too.''

July: "Forgit everything else on God's green earth 'cept backer. Git them looping shelters covered with limbs. Chop around the barns. Mend the furnaces. Find the thermometers. Clean up the lanterns. Buy the backer twine. Whatever hain't been done to the "guarden," do it right now. Won't be no time later. Got to git them sand lugs Monday morning. You thought your backs hurt when you were pegging out them backer plants. Well just wait til you've stooped down to the ground to git them lugs in 12 acres of backer, and you'll know something about the back ache. And Doan's Kidney Pills ain't going to do it no good, either.

"Bad enough to work all day in the mess, to say nothing of staying up all night and sticking wood in the furnaces. And how can anything grow as fast as them suckers? If them shoats would grow just half as fast as backer suckers, we'd have more meat than we could eat in a year. Good thing cotton ain't that much trouble after you git it laid by — that is — until it's time to git out there and pick it.''

August: "That big rain's done stopped backer from ripening. We ought to be through putting in, but that mess done turned green agin. I done wore backer clothes so long they smell pure sour. But you young'uns' got to run out and crap them bug-eaten collard leaves and throw them in the hogpen. If we don't git them leaves off and doctor the buds we won't have no collards for winter. Got to think about pulling fodder, too. Soon as we git through with backer, that'll be the next big job, and I can already hear every young'un here bitching.''

September: "Finally got all that backer put in. Them tips don't look like they were worth saving. Near 'bout green as grass in the barn. Young'uns fixing to start to school with nothing to wear. Well, they'll just have to wear what they got til we sell some backer and can go to town to git 'em some new overhalls and shoes and cloth for dresses. May have to keep some of 'em out to help house the crops anyhow. Been so busy I done forgot to git the turnip patch sowed. Wonder the old lady ain't been having fits about that. Fuzz, come here right quick. Go out there and break up the place in the "guarden" where nothing ain't growing. Got to sow turnip seeds. And if you see any "simlins" out there among the grass, save 'em. Some would be good stewed down with some onions in 'em."

October: Git in that packhouse and bear down to git that backer graded and tied and stuck up. We'll grade in the daytime and tie it at night when all the young'uns are here. Got to see about gitting hands to pick cotton, too. Shine, you take the old Ford and go to town the first of the week and round up some pickers.

November: Lord, Lord! That corn's still got to be housed. Why does there have to be so much work in farming? We'll have charleyhorse in our legs 'fore we git all that corn picked up off the ground and throwed in the wagon. Think I'll have a corn shucking this year. Anyhow, all the backer's sold 'cept one more barn. We will git to that next week. Cotton's picked too, 'cept for the scrapping around Thanksgiving. Maybe them boys will git to go hunting sometime. They're dying to git out there with their guns and dogs and mow down them partridges and doves and rabbits."

December: "Won't be long til Christmas! Most of the work's done for the year 'cept for all that wood cutting and hauling. But that's enough to half-way keep us busy. Hogs are fattening and hog-killing time's just around the corner. Been a long, hard year, and another is just ahead. Time to start all over agin. Ain't no end to it, and odd jobs ain't even been counted. They's enough work on the farm to keep everybody in the house busy 365 days to the year, and the extra day in leap year, too.

Night Of The Medicine Show

I liked to have forgot to tell you about the night the traveling medicine show came to the Hood Swamp School grounds. And I don't know why, for anything like that way back yander brought out the crowds in droves.

It was in late September I think. Anyhow, it was before cold weather. Folks hadn't been nowhere since they got through puttin' in backer, and old and young were ready for something — anything - to break the monotony.

There were two trucks with enclosed bodies and "Medicine Show" was stenciled in gold letters over the black background. Another flat-bed truck served as the stage.

Anyhow, 'bout dark they started flocking on the grounds and you could see 'em fighting skeeters and gnats that swarmed around their eyes. The banjo and guitar players climbed to the stage and got things rolling with "Frankie and Johnny" and "Turkey in the Straw." By then Joe Ben Blizzard was out there doing the Buck and others in the crowd were limbering up their legs. Joe Ben had already been sipping the bottle. Then the guitar player took up yodeling, and folks hollered and whooped.

The Medicine Man was on the stage in high-top hat, a black suit and string tie, and his old lady, or somebody's old lady, wore a hat with feather plumes and a red dress that sparkled in the light. A woman was heard saying she looked like a strumpet in that mess. But folks were clapping their hands to the music and it was evident the show crowd was looking forward to selling their potions.

Folks with half-grown young'uns were trying to keep track of them, 'specially them just-sprouting girls, but the young'uns were quicker than the old folks and there won't no way of keeping up with them. Boys were running hither and thither over the pile of coal beside the school building, then running each other into the woods, jumping over dog fennel and ragweed grown tall at the edge of the grounds, and darting in and out among the crowds, and the girls were giggling and looking at boys and the boys were doing the same to the girls.

Then the clown came out and did all sorts of crazy things and people were laughing and hollering and you could smell whisky on some breaths and some men had bottles in the hind pockets of their overhalls.

The fiddle player came on and said they were going to play a hoedown and for everybody to git out there and square dance. And they did. Men that I hadn't never seen do nothing like that got out there with the women that could dance, and they sashayed and promenaded and had them a time. One of the Medicine Show men was a good figure-caller.

By then things were really gitting lively, and the Medicine Man took over. He had a fine carrying voice that he had perfected over a long period of time.

"Let me have your attention, ladies and gentlemen," he began. "Please listen to what I have to say for it could change everything about your life."

He reached into a box and brought out a pint bottle, blue in color, and held it up for the crowd to see.

"I want to introduce you to my Elixir, ladies and gentlemen." He looked heavenward when he mentioned his Elixir. "It is the miracle medicine of all time, and I am the only person on earth that has the formula. I was the one that found the roots used in my Elixir in the mountains of West Virginia, and I didn't even know what I had til I mixed the whole thing together. I had rheumatism so bad I couldn't hardly walk, and two doses cured me! Yes sir.

"Then I got the gout and thought my big toe would kill me, and in no time I was dancing around like nothing had ever happened.

"There has never been anything on earth like my Elixir. As a matter of fact, it carries a 50-year guarantee. If you try my Elixir and it don't help you, all you need to do is get up with me and I will give you every dime you paid me for it."

"What else will it cure?" somebody in the crowd asked.

The Medicine Man had a broad smile on his face as he replied, "Ain't hardly nothing it won't cure."

"Constipation?" a woman asked far away in the crowd.

"Lord have mercy, lady, you can't be too clogged up for my Elixir to help you. One dose and the call of nature will be so smooth you won't believe you're in your own hide. On the other hand, my Elixir works both ways. If you're running off, turn the bottle up and take just one swallow and I declare you'll be well the next day."

"Now I want to say something to the men," the Medicine Man said as he squatted on the edge of the truck body. "Come up closer," he motioned to the men. Of course the women were as close up as they could get, too.

"Is your courage failing you?" he asked almost in a whisper. "Believe me, I know all about that. That is before I discovered my Elixir. And I know you recall the line in the old hymn that says 'Now I'm happy all the day,' except my happiness extends into the night, too."

"How much?" one elderly man asked.

"You won't believe this, brother, but one little old sixty-five cents will buy a full bottle of my Elixir and that's cheap enough to buy at least half a dozen bottles."

The man's old lady sided up to him and whispered, "We hain't got the money to throw away on that mess. You don't believe what he's telling you, do you?"

Old Jed looked hard at the old lady and said, "I don't know, but I'm shore God going to find out."

"Where in the world is them youn'uns? Zeppie Branch asked her old man when she could get his attention for a minute. "This old quack has got us so riled up we don't even know what our own young'uns are doing out there in the dark."

"What else will it cure?" somebody yelled.

"Lumbago, dizziness, chills and fever, cramps women complain about, bladder failure, flu, eases childbirth, cures sore eyes. It'll cure a sore throat before you can turn around almost. Just take a broom straw and wad a piece of cotton around one end, dip it into my Elixir and swab it around your throat, swallow twice and it's gone! It will near 'bout straighten a club foot!

"And please don't forget my bunion salve. Many of you know the torture of them things on the side of your feet. It will take them and corns away almost by the time it touches them. And I've got a special preparation for malaria. I tell you, I have everything you need for a new life. Your choice for thirty five cents."

The Medicine Man's old lady, or somebody's old lady, was handing out bottles of Elixir as fast as she could collect the money. They had timed the show exactly right, for farmers had just sold their first loads of backer and a little money was stirring. But the Medicine Man got a lot that was supposed to go for young'uns school shoes, overhalls and cloth to make girls' dresses.

Work, Work, Then Odd Jobs

No matter if we did just about work our heads off out in the country in the old days, there would come an occasional day in summer when all the crops were plowed out, when the grass wasn't growing because of dry weather, and there just wasn't anything to do in the fields. And those who never did all that work could ever appreciate the feeling among a pack of young'uns at such times.

To get up and eat a leisurely breakfast, then mess around for a while in clean overalls and dresses and bare feet and know you hain't got to hitch up a mule or grab a hoe and git down in them fields is almost too good to be true.

Lizzie Mae gets the dishes washed and goes down to the backer barn where she's got a "True Romances" hidden under the quilt on the bunk and turns to the page she's got turned down to find out what happened to the love affair she's engrossed in.

Shine and Fuzz feel good in their overhalls without any shirts and they take chairs from the porch to the side of the house where there's shade and watch folks passing along the road.

Sarah and Sis pull out their old dolls and go about making a playhouse, and as always, Little Bud is rolling his wheel and imitating the sound of an automobile, and slobbering.

Hank, the oldest boy, is sleeping late on account of he was out most of the night with some of the boys.

Everything's fine until the old man meanders out where Fuzz and Shine are laughing and carrying on. He stands silent for a few minutes, looking up at the thunderheads beginning to build up and sneezing several times while looking toward the sun. Then he blows his nose, holding it with his thumb and forefinger, slinging the mucous to the ground and wiping his hand on his britches.

"They's some things that have needed to be done around the house for a long time," he says, "and today is a good time to git them done. Them mules' feed troughs are loose and need to be nailed down. Ain't no nails, so you'll have to pull some from the studs under the shelter and straighten them. You can do that, Shine. I've got another job for Fuzz."

Fuzz and Shine have done and pulled the back of their chairs from the side of the house and are looking at each other with a look more disgusting than I can describe.

"Shine, them weeds' done and about took over behind the barn. You git a hoe and cut them things down or we'll have a woods back there. When Hank gits up I'm going to send him down to patch the old well at the hog pasture that we use to git water for the hogs. Cowwitch vines have wrapped around every post and you can't hardly git a bucket up and down. They's a rotten board that's got to be replaced too."

"Lizzie Mae!" the old lady yells as loud as she can, and the "True Romances" is quickly put back under the quilt. When she reaches the house her mother says, "Me and you's going to git in the smokehouse and check on the cabbage kraut and the cucumbers we've got in brine. We've been so busy I hain't had time to see if brine is covering the kraut and the cucumbers. We've got to check on the weights we've got in the barrels too. The brine has got to cover the pickles and cabbage or they'll spoil."

Sarah and Sis run by and the old lady stops them too. "I've got a job for you girls," she says. "Sarah, you take a washpan and go out to the shelter and git some of that lime out there and take it to the privy and sprinkle it good down in the pit. I mean sprinkle it good, now, to help cut down on the scent. And if the lime is lumpy, beat it up before you try to sprinkle it. And you go up in the barn loft and find a good tow sack, Sis. Bring it down and ravel it and less put up a new one to the privy. That old sack is pure wore out. And that reminds me, the leather that's used for hinges to the seats is wore in-two and the old man's got to cut some more from an old shoe and tack it on them seat covers. I've got a job for Little Bud, too. Anybody know where he is?"

Little Bud hears the yell from a quarter of a mile away down the path and rolls his wheel up to the house.

"I've got something for you to do, boy." the old lady says. "They is a dead hen in the henhouse under the roosts. She's got to be buried. You go git her out and take the shovel and dig a hole and put her in it. And dig that hole deep enough that a dog won't scratch her up before you git back to the house. And don't touch them roosts. I expect they's lice on them."

"I thought we had today off to play," Little Bud says as he looks up into his mother's face, grinning.

"They ain't no days to play, honey," the old lady replies. "They's something to do every day and when everybody is busy in the fields, some things just don't git done until days like this.

"And when you young'uns git through with that, I want you to go under the house where the ish taters are spread out and pick out the rotten ones. A rotten tater will cause another one to rot."

"They stink so bad I can't hardly stand it, Ma," Sarah complains. "Old rotten taters are the stinkingest things I ever seen."

"Anything rotten stinks," Kizzie replies, "but that ain't no reason to just let it lay around and stink up everything. I'd rather smell them than to pick them up and the mushy mess gitting all on my hands."

"You do it then, Ma," Little Bud says.

"Watch your sassy mouth, boy," his mother says. "Else I'll take you down a notch or two"

"Well, can we make lemonade this evening?" Little Bud asks as he starts toward the shelter.

"We'll see about that," the old lady says.

"Them confounded shoats are out," the old man announces as he looks down toward the hog pen. "Everybody git out there and less git them back in quick or they'll be running everywhere."

"I'm gitting out of farming right away," Fuzz says. "I swear, they ain't never a day that you don't have something to do. I'm just tard of working my butt off."

"Days like this are when you should be able to just lay around and let your galded legs cure up a little and make ice cream late in the evening and things like that," Shine says. "But no, it's the same damned mess every day to the week."

But he said this while the old man and old lady were inside and she had him cornered, telling him that one of the clothesline posts was near 'bout rotten through and she was scared her wet clothes were going to git in the dirt every time she hung them on the line and if that happened he could watch out. Wiping the corners of her mouth, she told him one of the legs to the wash bench had done rotted and she had propped up the bench with a piece of unslabbed stove wood and some brick bats and that one of them boys could fix that too, while they were catching up on things to do around the house, as well as replacing that sorry clothesline post, and he could cut some pieces of leather and git them seat covers back in place in the privy, too.

Mess They Used To Tell Us

They used to fill our noggins with a whole peck of mess when we were young'uns. Don't you oldsters remember how they'd say if we ate watermelon seeds, they'd sprout in us? Now just think about how many watermelons we ate way back there. By the time we could thump one and it didn't sound pure green, we'd start busting them, (the smaller ones) and they'd be slightly pink, and we'd pretend they were good. And by the time they got good and red, we were gobbling them down as fast as we could.

After we had eaten all the red meat (down to the green in the rind) there were a thousand seeds in the rind and a lot of juice too. Well, you know we'd take a knife and cut a "V" in the rind and turn it up and drink the juice too. And we swallowed seeds.

I remember that Marvaline Daniels was playing with watermelon seeds one day, lying on his back. That boy took a seed and put one in each nostril, and he got one of them down his windpipe, and they had a time with that boy. He was a mighty sick young'un for a while.

And I'll bet that every one of you that used to have watermelons in the house, usually close to a door, got your toe tangled up with that rind at least once. And let me tell you, that will just about kill you. What happens is that you go by barefooted and get a foot tangled up in the melon and the big toe dips into the rind, tearing up the flesh at the end of the toe and getting the rind about half an inch under the toenail. It's sore right then, but not half as sore as it is when infection gets under the toenail and just to touch it makes you scream.

They used to always pull watermelons and take them to the house so they would be fairly cool when they were cut. You must remember there were no refrigerators to put them in in those days, and no other means of cooling them off.

If bedstids were high enough off the floor, the watermelons were rolled under some beds, but some folks didn't want watermelons under there where the slop jar sat. So the best place most folks found to put the watermelons were beside doorways.

After we got through with the rinds, it was the chickens' turn. We'd put the rinds down at the edge of the yard and talk about pecking away, but them old birds had them one time. They didn't let up until the rind was thin enough to see through almost, and I've seen 'em just dry up after the chickens got through with them, before they were taken out of the yards.

You see little pieces of melon in restaurants today to go along with your meals. People cut off round pieces of watermelon and place them in plates today. But in my day watermelon was for the outside and with nothing else to go along with it. I shore would have thought it funny if I'd gone to the dinner table to eat my fill of vegetables and cornbread and pot liquor and seen a piece of watermelon on the table.

And they told us about babies coming out of old stump holes and had us out there like some pack of nuts digging and trying to find a crying baby.

They also scared us half to death about Raw Head and Bloody Bones. That was mostly the older young'uns, though. They had us so we'd shut our eyes the minute we got in bed and dared not open them. Them old skulls, or whatever they were, were right up in the loft waiting to come down and take us away if we didn't git quiet and go to sleep.

But back to something to eat. Today salads are big items in dining establishments. As a matter of fact, they're one of the biggest items.

People would have thought we were crazy if we had piled up a lot of raw vegetables in a plate when I was a young'un. People did finally git to shredding cabbage and making a little slaw, but that won't no big thing. All we knowed about lettuce was where folks planted seeds they bought when young'uns brought the seeds by every spring. Then all you got were big ruffled leaves with no sign of a head.

Just about everybody planted carrot seeds, but we thought of them as being rabbit food, and we'd eat a few raw, but no carrots were ever cooked at my house.

As far as bean sprouts go, ain't no way we'd et them. And tater salad was eaten as a separate dish. What we see in salads today would have been considered a pack of junk in the old days.

Besides, there won't no dressings to put on top of such mess. Mayonnaise was known back then, but I tell you few country hicks tried it. If we wanted onions, we'd go to the garden or to the shelter and get them, peel them and cut them up over what we were eating. We never did anything with radishes except eat them raw when they were pulled up and washed. I've eaten radishes when I thought my mouth would catch on fire.

I never saw no canned bell peppers in my childhood. The only kind of canned pepper we had was the kind that would burn you up. There was always a jar or two of hot pepper around with vinegar added and poured on collards and turnip sallet sometimes. Some people would cut up the pepper over their vegetables.

Celery was something else most country folks shied away from. It had a "quare" taste and had to be bought too, and there won't much buying at grocery stores in them days.

About the only vegetable we ever bought was cabbage. And that was when they were out of season. They were in our gardens until summer waned. But we'd get that hankering for something boiled, and the old man would pick up a good-sized head or two when he went to town for supplies. And that cabbage satisfied a longing that's hard to describe to anybody that won't brought up on soul food. Ever once in a while folks that et out of the garden just had a craving for boiled vegetables. Nothing else satisified them.

I'm thinking now about Pa, and what his reaction would have been if it had been possible to take him to one of these fancy salad bars with all the raw vegetables and how he'd have managed them prongs you use to pick up the food with. And the little plate to put it in. If he had gotten it on his plate, he'd have strewn it from the salad bar to his seat. But I wouldn't have had to worry about Pa. He'd have taken one look and just walked back and asked for a glass of water. And if he'd a tasted of the dressings they slur over the salad, he'd have spit it out of his mouth right there in the restaurant.

I'm sure he'd have asked, after leaving, if they had all that raw mess 'cause they didn't have no cooks in the joint. My, hain't times changed?

Fire Kills Teen-Ager

He was an 18-year-old farm boy. The son of a preacherman and a spirit-filled mother, he lived a quarter mile or so back in a field in a five-room house separated by a hall - two rooms on one side and three on the other - with a front porch and back porch. The house was surrounded by walnut, oak and chaney ball trees with barns and shelters and the usual layout of tenant-house grounds.

From the house back in the field, much of the community could be observed. There were the people chopping in the fields in early summer; men plowing and sending dust into the atmosphere; cows grazing on hillsides and endless acres of corn and cotton and tobacco growing in area fields.

He was one of four children. He had a brother and two sisters. He came along with the century and his world was filled with happiness. He helped to tend the land and found pleasure in farm life.

The mists of morning captivated him when he was caught up in the fog and wisps of thin clouds floating about him were touchable. Sometimes the fog would obscure the view of the neighborhood until midmorning when the sun would burn off the moisture.

He saw the hillsides come alive in spring as new growth filled in the naked limbs that had bared themselves to the fury of winter. The pastures and the rolling hillsides became green again and wild flowers sprang up and gave color to the landscape.

He loved the splash of color in the fall when some of the foliage was painted in tones of gold, pink, yellow, brilliant red and purple. From his vantage point, it was a circle of beauty.

The snows of winter isolated the little house sometimes and the neighborhood sparkled in a coating of white. At such times, smoke from the chimneys gave testimony to life in the houses scattered around him. And at night there were the dots of light signalling that all was well with the world and a community snuggled inside the homes for warmth and companionship.

Summer brought tall corn that obscured the view of the area and tobacco grew rank in the fertile soil and cotton patches shimmered in the summer sun.

Model T Fords were becoming popular, and he was popular. At age 18, the world is like a diamond in the sky. A young man's dreams are filled with wonder. He has all the powers of manhood, the advantage of youth, the promise of tomorrow and the fulfillment of young love. Pretty girls become angels in the eyes of 18-year-old boys.

There were box parties at the schoolhouse sometimes. These were always held at night. Dating-age girls would bake cakes or make candy or cookies and they would be placed in boxes and auctioned off to the highest bidder. And the young men would bid on the boxes of the girls they liked. If a boy and girl were going together, the boy always tried to be the highest bidder. He attended those parties and delighted in bidding on the delicacies and eating them with his girl.

There were the occasional rides under the stars in the Model T's and sometimes there were buggy rides, for automobiles were still new in the area and many people could not afford them.

The future stretched eternal before him. He plowed in the fields, cropped tobacco in summer, cured it at night, mowed and stacked hay, picked cotton and gathered corn, graded and tied tobacco and dreamed of marriage and a home and children.

His name was as common as the grains of sand that filled the wagon tracks in the path leading from the road to the house back in the field. The name George is as ordinary as the area in which he grew up. With a last name of Smith, he could have been one among millions across the nation.

George could not know on that morning in the eighteenth year of his life that his destiny was being sealed by the hand of fate. How little we know at best. We know nothing of the future.

George got up to build a fire in the cook stove for his spirit-filled Mama so she could prepare breakfast for her family. At his age, he would have been hungry and there is no doubt but that fried meat, scrambled eggs and biscuits or flourbread would have been served at breakfast that day. But there was no breakfast.

George placed the stove wood in the firebox, took the oil can and dashed the fuel over the wood, ignited a match and tossed it over the wood. There was an instant explosion and George was engulfed in flames. The can held gasoline instead of kerosene.

There was a well in every yard in those days, and George's first reaction was to run to the well. He jumped into the water to quench the flames, but the fire had already done its damage.

The family pulled George from the well and got him inside and on the bed. And they didn't take him to the hospital, although there was one in town. I don't know why, but I do know hospitalizations were rare in those days.

A neighborhood mourned and young and old cried openly. The handsome young man became a sight of horror. Burns covered a large area of his body. He became comatose, yet he lingered for weeks, hovering between life and death. Neighbors sat up with him at night and women helped with household chores during the day.

Caring for George in his condition created a great problem. They turned his body with sheets, and hunks of flesh and skin would peel off. His flesh rotted and blow flies invaded his room. They built a frame covered with screen wire and placed it over him to keep the flies away. The stench was unbearable. Camphor was used in the house in an attempt to eliminate the odor, but nothing worked.

Prayers were offered and a pall was over the community. The young people who admired George most could not face the reality of it all. He had been one of them and he had quickened the pulsebeat of many neighborhood girls. They took one look at the horror before them and fled the premises.

The Twentieth Century has waxed old and now creaks with age, but George was taken when the century as we know it in time was also in its youth. His body has rested in a lonely graveyard for more than 50 years, forgotten now by the masses, as we are all forgotten with the passing of time. His body rests where he once read the epitaphs on the stones and where the wind played among the trees and where he sometimes thought about those who had long since passed from the scene.

The fresh mound of earth settled with time. Life is for the living, and young people of George's age continued on that trail that inevitably leads to death. The wildflowers eventually bloomed above the ground where his body lay. Time healed the wounds and George only lives in the memory of those who remember him from the days of his youth.

There is no way of knowing whether George might have been able to survive if he had been a product of the latter part of the Twentieth Century under the same circumstances. Much progress has been made in treating burn victims with miracle drugs, the capability of growing skin in a dish, and special centers for treating burn victims. Even with those advances, many burn victims still die.

Zeb Mends Young'uns Shoes

Zeb backed up to the shelter post, rubbed his shoulders for a full minute, all the while twisting his mouth with his eyes half-closed. It was evident that the post had done its work in relieving him of the itch between his shoulder blades.

He propped his foot up against the post and watched the young'uns as they ran all over the yard, toting in stovewood and cutting splinters to start a fire as well as feeding up. The sun was setting on a February day.

The young'uns shoesoles flopping as they moved about got to the old man. They touched a nerve and he became irritable. He decided he'd have to do something about the shoe situation. He went directly into the house and to the closet in the back room and felt around until he found the shoe last. The largest metal piece that fitted on the last was attached to it, but the smaller one was loose in the closet and he had to feel under piles of rags and dirty clothes and such mess to find it, and that got to him too.

He rounded up the hammer and started rambling in the safe drawer for the shoetack box. He tore up everything in the drawer and the old lady walked in on him while his hand was still stirring up everything it touched. She snatched his hand out and asked him what in the name of God he was looking for.

"Them damn shoetacks," he replied. "Every young'un's shoesole is flapping about and it's time something was done about it."

The old lady wiped the corners of her mouth with her hand and told him he had been told about that a month or more earlier and he hadn't paid no attention to what she said. She reached in the corner of the drawer and brought out the box and shook it. "Not many tacks in there."

"They'll be enough to git a few tacks in each sole," the old man said. "Put tacks down on the list so I'll git some next time I go to town."

After supper the old man started with Shine's shoes. His shoesoles were really flapping out in the yard earlier. Reaching into the shoetack box, he took out a dozen or so tacks and put them in his mouth for easy access and immediately got to coughing and spit them out on the floor. Everybody looked at him and stifled their laughter, and all the old man did was tell them to git down there and find them.

Then all of a sudden he looked at the old lady and asked her when it was she had told him about mending the young'uns shoes.

"The same night you went to sleep in your chur while I was sewing and Sis got my scissors off the machine unbeknownst to me and crawled up in your lap and gapped up your hair so bad it will take it six months to grow out. That's when. Ain't no way I can do nothing with that hair now."

"No wonder I didn't hear," the old man said. "I was asleep."

"Huh!" the old lady replied. "I didn't tell you while you was asleep. I told you at the supper table."

Shine tried on the shoes and said a tack at the end of the shoe was sticking in his foot and the old man took it back and banged on it some more with the hammer.

The soles were not flapping on Sarah's shoes, but there were large holes worn through them. He told Sarah to run and find him an old shoe box to cut some inner soles to put in her shoes. "No wonder you've been going around with a snotty nose," he said. "You've been gitting your feet wet every time you went out."

"Can we parch some meal Ma?" Sis asked.

"No sirree," the old lady replied. "The far's gone out in the stove and won't be no far built in it agin til breakfast time."

"We can parch it in the coals," Sis replied. "Please, Ma."

"I tell you, you young'uns' going to drive me crazy 'fore it's all over with. But git the skillet and put the meal in it before you bring it in here and pull some coals out of the farplace and parch you some meal."

"I'd rather have sweet taters baked in the coals," Little Bud said. And Fuzz reminded him that there won't nary nuther good tater in the hill; that he had gone through every one of them and all had rotten places in them.

"I want popcorn," Lizzie Mae said.

"You always want to be different, Lizzie Mae," Shine replied. "Don't pay no 'tention to Lizzie Mae, youall. She'd be differernt or bust."

The old man looked at Little Bud's brogans after cutting pasteboard pieces to go in Sarah's shoes, all the while shaking his head. "They ain't worth trying to fix," he said, looking into the boy's eyes. "What on earth have you done to these shoes?"

"I just wore'em, Pa," Little Bud replied. "I couldn't help it if they wore out."

"You must walk funny or something," the old man said. "Here I have got to buy you a pair of shoes in February when there ain't money to buy flour with hardly. You done wore them shoes clean out, young'un."

"Git him some tennises," the old lady said. "They got them for 98 cent at the ten-cent store."

Zeb looked up at Kizzie like he thought she was crazy. "That's just 98 cent more than I've got, Kizzie. Does that git the message to you? Do you want to do without your snuff to git Little Bud a pair of shoes?"

Kizzie's only reply was, "Huh!"

Little Bud looked sheepish but he was ready for parched meal by the time it got to looking brown in the skillet. He took a spoon and dipped up a little and touched his tongue to it and pulled the spoon away immediately, blowing the powder all over the floor. Everybody looked at him and actually laughed. He had burned a blister on his tongue from the hot meal.

The shoetacks were gone by then, but the old man had gotten around to all the shoes even if there weren't adequate tacks for each shoe. Some young'uns said they felt tacks in their heels when he hadn't done nothing to the heels, and some said nothing. But all of them were thinking about how they had to pick up them shoetacks with the old man's spittle on them. They were disgusted, but you'd better believe they didn't utter a crying word about it to the old man. They knew better.

A glimpse into our personal lives more than half a century ago. And it seems like yesterday.

Old Zeb's Money Woes

I shore sympathize with Old Zeb Crebbins in his battle with his younguns' shoes. I sympathize with the young'uns and share in their joys too, cause I loved all that mess they et around the fireplace on winter nights. I had them floppy shoe soles, too.

I identify with old Zeb even today. I think I got that Depression-era mentality about prices in the 1930s when there won't nary penny of money circulating around in the sticks. I've taken that mentality with me right on into the 1980s too.

Once in a great while I have to go to the stores to buy me a pair of shoes or a pair of drawers or a pair of britches and mess like that. I will saunter in and look around and play like I'm just looking. But I'll glance at the prices, cause they are what I'm looking for. And once I see, I git one of them silly grins on my face and say to myself, "they've got to be kidding." I walk out and go home, knowing that whatever it was I was looking at was something I needed or I wouldn't of been there nohow.

I don't look for no tennis shoes. But I've huern from my grandyoung'uns that they sell for $35 to $40 (certain brands of course, and the only kind uppity young'uns will have today) and I immediately think about them brown ones and the white ones they used to sell at the dime stores for 98 cents. The ones with a round piece of white rubber on the inside where the ankle bone fits into the shoes. That's the kind a lot of women wear too, 'cause the cloth fabric stretched and was kind to their bunions. The word "Keds" was imprinted on the rubber. I just shake my head and think about old Zeb and I get consolation in knowing that he ain't around to see what has happened since his days.

But I reckon if I thought about it in the right sense I'd realize that if old Zeb could be around now at the age he was then, he might be making as much as a hundred dollars a week to feed his crowd, and buy a piece of clothes for them ever once in a while. (On one hundred dollars week?)

Anyhow, I go back and look at them britches agin. Plain gray or brown or blue with nary a thread of wool in them (thank God) made out of some manmade material we had't never thunk about in the dark age. I glance agin and the price tag says $49.95! For a pair of britches! And old Zeb didn't have 98 cents to git his young'un a pair of tennises. And I know I could find a pair of britches at a discount store, or somewhere, for a lot less than $49.95. But didn't I wear seconds and them $4.98 jobs for most of my life? By golly! I'm worth a good pair of britches for once, ain't I?

I say a little prayer and take them britches to the dressing room to see if they'll fit my "quare" body and notice that my drawers are ripping and that I've got to git some, like it or not. I can't find no shoes there, so I take the mess to the counter, and it don't look or sound nothing like the cash registers I growed up with. I see clerks slipping in some kind of little cards and hear them machines clicking for a full minute it seems like. Then they take out the little card and hand it back to you and ain't nary penny changed hands. Old Zeb would of loved that. Something like that was exactly what we needed way back there so we could of bought mess too. But no, we were denied all of that.   The clerk says, "Cash or charge?" and I've already got my little piece of plastic in my hand. I figger if everybody else is going to git anything they want without money, I might as well git in on it too. Seems good to walk out with a little package more precious than gold, and no money changing hands.

What really bothers me while I'm going from the dry goods store to the shoe store is that old Zeb Crebbins could of bought ever one of this family a new wardrobe with what I will eventually pay for one pair of britches. And I've still got to try to find a pair of shoes to git on my size 11 triple E foot, knowing that whatever I git will torment me and add to the discomfort of my poor feet. In the old days I paid from $2.98 to $4.95 for a pair of slippers.

I git that silly grin on my face agin, and start hunting for a pair I think I might be able to wear. I'm hoping the shoe salesman will be busy and will just let me alone so I can see what he's got. But no, ain't nary customer in the store and he's right under me with his slipper horn ready to git my feet into something with a pointed toe or this wing-tipped mess that I know I couldn't even git on. And with my feet sweating, my socks just crimp up when I try to slide them into the shoes and it feels like they's a pile of rags in the shoes. I hate buying shoes and wish sometimes I was back out there on some ditchbank as barefooted as a yard dog until I remember that I can't go barefooted either.

By now I'm feeling uncomfortable with that rip in my drawers. You men know what I'm talking about. I finaggle around a little and tell the clerk to let me look until I see a shoe I might be able to wear, and he looks at me like he'd like to kill me while I mosey around, even though I'm looking sheepish by then.

I finally pick out a pair of shoes (over $50) and the same rigamarole is played out agin at the cash register. There's all the clicking with that little card placed in just the right place, and in no time I'm ready to go home. It's fantastic! But we had some fancy mess at a few stores in the stone age. The clerks would put the ticket and the money into a little metal doohickey and put it in a slot and it would fly to the top of the store, shoot across, dip down and go out of sight to a cashier somewhere who would make change and send it back to the clerk. That was some years AE (after electricity in the cities) as well as a few years BEIC (before electricity in the country).

But you'd better be shore that the first thing I do when I git home is git out of them tore drawers. No drawers is better than tore ones. Then I slip the shoe box under the bed where it will stay for months before I dare even try to wear them shoes.

It don't seem like no time before that little card you used catches up with you. They's bills for everything I bought - three little items totaling well over a hundred dollars. I can pay part of the bill now and part later if I want them to add on then carrying charges for 18 percent or more per year. Or I can take my paycheck and pay it all and do without something else I need. And if I buy many items I've bought so much mess ain't no way I can pay for it all at one time. I can even add on more and pay more on a monthly basis if I'm a mind to. But after a while I'll be drowning in debt and the old car is giving out and a new one is more than the fanciest home cost when I was a boy. A house costs about as much as it took to run the county a full year back then.

When them bills came in is when it would have done Zeb and his crowd in. He'd a got by one month; then his crowd would have had to tie their little mess up in bedsheets, sling them over their backs and head down the railroad tracks to God only knows where.

If it were possible, I would love to go to old Zeb and say, "Old buddy, I 'preciate you and all the mess you had to put up with. I grieve with you. But cheer up, brother. You had it better than you think. Your young'uns are out there just like I am today, and they know what I'm talking about. All of us made it, Zeb, and the only reason you didn't is cause time run out for you.

You could go to bed at night with nothing on your mind, cause you didn't have nothing. You shore God had plenty to eat, cause I've been to your house many a time. I never saw your young'uns when they won't laughing. Oh, we think we're high and mighty in this "enlightened" age. But we ain't happy Zeb. We got too much to worry about. And money don't mean nothing no more. You dreamed about things you couldn't have then. We do the same today. In some ways, time ain't changed things very much."

Six-Foot Black Snake Had Eaten A Baby Turkey
Courtesy Louise Winstead

Working At Old Log Barn
Courtesy Lynwood Sharpe

Rest Spell For Farmers
Courtesy Lynwood Barnes

Milking Is An Every-day Job
Courtesy Louise Winstead

Early-Morning Chores

I n the east, there is a pink tint on the rim of the horizon where the summer sun will come swiftly in half an hour, sending its heat rays over the land that will increase as it climbs higher in the sky.

Out in the country, the day's activities have already begun. A family is busy with morning chores as they listen to crowing roosters who will venture from the chicken house with the first crack of dawn.

Hank is fumbling around in the stable to get the bridle on one of the mules and utters his first curse word of the day as the animal turns its head away from him. After bringing the mule out of the stable, he reaches up to the eaves of the shelter and gets the curry comb to run over the matted hair on the mule's rump from lying down in the stable.

Shine pulls the loop in the rope around the cow's horns and tugs at her to get her out of the stable. She has to be milked.

Fuzz is drawing water from the well, filling the troughs so the animals can have water before the mules are taken to the fields and the cow staked out on the hillside. It seems like they swill enough water to burst their guts. The well tackle squeaks as the water is brought up.

Little Bud is also at the well, awaiting his turn to draw up water in a wash tub to be taken to the woodpile and poured in the wash pot for boiling the clothes. It is also wash day. He's hollering for Sarah to come help him tote the water.

Chickens are out by now and nearby objects are discernible. Shine turns his back to the house and rolls him a Golden Grain cigarette and uses his overalls bib buckle to strike the match on. He blows the smoke at gnats already plaguing him around his eyes. The old folks don't know he's smoking.

Fuzz hears Shine say, "damn you!" and looks toward him. Shine has taken a lick from the cow's tail, already filled with cockleburs. Then the cow has to relieve her kidneys and Shine jumps up in a flash to get out of the way of the deluge and says, "damn you," again.

Hogs in the pasture are already squealing, and there ain't nary drop of water in their trough, and Fuzz fills a five-gallon bucket and hollers for Shine to come help him tote it to the hogs. Shine says he ain't through milking and Fuzz just waits until the old cow is tied to a tree. Then each takes hold of one side of the bucket handle and they start toward the hog pasture. Fuzz trips over a hard weed and water splashes all over Shine's overhalls, and they put down the bucket and Shine takes off after Fuzz and they tangle in the bed of weeds and fight for a good five minutes, with both of their faces rubbed in the dirt and with green stains on their faces from the weeds. The hogs are still squealing.

By then the sun has come over the horizon in a large orange ball and the old dog comes from under the shelter with a yawn, limping as he moves. A good third of his hair has come out since warm weather set in. The boys have promised old Black they'll dip him in burnt cylinder oil to git rid of the "scratchs" that are no less than red mange. But they hain't got around to it. The old dog coughs softly and the whole pack declares he's got distemper. After his ritual at the corner of the barn, the old canine just goes back and lies down. Shine wishes he were a dog so he could do the same thing.

After the wash pot is filled, chips raked around the pot and a fire started, Little Bud is put to totin' in stove wood cause he slipped around and didn't do it last night. His mammy tells him if he does such a trick agin he'll tote a whupping.

An old hen with a bunch of week-or-so-old biddies is all under the mules' legs scratching for food and one of the mules picks up a foot and planks it right down on one of the biddies, leaving nothing but a moist place when the mule moves his foot.

An old black-and-white she-cat emerges through the cat hole in the barn door with her sides no more than an inch thick. She's done had a pile of kittens, probably in the hayloft. An old tomcat's liable to relieve her of all the he-cats in the litter. She hadn't been able to come through the cat hole in some time. A rat suddenly comes from under the barn and that old cat pays no more attention to the rodent than if it were another cat. She meanders on up to the kitchen door and does her series of "meows" to git some handouts.

The old man is busy sharpening hoes under the shelter. Grass is green and growing and everything's got to be chopped. Every young'un will tote a hoe and will be watched by the old man to see they ain't slubbering and chopping down crops. Hank will plow with the cultivator after the choppers have made their rounds.

Shine attaches the long chain around the cow's horns, picks up the ax and heads down the path to stake her out in a new place for the day. He places the stake close enough for her to git under the shade of a "sweegum" tree when the sun bears down, but not close enough for her to tangle herself up around the tree.

The old man reminds Lizzie Mae and Sarah that them guano sacks in the loft got to be washed the first chance they git. He tells them they could have already had them washed; that they were told months before. He says they'll be needing guano sacks for truck curtains when they start puttin' in backer.

Insects are already stirring and chickens are jumping a foot off the ground to git them.

A thin coating of dew causes the crops to shimmer in the early morning sun.

The crowd heads for the field with hoes on their shoulders, a gallon jug of water in hand, and "meat and biscuits" in a paper sack. They go no more than a hundred yards when a yell comes from the house, "Sarah Ann and Sis, come back here right now!" Looking back, they see Kizzie at the peach tree, finding a good switch that she jerks free and strips off the leaves. They hear her mumble ... "had all the messing I'm going to take from them two youn'uns."

The girls run back to the house with fear in their hearts, and crying is heard and the boys, always glad for the girls to git their share of whuppings, smile as they head on down the path.

... A well-worn path that snakes slide over sometimes, leaving marks in the dirt; where birds pitch and peck at dead bugs; where ants work feverishly around their hills; where a red bird sits silently on her nest in a mulberry bush beside the path; where a graveyard sits nearby with bodies now forgotten that once toiled in the same fields; across a little bridge and through a marshy place and up a slight incline to acres and acres of corn and cotton filled with grass and weeds and cowwitch vines and bear grass and maypop vines to be chopped and uprooted.

One day among thousands in the fields half-a-century or more ago.

A Dream Becomes Reality

O bediah Letchworth is a name that hain't been laid on many people in this sinful world. And Obediah toted that name around until the year he entered the sixth grade. By then, he weighed over 200 pounds and had a full coat of beard, for he had never put a razor to his face. But that year, back in the 1930s, as he was taking his seat that was far too small for him, he dared anybody to ever call him Obediah agin. It was pronounced with the full O sound and the full B sound, and di, like Lady Di. He told the class from then on to call him "Obe" or not call him nothing. And the only times he heard Obediah after that were when a pack of young'uns was on the road and far enough from him to get away with it. Then they'd holler "OBEDIAH" long and plaintive.

But that ain't the point of the story. Nor is his wife's name. They laid "Kittie" on her and young'uns trampled that one in the ground, too. They'd meow when they got up close to her and say, "Kittie, Kittie, Kittie" like they were calling a cat.

Following their marriage, they did what came naturally and had ten young'uns as fast as they could turn them out. They were so loaded down with looking after young'uns and trying to make enough for them to eat, they stayed jaded all the time.

But as things worsened with each new baby, Kittie's faith in God grew like her belly. She was near 'bout fanatic about her belief in God. Every chance she got she went to church to hear the Word and to get spirit-filled. But there was so much to do she had to forgo church many times to get food on the table. But she heard about a camp meeting that was going to be held across the river, some 15 miles from their humble abode, and she broached Obe about it.

"I want to go to the camp meeting across the river," she told him one day when he came from the fields sweating and red-faced from the heat. "I hear tell they's going to be evangelists preaching all day long Obe, and I've got a pure craving to attend one day."

"Are you crazy Kittie?" he asked. "You hain't got nothing fitten to wear and them old tires on the Ford is wore out. Ain't no way we could make it over Little River and back. And I have all the sympathy in the world for you in wanting to hear the Word. Lord knows, about everything else you hear is the squall of a young'un. But I don't see no way to git you to camp meeting."

"I knowed the devil would git in the way when I mentioned it ," Kittie said. "He'll do it every time. And I was so hoping I could go."

Obe was feeling sorry for her by then and told her they'd see if they could work something out. Kittie said she'd sew up the dress that got ripped a few months back when she was bending to pick cucumbers for Sunday dinner.

"When is that thing?" Obe asked, and Kittie told him it was two weeks away.

So Kittie made her plans for camp meeting. The ripped dress was sewn up and she even went out and inspected the tires on the Model T. They were about as slick as her hand, and she said a prayer over them.

Her sister, Eva, that won't quite right in the head but who loved her young'uns dearly, would stay with the children. Kittie had finally got Eddie Earl off the breast and he was drinking milk from a cup.

Now Kittie didn't have but one indulgence, and that was her snuff. She felt guilty about that many a time and wrestled with God about it. She loved Salty Galenax snuff better than the food she ate. She had Obe to buy it by the bladder when he went to town for supplies. She'd dole out a day's dipping into a small tin box she kept in her apron pocket. And if she went to camp meeting, she couldn't dip all day long. But she'd trust God to help her if she could only get to the big tent.

And on a bright May morning they set out for camp meeting. Obe kicked the mobile tires before cranking the Model T, actually afraid that a kick would bust the things. Then he set the magneta lever high and the gas about a third of the way and turned the crank and the old car came to life. And Kittie was praying for a safe journey. They admired the corn swaying in the fields and young backer plants shiny in the morning sun and the people they passed on the road. And they made it to camp meeting without a hitch.

Obe told Kittie he'd stay on the outside, that he just couldn't stand sitting on them hard planks and miring his feet up in the sawdust used on the ground. He'd just have to while away the time the best he could. There would be other men there that couldn't stand to be inside and he'd talk to them.

Kittie didn't even think about snuff, for preaching was already going strong when she got there. The minister was telling about all the evils awaiting mankind if it didn't give up its sinful ways and she was in her glory.

It got hot inside and she used the fan with Jesus' picture on it that she had brought from home, and the next evangelist took the pulpit and talked about the sins of man that would bar them from heaven, and he was hitting close to home then, for her big sin rose up before her and she felt like she'd die if she didn't git a dip of snuff. He even quoted from the Bible about there was a way that seemed right unto man, but the end thereof was death, and she hung her head and asked God to please take away her sinful habit. But her prayer fell on deaf ears. She began to twist and turn and to fan harder, but she was listening with all her might.

The sun was beginning to head downward when they headed back home, and it won't no time before a front tire blowed out. Kittie pure jumped while Obe was trying to keep the Ford in the road.

"I knowed it, I knowed it," he said as he opened the door and stepped on the ground, not even touching the running board. He already had a block of wood sawed off of a pine tree in the boot, for the jack won't worth a cuss. He took the hatchet from the boot and headed for the nearby woods, saying, "I'll cut a pine sapling so we can git her off the ground."

He put the block of wood close up to the front of the car and ran the sapling under the front and told Kittie she'd have to hold the pole down while he tried to git the tire off. He was scared to look in the tire-patching box for fear the young'uns had used up all the cement sticking things on paper and the tire-scraper might not be there either. He had forgotten to look before starting on the trip.

The hole from the 10-penny nail was right next to another patch and Obe was afraid he couldn't make the patch stick. But it did, and they made it back home before sunset.

Won't no time 'fore he saw Kittie heading for the backer barn and she hollered and told him she was going there to pray and to git an answer about her dipping. Obe just squatteed on the wood pile and pulled a hunk of pine bark from a piece of stove wood and whittled away with his pocket knife and watched until Kittie came back toward the house. The first thing he noticed was the toothbrush in her mouth. She came up to him and said God had made clear to her through His word that it won't what went in the mouth that offended, but instid what come out — that that was in the Bible. That brown snuff juice was running down both sides of her mouth and she looked like she was near 'bout in a trance she had such a satisfied look on her face.

Rich-Girl, Poor-Boy Romance

Everybody loves rich-girl poor- boy stories. They are the sujects of novels and movies. It's romantic to think that a boy of low standing can attract a girl from a higher level in life and captivate her heart. It has happened to those in the limelight, and it has happened out in the sticks where most of the world knows nothing about. It happened out in my neck of the woods, too.

L.P. came from a background as lowly as mine. His daddy was a sharecropper and had a house full of young'uns like everybody else. They compared young'uns with doorsteps back there. They was a breast baby, a lap baby, a knee baby and the rest of the crowd that had done got a little age on them and could git out and work in them fields.

Edward was the oldest, then L.P., Joe Pope (they called him Joe Poke), Giles, Charles, Elousie, and I think there were others I didn't never know. (I can still see Giles, Elouise and Charles toting that ice sack on their way to and from the store to git ice for tea).

Well, L.P. worked in them fields until he got on up there in his teens. And he got tard of following a mule, so he got him a job at the store in the neighborhood, or filling station, or whatever you want to call it. And if I hain't fergot everything I ever knowed, his initials stood for Leander Pope. And L.P. was a nice-looking young man. The girls liked him.

Anyhow, he sold gas, cigarettes, pigs feet, soda crackers and block after block of ice for all us tea-drinkers, chipping it off in 5 and 10-cent pieces. And he sold them things teen-age boys bought and wanted all the other teen-age boys to hear when they asked for them, but not the old men. Them things they carried in their hip pockets. And of course he sold other mess, too, and might have toted a few bottles of white lightning 'fore it was all over with for all I know.

And it was ready-rolls for L.P. every day - Chesterfields, Lucky Strikes, or Camels. His smokes were a part of his salary, apparently. And the rest of us boys had to git Avalons or Wings on Sad'dy and Sunday if we got any kind of "real" cigarettes. I know we'd tell L.P. we wanted his ducks and we'd get several draws after he got all the nicotine he wanted. And sometimes we'd git him to give one of us a cigarette and three or four boys would smoke it. We had that thing down pat, man. We'd even take a straight pin and stick it through the cigarette after it got too short to hold with the fingers to git the last draw out of it. If we'd a had long beards back then our faces would a caught afire.

L.P. bought him some white shirts and white duck pants and sent them to the laundry in town, and he had the stiffest shirts and britches you ever seen. He didn't look like the country hick in his garb. His daddy, Mr. Pope, was still walking behind mules in them fields, as were Edward, Joe Poke and Giles. But Edward would leave soon, too. And it was a time with poor Miss Lony.

She looked like she was jaded all the time, and as thin as a rail. She acted like there won't nary bit of energy left in her poor body. I can see her today in them straight dresses they wore in them days, hanging loose so it looked like won't nary stitch touching her, with strands of hair blowing in the breeze. Incidentally, Miss Lony was sister to George Smith that lost his life as a result of the explosion in the cook stove. And Mr. Pope was brother to Miss Sadie that put on that out-of-this-world Easter party that time. He was also half-brother to Mr. Emmett who castrated all the neighborhood boars in the "Sharecroppers."

Across the way in another neighborhood lived a fine young woman named Ellen. But it won't too far away for boys in my neighborhood to go courting, and L.P. and Ellen became sweethearts.

Now Ellen won't from what you would call "filthy rich" people, but they shore had a lot more than L.P.'s folks.Ellen's mother and father were dead, but the oldest boy, Nick, and his wife, Inez, took over and became sort of parents to them. And there was a gang of them young'uns, too. They had a big store and sold all kinds of things. They could run farmers for a year, and the young'uns could git things out of the store and fared a lot better than us young'uns that didn't have no store with all that stuff in it, and no money neither.

Their house was across the road from the store, and even back there, it was an imposing house, kept in good repair and painted white with a big front porch and a lot of trees in the yard and buildings around the place with all manner of farm equipment. They were sizable landowners also.

Ellen was a sweet, pleasant, quiet, likable girl. She was average in looks with dark complexion, dark eyes, and I remember a few moles on her face. Ellen and L.P. were planning to be married.

About the only things Mr. Pope and Miss Lony could have given them would have been maybe a quilt and a hen or two and a rooster to git started in the chicken business, which was a part of every rural household in those days. I doubt that Mr. Pope could have given them a pig. I'll bet he was just like us and couldn't raise enough meat to last from year to year to save his life. They was too many mouths to feed to have any extras around

So, L.P., the former sharecropper, would go to see Ellen in the big parlor in the big house, and love blossomed and wedding bells were in the air. L.P. didn't have anything of substance to offer Ellen, for he was still working in stores and not making much money. Heck, they won't much money, no matter what you were in in them days, and clerking in a store won't much more than working in the fields. It was just cleaner and easier and you were out of all that hot sun. While most of us were slaving away in them fields, L.P. was under the fan at the store drinking Coca Colas. He didn't have to go for Pepsis or big oranges or RC Colas for the filling effect. Heck, he could have two drinks if he wanted them.

But Ellen had a problem with sore throat. She was a little peaked and thought maybe it was her tonsils, so she went to the doctor and in them days it seemed like every doctor wanted a person's tonsils removed. "Yeah, those tonsils are swollen," they'd say. "They have affected your adenoids and need to be taken out." So Ellen made an appointment to have her tonsils removed at the doctor's office. There wouldn't even be a hospitalization. And the appointed day came and Ellen went in for the tonsillectomy. Her tonsils were removed without incident and she was placed in a room to await recovery from the anesthetic.

The doctor was busy with other patients, and Ellen was left alone in the temporary recovery room. But blood from the surgery got into her throat, and there was no one to remove it, and while she was unconscious, she strangled to death from her own blood. It happened on June 19, 1935 and it was recorded in that 51-year-old diary. It was an unhappy ending to a poor-boy, rich-girl romance that had the blessings of the community.

A Family Grows Up

S pring brought its profusion of flowers with plenteous moisture and fruit set on the trees and fresh growth flourished. Soon tiny peaches and apples and pears appeared and stray petals from earlier blooms flew in the wind.

Wild cherries appeared on the trees along the ditch bank and in time they ripened and turned black and the birds feasted and scattered the seeds on the ground.

Miniature strawberries were red on the hillside and along the path to the back fields and our feathered friends feasted.

The wild plums ripened and glistened in their red and yellow skins, then fell to the ground. Yellow jackets and wasps hovered around them.

Brierberries became purple and awaited human hands to be pricked by the thorns that grew on the bushes as their protection. They were left for the birds, too.

The land was tilled but the maypops flourished. Plants came up where plow sweeps couldn't uproot them and the vines became heavy with fruit and the blossoms shone in the rows of cotton, corn and tobacco. In time the fruit yellowed and remained on the vine until frost claimed the plants.

The forests were left to the wildlife and foxes sometimes darted from the woods and scurried across a field and possums and rabbits and squirrels played at the end of rows. Wild fern grew beside the paths and flowers sprang up among the underbrush, but nobody noticed.

At eventide, fireflies congregated in the yard and competed with the stars in lighting up the night, and their fragile bodies were unharmed.

The crows arrived with the spring flowers and they cawed and pitched on the scarecrow in the rosen'ear patch, picking at Zeb's old felt hat atop the stick, but nobody seemed to care anymore.

A family had grown up.

The world had survived the 1930s and a new decade was well under way.

Hank apprised the old man of his plans early in the year. He was the oldest and the first to decide to leave the next. He said that after four years of not paying out of debt and with no hope of making any money again, he was going on up the road next year in search of something besides farming. But he was realistic. He said he knew he wouldn't be able to find a job that paid good money. He'd have to take a manual job, but if he could work in a factory or a mill or some such place he'd at least have a dollar or two a week for himself.

Fuzz was tall and broad-shouldered and approaching 20. He was getting itching feet.

Shine was 18, ruggedly handsome with auburn hair and black eyes and the girls were swooning over him.

Little Bud was 17 and pimply-faced and stouter than the others. He was anxious to leave the farm as soon as possible.

Lizzie Mae was as pretty as a speckled puppy with curves in all the right places and a winning smile. She had applied at the dime store for work.

Sarah was 15 and dreaming about boys. She had long-since discarded her dolls and where playhouses had once dominated her world, weeds grew.

Sis was 13 and self-conscious and gangly and she cried a lot in secret because of her ugliness. She still wanted to play with dolls and make playhouses but Sarah refused to play with her anymore, and her world was filled with loneliness.

Everyone felt change, but it was something intangible, too far away to have an effect on the present, too elusive to lay a finger on. Something was blowing in the wind but there was no sense of direction.

Sharecroppers all, they were like most of the others in the community. There was a restlessness in the land and the younger generation was ready for a change even if they were unprepared. They knew they were facing an uncertain future and that they would never reap the richer rewards in life, no matter what came.

Born and raised on the land, that was the only life they knew. They could learn if given a chance, but they were lacking in credentials when they thought of other ways of life.

The old man assessed the situation with some head-scratching and he realized that a way of life was coming to an end. The years had slipped up and he no longer had the hands to tend a large farm. He had lived on the same farm and in the same house since the day he and Kizzie were married. After the children came and grew large enough to work in the fields, more land was rented and their pattern of life remained the same. The old house became home to all the young'uns and things went along as smoothly as they had gone during all the years of his and Kizzie's marriage.

Zeb talked it over with the old lady and told her they'd have to start making plans for a drastic change. They would have to move from the old place and find a one-horse farm that maybe he could tend. The young'uns were all about grown and what was happening to them was what had happened throughout history. A generation grows up and has to leave the nest and find its own way in the world.

Kizzie shed a tear and said it was sad that the family was growing up and opined that the years when they were around her coattail had been the best; when they stood around her chair and looked up to her like they thought she was really somebody. She asked what had happened to the years? She couldn't put her finger on them.

"There ain't even no carts out in the yard no more and I hadn't hardly thought about it. I did see one with a fish-box body and one wheel in front like a wheelbarrow is made, lying on top of a pile of backer sticks under the shelter a while back. I miss them now, and the wheels and the playhouses and hearing the young'uns hollering in the yard and running everywhere and hearing them holler 'hell-over' when they throwed the string ball over the house."

"Old Black ain't the same either," the old man said. "He's content to just find a place in the sun these days, whether the weather's hot or cold. He's quick to wag his tail when we walk by, but all the bounce is gone from the old boy now. There didn't used to be a white hair on him, and he's done turned white all over his head. Do you realize how old that dog is, Kizzie?

"Shine was a baby when Hank toted him across the field and told us he had him a puppy." Kizzie said. "Shine's 18, so that's how old Black is."

"That old dog run all over this farm with every young'un," the old man said. "He used to run all day long in the fields, going from one to the other when they were working in different places. That's how fast time flies, Kizzie."

"Which one will go next?" Kizzie asked.

"Fuzz, probably," the old man answered, "that is unless Lizzie Mae goes hog wild over some upstart in the neighborhood. She bears watching, Kizzie. She's too pretty for her own good."

Kizzie sat down and cried quietly for a while, then went to the kitchen and made a fire in the cook stove to prepare supper for her large crowd.

A Mother Remembers, Cries

K izzie bent over the washtub, rubbing lye soap generously over a nasty shirt, then dipping it into the water and scrubbing furiously to remove the dirt. A cat came up and rubbed her tail over Kizzie's skirt and a bluejay from the tree above swooped down at the feline, causing her to hiss and bow up her back. The second swoop by the bluejay got the cat moving.

Kizzie had a lot of things on her mind. The fact that the young'uns were grown up caught her by surprise. She knew it was happening, yet she refused to accept it for what it was.

She thought about God's plan of creation and about her and Zeb; how the children had come without any planning; how they had given them instant love and more work than they could hardly do; how as more and more unplanned children came, it was the same love after they arrived.

All the others were in the fields working, and the loneliness made her melancholy. Her tears mingled with the dirty water. She was remembering the children's antics over the years.

There was the day Hank brought home the little black puppy that had meant so much to all the family; the time Lizzie Mae came up with a kitten, grasping it around its neck until it was lifeless when she released her grip to show it to her mother; the day a gander guarding the nest of its mate while the goslings were hatching got hold of Little Bud and whipped him to the ground and his screams had brought her running down the path to the ditch bank and her fight with the gander before getting Little Bud free;

The little green snake Shine brought up one day, held tightly by its head and his pride in capturing the reptile; the time Sis climbed up the well curb and was looking down into the water when Hank grabbed her;

Captive butterflies seeking escape from strings attached to their fragile bodies; toad frogs brought up in buckets; lizards and scorpions in homemade crates; injured baby birds; caterpillars squirming in tin cans; crickets and june bugs and crawfish and worms and other insects to satisfy rural childrens' curiosities;

Wild flowers, damp with dew, picked with care and taken home to the one person who reigned as queen at that special time in life. Wild flowers that became giant rainbow-colored bouquets in remembering.

The time when the old hound was having puppies under the shelter and two or three of the smallest young'uns found her chewing off the umbilical cord close to the puppy's stomach and thought she was eating her puppy and they took several puppies still wet from birth and brought them to her in an effort to save them; the time Fuzz took a swallow of kerosene and they had to find somebody to carry him to the doctor to have his stomach pumped out; the times one of them would stick nails deep into a foot and their piteous cries as they were doctored; times when they cried because they wanted to do things that would have been dangerous or because they couldn't go to another child's house to play when there was nobody at home to look after them.

The laughter that rang over the premises came back as a song in remembering; the girls garbed in worn-out clothing from the ragbag with an old pair of worn-out Sunday shoes with a heel an inch and a half high that dangled on their feet, causing them to have to slide their feet as they walked, with the old handbag they had found in a trunk in the loft; the boys building carts and dragging old boards to their "workshop" and searching for wheels and pulling nails from old boards; children playing on jump boards and the merry-go-round Zeb had rigged up for them;

Cries in the night from bad dreams; children standing around her when she was making a cake, waiting for the scrapings from the bowl; how they all gathered on the porch on summer evenings and watched the stars and the moon and listened for night life in the woods; taking them to Sunday school and church and getting the girls dressed up and the pride they showed in a new dress or a new pair of shoes that were seldom in coming; how the boys griped at their Sunday apparel; how they pretended they knew nothing about Santa Claus being a fake long after they had learned about it at school; the pleasure it gave them on Sunday not to have company and to be able to sit at the table and eat of the good parts of the chicken; the songs and poems they made up and recited to each other and the games they played — blindfold, hiding, hopscotch, jumping rope, stick frog, horseshoes.

Kizzie would sob occasionally as she remembered how they had started growing up and their reactions to the changing process in their bodies. She had noticed the results of puberty among her boys. She wondered what caused such passions boys were possessed with. The girls had been timid at first as their busts began to fill out and she recalled how they were ashamed at the bulges they were unable to hide; how the boys' voices were gawky and how the hair on their faces embarrassed them until they pleaded with Zeb to let them use his straight razor to shave it off.

She loved them so much, the children that had come from her own body. She thought of every one as a living miracle and would have given up her life for any of them without question. She thought of the hard struggle to get them through babyhood and on the road to becoming men and women; all the sleepless nights when one was sick; the patching and sewing, cooking, washing, ironing, canning, working in the fields; defending them when she felt Zeb was too rough in meting out punishment; crying with them when their worlds were shaken; praying for them when they were finally in bed and her world became quiet for a little while.

The girls' playhouses seemed more real as she remembered them; the carts and other homemade toys more like the real thing than in just fulfilling the desires of boys to create something to entertain themselves. The green cherries and apples and peach leaves and poke berries became real food in remembering the children's happiest days.

The cold days of winter seemed best of all, for they were together then in one room, a family laughing together and playing together. No, they hadn't worried her as badly as she had told them they did. They had made her happy — happier than anything else on earth could have done.

New tears flowed when she recalled Christmases past. They were so simple, yet so beautiful; the egg hunts at Easter when two or three dozen eggs were boiled, dyed or painted, and hidden among the bright green rye; the reunions they attended every summer; making ice cream or lemonade; going fishing; hunting for yard brooms; searching for toothbrushes; huckleberrying; nights at the backer barns. It was all ended. Her days with the children, as children, were over. For a little while she longed to be the young mother again, sharing and watching over them and being the star in their lives for a little while.

She had finished the washing and hung out the clothes before all the tears were gone. She said a prayer and asked God to help her accept life as it was, not what she would have it be.

Turn 'Em Loose, Let 'Em Fly

Kizzie was putting a bottom in an old back-porch straight-back chair. The straw bottom had become ragged over the years, and it wasn't doing anybody any good in its present condition.

She was out under the oak tree near the smokehouse with her tub of hot water and a pile of shucks. She'd dip the shucks in the water until they were soft and pull off two or three of the husks and twist them together until they were strong enough to go across the width of the chair and attach to the bottom.

Kizzie was still thinking about all the young'uns being grown up, and she talked to herself in her mind without uttering any words.

I'm going to turn them loose and let 'em fly, like birds. If birds don't fly when they git old enough, they're pushed out of the nest. Course they're pushed out cause there are going to be more birds. But with Zeb and me, won't be no more babies.

No different than it's always been though. No different than Zeb and me. Ain't nothing new about it. Just hits home when it comes.

Funny anyhow, the way it works. You work and slave to raise a gang of young'uns. They're your whole world. Ain't time for nothing else and if there was ain't nothing else you want to do 'cept mother over them and try to please them and make 'em happy. It's a hard job.

Bunch of young'uns grow up knowing mostly what's carried on in the family. You'd think they'd all see the same way. But that shore ain't the way it is. Look at how different ones turn out. Drunks sometimes coming from sober homes. Loose women coming from mamas that show nothing but purity before their daughters.

Never know how they'll be nohow. Try to learn a girl how to sew, she may never set down to a sewing machine. Show her how to cook, she may remember a few things you show her. She may not remember nothing. Oh, there may be some pie or something like that she'll want to bake 20 years or so later and she may wonder what ma done to it to make it so good. You try to show her that it's just a knack for things like that; not something you set down on paper.

Once they git grown they can turn clear around from what they used to be anyhow. Ma and Pa hain't got no sense. I declare it's like that ever time. How come is it that young'uns that thought the old man and old lady was pretty clever folks when they was little all of a sudden put them down so low?

Sometimes all the love you feel for them is put to the test when they start sassing you and deciding to do what they want to. It hurts so bad way down inside it near 'bout makes you sick. You think to yourself what will become of them and what it'll be like when they start having young'uns of their own. No matter what they think, having their own young'uns is the only way they'll ever learn what it all means.

Course they probably won't have a bunch of them like has been the case in the past. Things is changing. We always thought of a house full of young'uns in terms of having a big work force in the fields. We thought of it as an act of God. But these young'uns ain't even aiming to farm. They'll be trying to forgit all the things we tried to stress to them.

Love's still there as long as there's breath, but it seems like the older the young'uns git that love gits to hurt more and more sometimes and there's more to overlook, no matter how bad it hurts.

By the time Zeb and me's rotten in our graves, the young'uns will have just about forgot us 'cept for the times they'll remember some sort of what they call "mess" we told them, like we didn't know nothing about what we was saying when we told them.

And somewhere down the line when more and more gran-dyoung'uns come along, or their young'uns, there'll be a few that they'll point to and say, "Ain't that another Zeb Crebbins if you ever seen one? Look at the back of his head and his walk." Or another might have a chin like mine — kinda peaked — or one that turns her head a certain way and I can just hear 'em say, "All right, Miss Kizzie, stop acting like Ma." But I know one thing: They shore won't name nary girl Kizzie. They've poked enough fun at my name as it is. But I reckon I paid them back with the names I slung on them. But I shore didn't intend it that way. It just seems like that nobody don't like their names.

So they's a few things only God almighty can change. They can grow away from you and go their own ways, but nature sees to it that, for good or bad, something that you had a hand in creating will carry on in the future.

I got to let 'em go. I've finally learnt that you can't keep 'em tied to your apron strings. But I want to have enough gumption to let them find their own ways without putting my mouth into it. I feel like I've done my duty and God knows it was something I done out of pure love. He knows I tried. And somehow I feel like they'll have a little respect for me when they look back on their past. And

Zeb too.

Sometimes over the long haul, when people look back on their ma's and pa's they may change their way of thinking. That's after they've been through the same fire and know more how to judge. The one thing that teaches better than anything else is experience. Some of them git to thinking that Ma and Pa weren't so crazy after all. They knowed a lot more what they were talking about than we give 'em credit for. But that's over the long haul, mind you.

I done got this chur bottomed, and it looks right pretty if I do say so. Now I'll turn it bottom upwards and be sure all the shucks are tied so they won't come loose. This old chur will last mine and Zeb's lifetime, or what years we got left. It'll come in handy to sit in and work on vegetables.

Zeb, Kizzie Share Feelings

B rown leaves floating on October winds. A red sun hovering low in the west. Butterflies soaring aimlessly. Brown corn stalks contrasting with rank green soybeans between the corn rows. Coxcomb and marigolds, and zinnias with dying leaves. Chaney ball trees with fading foliage and yellow pods of balls cluttering the yard. A little pond in the distance reflecting the blue skies and an almost-unearthly quietness. A rare Sunday afternoon when Zeb and Kizzie are alone.

They're on the back porch, Kizzie sitting in a straight chair and Zeb lying on the floor with a quilt for a pillow. Kizzie dips her snuff and spits in the yard while taking in the scene. Zeb turns from side to side occasionally to rest his back. He looks across the cotton field in the distance, now white with open bolls. "Time to git that cotton picked," he says as he gazes in the distance. Kizzie says nothing.

"Time to git everything harvested 'fore the winter sets in," Zeb says as he leans his head over and spits on the ground. Kizzie says nothing.

"You're mighty quiet old lady."

"I didn't know you wanted me to say anything."

"Naw, we don't talk too much," Zeb says. "We ain't never talked too much to each other. Maybe we ought to talk more."

"About what?" Kizzie asks.

"About us if nothing else," Zeb replies. "How we feel and all that."

"How do you feel about everything?" Kizzie asks.

"A lot more than I've ever said. I don't know Kizzie. Folks just git started a certain way and they just stay in that same old path. But some things ought to be said."

"Like what?"

"You know something Kizzie. We been married going on 25 years, and if either one of us has ever mentioned the word "love" to each other I can't recall it."

"Well, I thought we understood each other about that," Kizzie says, "I tell you one thing, Zeb Crebbins, it won't just for fun I took on the job 25 years ago that I'm still filling. It had to be something stronger than anything else I've ever felt in my life. But you know what I think Zeb? I think that just because sharecroppers are so low-down they think they ain't supposed to do like other people. There ain't no difference, Zeb. It's 'cause we think that way."

"I know," Zeb replies. "We think 'cause we ain't got nothing we ain't supposed to live like people that have a little something. But we may think even deeper than them. And you know something else. I wouldn't be happy no other way. Happiness means different things to different people. I couldn't never be happy high up in some office building. I'd go crazy Kizzie. I love the land. Sometimes I think I'm in some kind of kingdom when I'm out there on that land I've tended all these years that ain't even mine. I love the smell of the land. Why sometimes when I'm plowing I'll pick up a handful of dirt I've just turned up and hold it to my nose. It smells sweet and shines near 'bout like gold to me

"And I'd of loved to have had a better house for you and the young'uns and all that, but it ain't never bothered me that I was just an old sharecropper. I reckon that's because I don't know no different. And I do 'preciate all you've done, Kizzie. God knows I 'preciate it. You won't never know how I've depended on you and you ain't never let me down. And I'm going to say it right now. I love you, Kizzie Crebbins."

"Is something wrong with you Zeb?" Kizzie asks. "Are you going to die or something? You're doing the quarest talking I ever huern you do."

"I'm all right, Kizzie. I just had these things on my mind and I had to say 'em."

"You didn't have to tell me you loved me, Zeb. I already knowed that. But I 'preciate you telling me. I never heard Ma and Pa talk nothing about love either. I never saw them kiss each other and I heard Ma say Pa had never seen her stark naked in her life, nor she him, and I could say the same about us. But I know they loved one another and I know you and me love one another. We just ain't the kind to show our feelings."

"I reckon I'm doing more thinking on account of the young'uns all being grown now," Zeb says. "I never really took the time to think about what you and the young'uns mean to me. We been too busy to take up a lot of time with them. Maybe we'll have a whole lot of grandyoung'uns so we can cater to them now that we won't be hustling to put food on the table for our pack and trying to keep the wolf away from the door."

"But hit won't never be the same no more," Kizzie says. "Young'uns is changing Zeb. They are learning what's going on everywhere else and they are restless. I watch my own crowd every day and other young'uns that come around, too. And they don't act like they used to. They're gitting so they have minds of their own more and more every day. And that may be good in a lot of ways, but it might not be so good in the long run. They're gitting more knowledge, and you know what happened to Adam and Eve in the Garden of Eden when their eyes was opened. But they's one thing about it. For better or worse, young'uns can't be held back. We couldn't hold them back no more if we tried. They's a new breed out there now Zeb, and they're what we got to depend on to carry on in the future. But back to what you was saying.

"You been a good man, Zeb. I ort to of told you that many a time when I got after you about something. But I want you to know I look up to you and I have respect for you, Zeb."

"Just look at that sunset, Kizzie. Ever seen anything any prettier, 'cept for the young'uns coming up the path to feed up? They're ourn, Kizzie. Yourn and mine. They're all right for sharecroppers' young'uns."

"Being poor ain't got nothing to do with it," Kizzie says. "It's the way people are brought up and the principles they learn as young'uns. That ain't going to make saints out of folks, but it gives 'em a pattern to go by. If you try to make something without a pattern you end up with a mess, and people that don't have no pattern for their lives end up the same way. I expect as much from my young'uns as people do that live in them big houses in town. Poor hain't got nothing to do with sense. Thank God for that. I think our young'uns could learn anything any young'un could learn — some of them anyhow."

"I finally got you to talking, didn't I old lady?" Zeb says, laughing. "I tell you, talking is good for the soul sometimes."

"It's gitting cool out here,' Kizzie says, shivering. "I'll go in and put the left-overs from dinner on the table. I shore ain't doing no cooking on Sunday night."

Change Merciless In Country

C hange was slow in coming. Subtle at first, it manifest itself in disguises that poor people in the country accepted as a part of life without fanfare or comment.

Power lines found out-of-the-way houses in back fields, stood along highways, along railroad tracks, gutting through forests and finding the isolated places to bring light to a light-starved people. Dangling receptacles hung from the center of rooms and with electricity at a giveaway price, people still bought low-watt bulbs and remained in dim surroundings to keep down the cost.

The public began buying refrigerators when money was available to make the monthly payments. Electric irons were almost luxuries after ironing with flat irons over a lifetime. There was a place for ice in the refrigerator, although there was far too little space to make enough for large families. But electricity brightened the rural world.

Years after World War II ended country people were still struggling to overcome the Depression throughout the 1930s and the sacrifices necessitated by the war. Many remained under the yoke of debt.

Supermarkets were on the scene and rural people, as well as city dwellers, flocked there for a variety of foods and many other items that had never been available to them before under one roof. The supermarket was bringing items to the people at a cheaper price than they were able to raise them. Many former farmers were working in plants or retail establishments and had some weekly income, although small. Well into the 1940s the average weekly salary for many workers was around $12.50.

Many cow stables were empty after milk and butter became available at the large grocery chain. The stables eventually dried out and children sometimes made playhouses in them.

Tractors were becoming popular, and every farmer who could afford one got rid of his mules and left the stables empty. Hauling stable manure in spring became obsolete.

Eggs were cheap and there were fresh dressed chickens in the meat departments, elminating the need to wring a chicken's neck, scald and dress it. Many chicken houses also became empty and fewer and fewer barnyard fowl were seen around country homes. The colorful sight of a variety of chickens in green rye fields became a memory. Few roosters were crowing to welcome a new day.

Hogs weren't squealing in pastures anymore. Meat was available at the supermarket, ready to eat. No more shucking corn, toting slops and water and mixing wheat middlings for a pack of hungry hogs.

People living in country homes that had a variety of shelters and barns to accommodate their livestock and farming implements found themselves with an excess of buildings. Once they were not used, the deteriorating process began, leaving reminders of the past that had no place in the present. Many were torn down or neglected to allow nature to take its course.

Change was more evident along the highways. Trailer homes were cropping up everywhere, a sight entirely new in the area. Small businesses were operating along the roads where traffic was much heavier than in former days. Occasionally a landowner would build a new house near the old homeplace and leave the old house standing forlorn in the background, an eyesore now that had been revered as home in the past. The old places became storehouses or packhouses for tobacco, or just left for time to take its toll. Only memories were left of days when the old house was habitated by many children and everyday chores were done year-round; where the pot had boiled on the cook stove seven days a week; where voices were heard at nighttime with laughter and singing and whispers; where boys and girls had learned about life, worked in the fields, dreamed about a time when there would be other ways of life.

There was still plenty of country life. Children roamed over the countryside and explored their world about them, but something was missing.

It was so lonely sometimes to walk to the old houses and see the results of neglect. Empty stables and hog pens and hen houses brought a feeling of sadness and a longing to see it all again, so soon after those things that had had a profound impact on our lives were forever gone. We had played under the trees, but even they didn't look the same. They, too, were deserted. Their strong limbs had held us when we climbed high and gazed on our world from their branches. It gave a feeling that the trees also were missing all the attention they had been given.

The songs of the birds sounded muted. The whisper of the wind was different.

Something that had been a part of the people's lives was gone, leaving a void. Oh, there were many who were happy to be done with milking cows, feeding mules ar hogs, tending to chickens and getting in something to burn, for oil heaters had become popular and many people had 55-gallon drums attached to their houses to hold kerosene to burn in their heaters.

People were also buying electric stoves, eliminating the need for stove wood. Menfolks were even happier than the women to be relieved of the responsibility of cutting wood for the fireplace, the kitchen stove and the tobacco barns. Tobacco barns were being heated with oil also. Some people said it just made the menfolks lazier for it didn't lighten a woman's load all that much.

Old buildings that weren't used seemed to start swaying in a hurry, as if emptiness took away their spirit also. A shelter would sag or a barn would drop in a corner and the rotting process was hastened. The old buildings became nuisances, and over a period of time when people renovated their homes and grounds they were just torn down and thrown away. It left large gaps in the surroundings and something was gone forever that had been an intimate part of life. The "heart" had been cut out of country living, leaving a hollow place that would never again be filled.

Once change got rolling it was swift and merciless. So much of it only lives in the memory of those who lived in the old days.

Proud, Doting Grandparents

I n the natural progression of life, grandchildren were added to the homes of the Crebbins family. This pleased Zeb and Kizzie. They doted over the babies, observed all their antics when they were around them and watched as they went through the various stages from infancy until they were observant of life about them.

Some of the grandchildren always wanted to go to Ma-Ma's and Pa-Pa's, while others preferred to stay at home or go other places. But all of them showed love for their grandparents.

Hank's oldest son, Robert, who was called Bob, was intrigued by the quaintness of life at Pa-Pa's, as were Lizzie Mae's second child, Anna Maria, now eight, and Shine's boy, Chad, 10. Pat, Sarah's oldest girl, 7, also loved to go to Pa-Pa's. And Zeb and Kizzie looked forward to the times when several were there together.

Upon their arrival, they always let Ma-Ma know they wanted

something from the safe. Almost by the time they entered the house, they were asking for something to eat. And Kizzie would go with them to the kitchen and start giving them handouts.

"Why don't we have a safe, Ma-Ma?" Pat asked.

"Them old things are not for people today, honey," Kizzie replied. "That old safe was my mama's, and her mama give it to her and she didn't have no room for it because she already had one, and it was stored in an old barn, and when Zeb and me was married she told me to git it to help git us started off house-keeping."

"I wish we had one," Pat said.

"Me too," said Anna Maria, and Chad said the same.

"This chicken's good," Anna Maria said as she tackled a thigh. "Know where we get our chicken, Ma-Ma?"

"At the grocery store," Kizzie replied.

"Un uh," Anna Maria said. "At Kentuckey Fried Chicken. But it don't taste like yours."

"I want some of that gravy in the pot on the stove," Chad said, "and a biscuit so I can sop it. We don't have gravy like that at home."

"Ma-Ma's got some apple jacks!" exclaimed Pat. "Can we have one, Ma-Ma?"

All these things pleased Kizzie. All the grandchildren had so many things she and Zeb had never had and handsome homes and conveniences that made her old house seem out of place. Despite their disadvantage at being country young'uns and sadly lacking in education, they had done far better than she or Zeb expected. But the children's exuberance and the pleasure they got from her cooking made her happy, and she remembered the past. One day when they were all around her, she said, "You ought to of seen your mamas and daddies when they was young'uns and their carrying-ons about something to eat." A broad smile was on her face. "They were pure foolish about some things that people don't eat no more. Why I remember when a nanner sandwich was something sweet to them. When they was nanners at the store and there was any eggs around, I'd send them to the store and git some nanners and light bread."

"What's light bread?" Maria asked.

"Oh, they call it loaf bread today," Kizzie said. "And at first there won't no sliced bread. You had to cut the slices and we'd take a heated knife and cut slices, and the young'uns loved it better than cake. And on Sunday I'd mash up some nanners and sweeten them and just smear them on the bread and that would be the only sweet we had for dinner."

"Yuk," Chad said.

"And when they was big dinners, the young'uns always wanted fried weenies on the table. We didn't make hot dogs at home in them days like they do today. But at them dinners several women would have fried weenies. They were wrinkled and juicy and the young'uns grabbed them and a fresh cucumber pickle and had them a time. And they was good to me, too."

Chad would follow Zeb out in the yard and they'd walk over the grounds and down to the rotting tobacco barns. Zeb would point out places where the hog pasture used to be and where the young'uns played baseball and they'd open the shackly doors to the barn and stables and peep in and Zeb would tell Chad stories about when (Chad's) daddy and the others were young'uns, and Chad said he wished he'd been born then and could have grown up with them. He picked up a clod of dirt, looked into the sun and squinted his eye and threw it at a wild cherry tree in the distance.

Zeb observed as Chad wound up his arm and the way he squinted. "You know something boy. You ought not to be named Chad. You're another Shine if I ever seen one. You looked just like your daddy when you was throwing that clod of dirt, and acted like him too."

"Daddy says I remind him of you," Chad replied.

"Naw, you ain't like me, Chad. You're like your pa."

Bob usually visited Zeb and Kizzie when the younger children weren't there. He would stay for several days sometimes. Bob was studious and showed a great interest in his ancestry. He'd ask Zeb all kinds of questions about what he had been like as a boy and how it was when his children were growing up. The surroundings were so old-fashioned, so unique he found them intriguing. He'd look over the house and marvel at its simplicity. Something about it seemed more solid than any place he could remember. The furniture was old and scratched, and it was evident it hadn't been acquired for good looks. Yet, it was something he treasured.

"It seems a little bit strange out here," Bob confided to Zeb. "It's different and something you don't see much of anymore. But you know something, I like it."

"It's something just about faded from the scene," Zeb said. "Better take a good look at it boy, for the mess you see around here is the way we've lived all our lifetimes, Kizzie and me, and millions of others before us. But it's done got modern now, and it's put us in our places all right."

"Don't you want any of the modern things we see everywhere now, Pa-Pa?"

"Don't bother me none that I don't have'em, Bob. I done growed old in this way and I ain't pining about what I'm missing now. I'm glad all of you have these newfangled things but they's sort of out of place for me and Kizzie."

Anna Maria came up as they were talking. She looked at Zeb and said, "You talk funny Pa-Pa," laughing.

"How do I talk funny, baby?"

"You say everything the old-timey way, like 'don't bother me none' and they's for they're' and things like that."

"That's just an old sharecropper for you, baby. Done got old and growed up ignorant and spoke like everybody else I was around. You done learned to talk right prissy-like, little girl, and I'm mighty proud of you. Don't you pay no mind to your old grand-pappy just 'cause he sounds like some kind of nut. I've thought about a lot of things I couldn't never say, 'cause I didn't know how to say 'em. But I'm mighty glad you grandyoung'uns are coming up the proper way. But Lord, you've missed so much! Having all of you around makes me young and I can see all my own young'uns in you all over agin. I just wish things out here was like they used to be so I could really show you something. But it ain't the same. Yeah, you've missed more than I could ever tell you if I was to sit down right now and try to tell it like it was. You'll just have to ask your own ma's and pa's about it."

The Last Family Reunion

J une bugs singing in the old oak trees. A yard swept clean and looking good enough to eat off of. Smoke from a barbecuing pig wafting over the grounds with the scent of vinegar and cooked pork making everything hungry within its range. Even the dogs are sniffing the air. Long folding tables sitting under the trees and a wooden tub filled with lemonade.

It was the Crebbins family reunion. At the same place Zeb and Kizzie had lived since their marriage. When tractors replaced the mules, farmers needed more land and the farm Zeb had tended was rented to other sharecroppers. They were allowed to continue living in the old house.

Kizzie was busy in the kitchen, surprisingly spry for her years, cooking a big pot of summer collards and making her chicken pie that she had become famous for in the community. She used half-size fryers and a large, deep pan. There was plenty of broth

An Old-Fashioned Barbecue From Long Ago
Courtesy Peggy Dew

and she added boiled eggs, garden peas, a few onions, and those bite-size thighs and pulley bones and gizzards; in fact all the pieces of chicken, and cooked the pie in the broth, adding enough pastry to give it consistency, and cooking it in a Kizzie-only crust that always melted in your mouth by the time you tasted the contents of the pie.

She kneaded dough as if she were going to make biscuits in the old days. She had to make the young'uns some "cinniment buns." She rolled the dough out on a white sack she used for that purpose, then spread half a pound of butter on the top side of the dough. Opening the sugar stand, she used a tablespoon to spread sugar over the butter, then took the cinnamon box and sprinkled the powder generously over the top. Starting at the outer edge, she rolled gently until she had a roll almost two inches thick. With deft fingers, she closed up one end of the roll so the contents would not escape, and placed the buns in the pan. When the crowd got to eating good, she'd slip in and put them in the oven and they would be steaming with the juices oozing to the top and the odor filling the yard when she brought them out. The young'uns would have had a fit without the "cinniment buns."

Zeb was out at the pit where Hank was cooking the pig. He'd bend over and pick out a morsel of the meat, waiting for the skin to get crisp.

They started coming early, bringing dust as the cars rolled into the yard. About all the family was there with the exception of Lizzie Mae's second boy who was a student at the University of California in Berkeley, and Sis's daughter that was expecting a baby any day. One of Shine's girls wasn't there for she was living with a man in town and she didn't want to hear tongues wagging about her.

They toted in gobs of vittles, like they were going out of style, and the young'uns were picking at each other, even with silvery heads, as they had done in childhood, and Zeb and Kizzie were filled with pride. So much was going on it was hard to get the attention of anybody. The boys sat together under a tree and you never heard such laughing as they were doing, and everybody knew they were telling about carryings-on on the same spot when they were young'uns. The girls were doing the same thing in their little circle.

Grandchildren who didn't hardly know some of their cousins got into the act also. There were college graduates and high school students. One was a doctor. One a teacher. A few were farmers. A few looked like typical hippies of the era with long hair done in pony tails. Some were pretty; some plain, but all had a common interest. They were descendants of the two old people being honored.

Zeb asked the blessing and thanked God for giving him and Kizzie a fine family and all the bountiful blessings in life. Kizzie stood and said she would never have believed there would be so many in the same family and she told them how much she loved them.

The young folks took their paper plates to the barbecue bowl first, but not nary one of Kizzie's young'uns did that. They lined up where her collards sat and dipped into them generously. Next, they took small bowls and filled them with chicken pie and reached for the baked cornbread to go with the collards, and bowls of fresh hot pepper to cut up over them. Some of 'em didn't even taste of the barbecue. Fuzz saw something he thought was country ham and made a bee-line for it.

Kizzie had already got the "cinniment buns" in the oven and Sis said unless she was mistaken there were cinnamon buns somewhere around and about that time Kizzie came out of the house with the steam rising in the air as she brought them to the table. Kizzie's children that were not through eating took them a bun before anybody else got a chance.

After dinner they went through the house, into every room, pointing out the beds they had slept in to their children, where they had sat at night and got up their lessons; the place they had sat at the table; remembering little incidents during childhood.

Some of the grandchildren said they didn't see how anything they were told about it could have been exciting or made them happy, and the children just shook their heads, remembering a million things it seemed like, all of them parading before them in a moment's time. They went back under the trees and showed their children the limb where the swing was attached and where the woodpile had sat and the spot where the wash pot was placed. They got into an argument about that. One would say it was sitting a few feet one way or the other, and in the final analysis all agreed the wash pot had sat on the woodpile. The young folks were shown where the fence had stood and the post at the end where the slop jar was hung every morning.

They began leaving fairly early, for some of them had quite a distance to travel, and finally Zeb and Kizzie were left alone. The sun was beginning to get an orange haze by the time everyone was gone.

"Might be the last reunion we'll have with that many of us together," Zeb said.

"Probably so," Kizzie replied. "But this was a good one. But I ain't worrying about the future, Zeb. We done done our best and our young'uns are doing all right. They comes a time when you just don't think that much about tomorrow. That's bound to be old age, ain't it?"

"Yeah," Zeb said. "I'm like that too, Kizzie. I think too much about the past to be all that concerned about the present. Time's just passed us by, Kizzie. We're old folks."

Kizzie died a few months later of a heart attack.

Zeb's Last Prayer

Old Zeb sat looking out a window of the house that held a million memories. The sky had turned from gray to a lead color and snowflakes were beginning to fall. They were hardly discernible at first and only showed when drifts of wind would bring them swirling around the house. The wind played on the tin roof but inside it was warm.

Zeb had an old chair pulled up to the window and he draped his body over the chair bottom with the rungs facing him. He placed his hands on the rungs. Looking toward the road, he saw people milling around the supermarket, gathering groceries in anticipation of a snowstorm. The supermarket and surrounding buildings obscured the view of much of the community that had been landmarks during most of his lifetime. He felt like a stranger in his own land.

He had grown old with time. It was the 1970s and Zeb was 77 years old. All of the former Zeb was gone. His health had failed. He was plagued with pain. It was an effort to get about. It had been bad when Kizzie was there to help him, but she was gone, too.

The children had asked him to go live with them, but he had refused, saying he wanted to be independent as long as possible; that they didn't need an old man around to upset their lives and cause a stir all the time. But time was taking its toll, and he realized that he would have to make other arrangements in a short while. He was losing his grip.

It was praying time for Zeb.

He closed his eyes and lay his forehead over the old chair and prayed silently.

Oh Lord, I come to you today to lay open my soul. I've done it before, Lord, but I ain't never said it like I'm saying it today. I'm burdened, Lord, with the cares of life and the pitifulness of old age. I've come to the end of my rope, Lord, and I'm ready to leave this old world.

I want to thank You, Lord, for a million blessings You've showered on me. And I didn't deserve them and You know that. You've just been good to me and propped me up when I would a fell. Don't think I don't know what You've done for me, Lord. And in thinking about it, even with my infirmities, it makes me feel good.

I'm reliving all of my life, Lord, and when I look back on it, I wouldn't have traded places with a king. And I ain't saying I wouldn't have 'preciated some of the things kings have, but You know I ain't built that way. I never looked back on what I missed by being a poor farmer and never felt no envy for them that was above me. I've thought sometimes I had it better than them.

I think about it, and I know there never could have been no better way for me to live my life than right here and in the way it's been lived. And I shore ain't trying to make no saint out of myself, Lord. You know every fault of mine, and I'm ashamed for You to know some of the things I've thought and done in my life, but I'm glad You're the one that's going to judge me. I shore wouldn't want it to be no man.

I hain't tried to make no show, Lord. You know that. I've tried to be a daddy to my young'uns and a husband to my Kizzie. And I know they ain't always seen me as being somebody to pattern after. I've had to beat the young'uns, Lord, when it hurt me a lot more than them. I had to try to point them in the right direction. I've had them in the fields when I know they hated me and thought me the quarest old man in the world. I had to do them things, Lord, to try to make ends meet and to keep things together. I've felt alone a lot of times, Lord — left out — when the young'uns didn't come up to me and say something kind. I wanted them close to me, Lord, so I could put my hand on their heads and look into their eyes and just let them know I was proud of 'em.

Whatever I've been, Lord its been right here at home and in the fields that surround me.

Ain't many people ever loved the land better than me, Lord. It has been a privilege to be out there where it always seemed clean and refreshing to be plowing the dirt and watching things grow and listening to the birds that have sung for me for a lifetime. Thank You for the birds, Lord. Thank You for the plows and the rakes and the cultivators and all the things I used in farming to help tend the land. Thank You for the chickens that run up and down the rows when I was plowing near the house and they'd follow behind me picking up the worms turned up with the plow.

Thank You, Lord, for every person I've known in my life. I feel like every one of them have had an impact on me. Good folks. Plain, simple, God-fearing folks that believed in work and decency and principle. Thank You for my neighbors. They've helped me in times of need, and I've tried to do the same for them. We've lived in harmony for the most part and the few times there have been words between any of us, it was something that blowed over in no time. We are of the flesh, Lord, and all of us are sinners.

Please forgive us.

You shore knowed what you was doing when you give me Kizzie, Lord. I wouldn't a been worth a dime without her. That woman put up with enough mess from me to have killed some weaker women. And I don't mean I beat her or nothing like that. But you know my hot-headedness, Lord. I was always a minute man. I wanted things to happen right now. No waiting. No nothing. No thinking things out. But thanks to my Kizzie, she kept me from doing foolisher things than I did because of her level-headedness. I hain't had no world since my Kizzie left me two years ago, Lord. That finished me up.

I feel a smile coming on my face, Lord, when I think back on our young days, when the young'uns were coming along. I know now that I had the world in the palm of my hand then. Right out here in the middle of nowhere. Just an old sharecropper with nothing to speak of, yet I had everything. We was all together, day and night. Won't no thought of being nowhere else. We tended to the young'uns, got them fed in the morning and watched them play throughout the day, fed them at night and got them bedded down, and it was a peaceful world.

Oh, I know today folks say we was pitiful back there with no money or nothing and full of ignorance and all that. But folks to-day look for what we had then, and it ain't to be found. They run here and yander trying to find something to satisfy them, when there ain't nothing. Money don't buy a minute of happiness. Folks want to think of everything in terms of dollars. And the Good Book says the love of money is the root of all evil. Seems like folks today are thinking of the mighty dollar rather than each other.

Only You know the love I have for my family, Lord. I won't never able to tell them like I wanted to. Maybe I didn't show it like I should have. I've always been a shy man in some ways. But You know the love I have for them Lord, young'uns, grandyoung'uns and great-grandyoung'uns. 'Course, it's different now. The young crowd don't know how to deal with old folks. They live a different life than what me and my own young'uns lived. They can't know how it was, for none of it ain't out there today. They look upon us with pity, too. But my own young'uns seemed a lot happier when they was running all over this place and the neighborhood than the young crowd today.

I ain't proud of everything my own young'uns did, Lord. They are like everybody else. Each one is a person on his own. When Hank was running around and drinking and all that mess it wor-ried me and Kizzie near 'bout to death. And when Shine got tangl-ed up with that woman it weighed heavy on our hearts. When

Sarah had to git married, that tore us all to pieces. But we won't the only ones that had troubles.

Lord, I don't know why all these little bitty things are coming to me today. It just seems like I'm seeing everything all over agin. The past is rolling before me like it hadn't never happened before. It seems like they're happening right before my eyes, when You know they happened so long ago, Lord.

I can see a calm spring day when we burned off the fields and the hillsides with reed beds burning and I can hear the stalks popping and see little bits of ash rising in the air and hissing as the smoke dies and the particles falling back to earth.

I can see the stump of an old dead tree burning in the night after it caught afire from burning the grass, way off down in a field where it lightens up the night and the ebb and flow of the light as the wind blows.

I can see a yellow cast over the land after a rainstorm when the sun is out behind the cloud and its glow gives the landscape a quare look for a little while.

I can see the lights being lit and the glow in the windows as darkness falls. I can hear the bark of the dogs and the meow of the cats. I can see starlit skies with a million diamonds sparkling from above and moonbeams and shadows and hear eerie wild cries from the woods.

I am now out in a gray dawn, waiting for the sunrise and hoping the eastern skies will have a few clouds around so the sun will paint them in pink and orange and purple. I am able to discern that old pine tree way off yander that stands above everything else in the circle about me.

I can smell the mule lot, Lord, and it's miry from winter rains and snows. I can hear the boards that we use to git to the stables sqush as we step on them and they sink down in the mire. I'm thinking about them old mules, Lord and how I loved them almost like they was my young'uns. They were so faithful all them years — pulling plows and cuarts and wagons — and never complaining- I hope them old mules didn't never thirst for water because the young'uns didn't keep them at the trough long enough or carry them to the stables at night without taking them by the well for their swills of cool water.

I remember all the days, Lord, before we had anything like a bomb to worry about. There was no thought of anything falling out of the sky to kill us. We thought of war but weapons were something we thought was pushed out on battlefields on mobile units. Oh, how simple was them days, Lord!

I want to thank You agin, Lord, for bringing Little Bud through

World War II and bringing him back home safely. Thank You for bringing back Sis and Sarah's husbands.

I can see the little creek I remember so well, and I'm there agin right now. The trees are overlapping over the stream and there's deep shade over the water. In places where the sun comes through, I can see thousands of little tadpoles wiggling around — little tadpoles waiting for their turn to be toadfrogs. Lord, I know won't hardly none of them survive to be frogs, for other kinds of life going to eat most of them.

Thank You, Lord, for letting me hear the trains right now, sending out their waves of sound as the cars run over the ties. It's nighttime now, Lord, and the old train passing through is making me lonesome, and sleepy. Old train passing through the night, going to faraway places I ain't never been, rocking its life away on them railroad tracks.

These little things are all I can lay claim to Lord, after living beyond my allotted three score and ten years. Ain't much for a man to lay claim to and nothing of importance. You live it and you look back on it, Lord, and you wonder what it was all about. When you look back on it at the end of the road, it seems like you hain't done much to make this old world no better. Seems like everything you've ever done has been in preparation for this day — the day of reckoning.

It's all because I'm of the flesh, Lord, and a sinner in every way. It's all I've known to think about and to build my life around. But as I've already told You, I'm thankful for that little bit of heaven You've let me live here in the land that I love.

Lord, I ain't never been as glad of nothing as I am in knowing that You ain't going to judge me for what I've been able to lay up in this world like land holdings and money and a high standing among people. If that was the case, I'd be headed for the bottomless pit of hell. I always thought how nice it was for them that had them things. I always loved to look up them paths with trees on each side leading up to solid-looking houses with them big front porches and yards filled with trees and shelter after shelter in the back with all manner of stuff to farm with and 25 or 30 bales of cotton out in the yards in the fall. Then I'd think about all I had to contend with in gitting my plows fitted with the right plow points and sweeps and finding bolts and nuts to fit and the kind of wrenches I needed.

And I know that in this old world a man is judged by what he has and that's the kind that make the leaders cause they have influence. It's shore good that there is somebody to lead. What would an old sharecropper like me ever a done if I'd had to try to lead anybody?

Ain't nobody on earth that can know what lurks in the heart of man, Lord. We can pretend to be one thing and make the world believe it. We can pretend we're good when in our hearts we got all manner of sinful lusts and hatreds and biases. And they ain't many of us that don't have them. If it won't for forgiveness, Lord, I wouldn't stand a chance with You. I've done my share of bad thinking and bad deeds, but that's all behind me today, Lord. It makes a big difference when you know they ain't no more trying to fool the world, and they hain't never been no fooling You. Any man that looks into his conscience knows that You are all-seeing, all-knowing. I would be in the worst fix I've ever been in in my life right this minute, Lord, if it won't for faith.

They's many people that say there ain't no way of knowing beyond the grave and they don't believe in no being beyond man. I shudder to think what kind of fix I'd be in today, Lord, if that was my case. This separates everything I've lived and thought from tomorrow, for in this world, there won't be no tomorrow for me.

It's all running through my mind today, Lord, from the days when I was a young'un and helped Pap split rails and do a lot of other things; the one-room schoolhouse and the long walks to and from school; the day I met Kizzie when I was still a strapping boy and knowed right then that I had to have her for my own; the day we was married at her Pa's house and I took her right here where we started housekeeping.

Won't nothing on earth like that little Hank when he finally got here. Thought sure Kizzie would die before he ever made it into the world. I suffered the torture of hell that day, Lord, but You made everything all right. And when every young'un came along I was just as foolish about each one.

I remember the struggle, Lord, the gitting up before light in plowing season and being in the fields by the time the sun came over the trees — feeling the cool dew on my feet and listening to the birds sing and watching people in other fields. You know that I've plowed til I felt like I couldn't make another step. I've crapped backer til I fell out and had to set down under a hill of backer and try to git my senses back together. Pure passed out. I've been so jaded I couldn't hardly git my body on the old mules' backs to git home at dinner time.

I've sawed wood til I felt like I couldn't raise up after bending over them old trees all day long. I've pulled fodder and picked cotton and toted a soda bucket and got up taters and all manner of things, and I used to think I wouldn't make it til my young'uns got old enough to take over and do some of the hard work. But You helped me, Lord. Thank You for all Your blessings. And the good part is I never felt like I deserved anything better.

Then, lo and behold! When this old world got modern they started bringing in workers from other countries to do all the work we used to do in the fields. That let us know right quick that we was as near nothing as you could git. Here we had done all them things for hundreds of years, and all of a sudden that kind of work won't for none of us. I shake my head, Lord, when I think that a time may come when we can't git foreigners to do our manual labor. What will we do then? But that ain't for me to worry about.

I don't dwell on the hard work, Lord. I dwell on the pretty part. I see all these pretty pictures on television and I have a longing to let the world know how pretty it was out there in the open and the kind of life I've known. 'Course, I reckon folks would say it was showing torture and all that kind of mess. But they can't know what it was like to hear the darkies singing at sunset when the cotton was being weighed in the fields and the sun the color of an orange and all them sheets of cotton around the weigh horse and people proud of their day's work. Or men singing when they were crapping backer and making something pretty out of hard work; telling jokes and laughing and eating watermelon and talking about what they were going to do Sad'dy night.

I remember all the times I went to town on the wagon to git flour and sugar and white meat when ourn give out, 'lasses and syrup and sewing thread and mess like that for the old lady, and how pleasant it was sometimes. I'd watch people in the fields and around their houses and look at all the crops growing and it seemed like the world was turning the right way and everything was in its place. I remember how I'd pass womenfolks in their yards in town when they was out working in their yards and I'd tip my hat to them and they would nod their heads to me and how friendly they seemed. But I always felt a little "jubious" when I passed cause I was scared the old mules would want to spread their manure all over the streets or worse, have to stop and make water. Sometimes they did both, but I just tried to ignore it and they didn't take no count of it.

I remember when I've had to go up to the courthouse to talk to the big boys a few times, or go up in the bank building to talk with the learned men when I needed a little money and didn't see no way to git it. At such times, I always thought it would be nice if I could a had on a nice suit of clothes and a good hat. But that didn't keep me from doing my business with them. And they was always nice. They never made me feel low-down cause I was a poor, ignorant farmer. Sometimes it took a lot of courage to do some of the things I had to do, but them things just test the strength of a man. I didn't never want to shirk my duty, Lord, and I've been proud of my manhood every day since I growed up.

You've shore cut me down to size today, Lord. No matter how near a nobody I've been, I had my pride too. Its all been stripped from me now, Lord. You've let me know that it don't matter about nothing else in life except what's inside that heart. It don't matter what church we've been to, who we've heard preach, what kind of show we've made in the world. It don't matter what we've told anybody else to do. It don't matter about what we've said. It's the sermons we've preached through our everyday lives that count.

I've tried to help my fellowman in all the ways that I've knowed. When one of the brothers was sick, I was there to help plow the fields or whatever needed doing. I was just one of several men that pitched in in times of trouble to help out a friend. I know when Albert had that stroke that everybody thought would kill him us men tended his crop the rest of the year, and he was crippled in early April. He lay there for a month and couldn't even move and it got his speech so he couldn't never talk hardly plain enough to understand after that.

It done something to Albert's mind, too, and when he finally got out of bed and got him a walking stick with the useless arm in a rag sling around his neck everybody thought he was going to kill hisself trying to git about. And that done old Albert in as far as farming goes. He finally had to go to the Poor House to live out his last days.

I've been to neighbors' houses and helped set up with the sick. I've been called on many a time to lay out a corpse and I always done them things gladly and always felt sorry for them that was left to grieve.

We've fed and bedded the preachers and always tried to show them the respect due the men of the cloth.

I've had a few young men come to me to talk about their problems when they got in trouble with the law or women, or whatever, and I always had a special feeling for them, cause I had boys of my own that went to others stid of me when they had problems.

And I see all them things wrote down in that Book of Life, but I know it ain't them things that's going to take me to heaven. It's all between You and me, Lord. It's them sins we committed and let the devil make us believe we hadn't done nothing wrong.

I've thought about death all my life, Lord, knowing that one day I would be the one that would face You in all Your majesty. But I never knowed it would be like this, Lord. I never knowed how near a nobody a mortal man could be til I faced this moment. Lord God Almighty, have mercy on me! Please, God, have mercy.

I know now that man ain't nothing but chaff in the wind. You made him after Your own image, Lord, but he's flesh and blood and a sinner all his life. You give him a body as a temple for his soul, but he has defiled that body, Lord.

I know that if I had a million dollars to lay at your feet, it wouldn't make nary bit of difference on this day of all days, Lord. When man confronts that Book of Life and sees what's put down there in his name, he's the lowest thing that ever crawled on this earth in his heart, 'cause there ain't no gitting around that one. My Lord, my heart is heavy for the whole world today. If I could only warn 'em and let them know what I'm facing this day, it would mean so much to me. But all I hear is "too late, too late, too late."

I'm in a state, Lord, where I'm beyond all human understanding. I know that what I'm experiencing ain't from thinking in the way I've done all my life. This is beyond the realm of man. It's my whole life flying before me in an instant.

I always thought of the big, black sins as the ones that really mattered, Lord, but that was before I saw that Book of Life that told everything about me. You know that You and me straightened out the big black sins a long time ago, cause they're blacked out in the Book, but so many little ones are wrote down.

I'm so ashamed, Lord, when I see the black marks where we set down at the table so many times and failed to give You thanks for the som'n 'teat that sustained our bodies. We just turned our plates over as fast as we could and pushed them up to the bowls and started raking out the vegetables and stuff like we was perishing to death. I'm guilty, Lord, and I know now that I couldn't a set a poorer example than that before my own young'uns.

And there were the beggars I passed by on the streets over the years and the ill-deformed people selling their pencils and stuff and I've passed them by and not given them nary penny nor bought the little things they was selling. I didn't never feel like I had a extra penny, but just one penny might have helped them back in the days when they won't no money. I know they was times I questioned whether they really needed handouts from the public. I was judging them, Lord, and I know now that it ain't up to us to judge nobody. I know it's better to try to do something for them worse off than us without trying to figger out their needs. It ain't up to us to judge.

Have mercy on me, Lord. My mouth's so dry and my eyes ain't focusing. Seems like I'm seeing everything backwards. Seems like my eyeballs are in the back of my head.

I'd call on you with pretty words if I could, Lord. You deserve better than I'm able to say to you. I'd make my words sound like a poem if I could, like the Psalmists in Your holy Word. But I hain't got it in me, Lord. A third-grade learning ain't much to plead with. I've huern people that could say things so pretty, Lord, all proper and everything. But I thank You, almighty Father, that You always had mercy on the lowly when You was on earth as a man. And I know You can hear me and understand what's in my heart just as good as if I could say it like it ought to be said. It's just in Your honor that I'd like to say it in a pretty way.

I feel the sting, Lord. Oh, that sting, Lord, it's different from anything I've ever felt in my lifetime. Nobody can't know, Lord, not til they've reached this state. It's real, Lord, and it's so dark. Darker than any midnight I've ever seen. Ain't never been no valley like this one, Lord.

I'm being judged, Lord, cause the Book is open and I see it all. You put it all down, didn't You, Lord, just like You said? Every time I've beat the young'uns, every time I've said things I shouldn't, even them evil thoughts are here right before my eyes. They's some checks beside the whuppings I give the young'uns, and some cross marks too. I thought I was doing right, Lord, but I was justifying my own feelings. So that time I beat Hank about killing that biddy with a clod of dirt was a big cross mark. And the time I kicked Shine so hard he fell to the ground won't nothing but my own anger rising up. Shine cried, Lord, and he looked up into my eyes so pitiful, but I pushed it aside and just let him go and git hisself straightened out without any sympathy from me.

And I talk about how I loved them old mules, Lord, but nobody would a guessed it that day I showed myself with old Cindy down in the mash. Nobody saw it but me, but I see it's right there in that Book. And it was my fault to start with. I went down in the mash to plow shoulder-high corn and forgot to put a muzzle on Cindy, so stid of going back to the house and gitting a muzzle, I said I'd keep her from biting off stalks of corn. But Cindy loved that green corn, like all mules do, and she'd reach down and bite off a stalk and eat it while plowing, and I got tard of her doing it. So the old devil rose up in me big, and I stopped the mule and took a plow line loose from her bridle and beat and cussed her and she tore up a lot more corn jumping around when I was putting the rope on her than she'd have et.

And Lord, I don't want to face what I done to that old hound-dog even now. I'm lower than that dog and that's a pretty black stain on Your holy Book. Just an old stray hound dog that come up to the house one day so heavy with puppies she couldn't hardly walk. And that old dog went up under the house and had them puppies, 13 of 'em, and we could hear 'em crying and squirming around under there, and I didn't want no old stray dog hanging around. The next day the old dog come up to the back door with every rib showing and her hip bones sticking up a full inch, and she was wagging her tail and whining for som'n teat. The string beans and ish taters boiling in the pot were smelling high. And that old dog was so weak she was wobbling in her hind legs. And Lord, if You forgive me for this one, You'll do more than I would do for anybody. I run down them doorsteps and kicked that old dog on her hips, and she fell down and acted like she was paralyzed for a minute. Then she just got up and looked at me with them sad eyes and put her tail between her legs and went back under the house to them squirming babies, with no milk for them.

I made the young'uns go under the house and put them puppies in the basket we tote corn to the hogs in and carry them to that old half-rotten backer barn across the branch and dared anybody to give her a mouthful to eat, cause I knowed if she was fed at our house she would take up there and wouldn't be no gitting rid of her. I didn't see that old hound agin until right now, Lord and I just know she died in that old backer barn and every one of them 13 puppies. You made animals too, Lord, and why does anybody mistreat them? Is it cause we want to show power over something?

And I killed that cow that time just as dead as if I'd a took a shotgun and blowed her brains out. That cow was small and had a hard time having her calves. The last time she near 'bout died and the calf was dead and she never done nothing hardly on that freshening. Didn't give but about a gallon of milk a day and dried up in three or four months. But the next time she was in season I put her right back to the bull, and when her time come she just lay there and grunted and lowed and didn't do nothing and just died right there in the stable. We had to tear down a side of the stable to git a trace chain around her neck to drag her up in the woods for the buzzards. But I put all them things out of my mind, Lord and didn't feel too bad about them — until now.

And there's a cross about something I didn't do. That time Little Bud lied to me and I knowed he was lying, but I just overlooked it and didn't lay a hand on him. I see now that he should a got the rod, Lord.

If there was one thing I wanted to do, Lord, it was to set a good example before my young'uns. I wanted my young'uns to be all the things I was not. I wanted them to look up to me and respect me and think of me as a decent man. But when I look at that Book of Life, I got many doubts. I loved them, Lord, and You know that. But I thought love was trying to keep them in line and keeping a tight rein on them. I just hope that time has let them know that whatever I did, it was what I thought was best for them. I hope they'll remember me with kindness.

I'm so ashamed Lord. I'm looking at page after page of nothing but one or two words where I started to offer my thanks to You at night and dropped off to sleep without saying anything hardly. And many blank pages. I didn't even kneel before You, Lord, to show my reverence. Just fell on the bed and said I'd say my prayer after my head hit the pillow.

But just let my heart git troubled and there's page after page where I poured out my heart to You. In the bad times I was calling out to You with all my heart. Let one of the family git sick and I was pleading day and night for You to look down upon us. When the droughts come and it looked like the backer and corn and the hay was going to dry up, You heard my cries. When I felt like I had to have a few dollars to git things we needed so bad and didn't see no way to git it, I was down on a hillside pleading with You.

I've been a bad times Christian, Lord. I see now that when the corn and backer and cotton were green; when the rain was plentiful; when the taters growed and cracks showed around the hills and the backer cured up pretty and the boll weevils didn't eat up the cotton bolls and all the family was all right, I didn't do no praying at all hardly.

I remember the good times at the house when the young'uns were singing and playing and the nights by the fire in winter and all of us eating around the dining room table and Sundays and preaching and hearing the Word and family reunions and all-day meetings at the church, and my cup runneth over when I think about all of it.

I've seen all this space stuff on television that seems as fer out to me as anything can git, and men riding around on the outside of the earth and I've never wanted none of that. When I ride into space, I want to set a straight course to where You are, Lord, no round-and-round and then coming back to earth. I want a one-way ticket, Lord, with You the pilot, cause I know You'll direct the ship to the right place.

Bless every one of my family, Lord. I place them in Your hands and trust You to direct them in everything they do. If I've failed them in any way, forgive me, Lord. Look into their hearts and show them the right way. I done all I can, Lord. They got a lot to face in this old world.

They had it tough when they was young, Lord, but they got it a hundred times better'n I ever had it today. They got nice homes and big cars and good jobs and everything I hain't never had, but I can't say they act any happier now than they did when we was living the hard life. Seems like sometimes that they've lost sight of the real pretty part of our lives.

Maybe they just don't see it like me, Lord. I know that what I've seen that was so pretty to me came from the heart, not seeing it through the eye. Else, how could the kind of life I've lived, out where they'd call it the wilds today, with field after field of crops and bushes and trees and hillsides and gray buildings with no paint on them be pretty? I know, Lord. It's because it come from deep inside me. It come from the heart, Lord.

Zeb raised his head from the chair and appeared to be in a stupor. He looked out the window to a world of white. Snow was falling so thick he couldn't see the road and every tree was etched in white and the wind would sweep around the house, blowing the snow from the porch where it piled up in drifts. He looked up, and the snow was coming under the eaves of the house and dusting the bed in white.

He gazed out the window again, and scenes from the past came alive. The young'uns were running over the yard, laughing and hurrying to get in something to burn, milking the cow, feeding the mules and cow and carrying a basket of corn to the hogs. They were excited about the snow. Their faces were pink and their toboggans covered with snow. They saw him and waved at him and he smiled.

Kizzie was busy in the kitchen, preparing supper and getting things ready for a long winter's night. They'd pop corn. They'd make snow cream and young'uns would go out and git balls of snow and bring it in and smoke it in the fireplace to give it that smoky taste. Kizzie wouldn't even fuss at the young'uns for toting in snow on their feet that would turn into water. They'd tell stories and jokes and everything would be just like it ought to be.

The snow scene was replaced by spring and everything was in bloom and Zeb could smell the fragrance of the flowers and crops were up and the landscape was turning green. Then came summer with deep shade in the yard and everywhere he looked crops were tall and people were at work in the fields. The little children were playing and the sun shimmered over the waters and the pastures were filled with cows and hogs and mules and horses and the grass was lush.

Came fall, and the golden hues of autumn showed over the land. The trees turned and the crops were ripe. Foot-long ears of corn hung from the stalks and mown hay patches were the color of honey. Cotton fields were white and the leaves on the stalks had acquired a purple color. Zeb stood in the middle of the 15-acre field and marveled at the sight. The sun was golden and the skies a dreamy blue. Gentle winds blew about him and he took in the scene through his eyes, mingled with the depth of feeling from his heart, and it seemed like heaven on earth.

Then they were all around him, showering him with kisses and feeding him all the things he liked — collards fresh from the pot with crisp, oven-baked corn bread; corn, tender and sweet; mouthfuls of fresh field peas, still steaming from the pot; tender barbecue; bites of country ham with biscuits dipped in the gravy; lemon cake with grated rind showing in the icing — and he was filled with food — and happiness. The telephone nearby was ringing but it seemed to be in another world.

All of them knelt around him and the children were the same age as the grandchildren and all were young and beautiful and Kizzie was the teen-ager again with a flawless skin and deep, penetrating eyes. She was so fragile he could place his hands around her waist. She dominated the scene and the sun coming in the window shed its rays on her hair and hues of gold played about her face. She was dressed in white and held a bouquet of cotton blossoms and scattered them around him.

Hank brought him the collar one of the mules had worn. He was smiling and handsome and his cowlick showed. Fuzz had polished an old curry comb until the handle glittered in the light. Fuzz was getting heavy down around his mouth. Shine's freckles were prominent and his hair the color of burnished gold. He was wearing a broad smile as he placed a tobacco thermometer in Zeb's hands. Lizzie Mae had always been the prettiest young'un in the crowd and she was radiant as she brought the old coffee grinder and placed it before him. She reached over and kissed him and patted him on the shoulder.

Little Bud brought a pair of worn-out shoes he had owned and found in a box in the loft. He said, "I love you, Pa," and Zeb cried aloud. Sarah had the shoe last and Zeb remembered all the times it had been used over the years. Sis brought an old rag doll Kizzie had made for her and she hugged her father and he wept again.

The grandchildren and great-grandchildren brought in flowers and fancy gourds and colorful leaves and there were fruits and nuts and a carpet of color around him.

***

Then they were gone, and Zeb sat alone. He resorted to prayer again:

Lord, You give me some high hills to climb, and there was times when I couldn't see the forest for the trees. I been down in one of them big fields more than one time when I felt like I was the only person on earth. I've looked across at the woods and it looked like the trees was bowed down and it seemed like the birds won't singing no more. I've just stood there and cried like a baby and wiped my tears on my shirt sleeves til they was pure wet. I felt less than a man then, Lord, and I'd a been ashamed for anybody to see me. Didn't nobody see me but You, Lord. Not Kizzie. Not the young'uns. Not nobody but You. That was when I didn't look up, Lord. That was when I was feeling sorry for myself.

But them cries cleaned out my soul, Lord. I'd git up to a pretty sunrise and everything looking bright agin, and it looked like a whole new world.

I thank You, Lord, for taking a nobody and letting me be able to see something pretty on the low side of life. I thank You that most of the time I was able to see the good side of man without looking down on the ones that was poor as trash like me. I'm glad I could think of my own class of folks as high as if they had been high-ups.

And now, Lord, it has come down to just You and me, and nobody else on earth. It's like there never was nobody else. All the pretty sights I just seen was in another world, in another time. I'm looking into Your eyes now, Lord, asking You to see me for what I've been.

Lord, am I damned to hell? I need a hand Lord, just a hand to hold on to right this minute. How deep is this valley, Lord? Where is the light? I can't move, Lord. I can't do nothing. I see the Book closing, Lord. And I'm standing on nothing but faith. But I feel a hand, Lord! Thank You, Jesus. I'm seeing a light, Lord. It's so far away, at the end of a tunnel as long as my life. But it's LIGHT, Lord, beautiful LIGHT. I see bright places and dim places where I can't hardly see nothing. But some of the tunnel is so bright it has to be a heavenly light. Thank You for forgiveness, Lord.

I......commend.......my spirit.......

A half-moon appeared to be sailing across the sky as white clouds, spent of their fury, drifted over the heavens. The clouds had come in swiftly, sifting the white powder over the area and making a postcard picture for camera buffs. The gray clouds of daylight were gone and stars were appearing in the heavens. But wind howled around the house and the tin still rattled on the roof.